To Thom
From one wh
your scholarly dedicat
contribution.

Oct. 86.

ENFORCING INTERNATIONAL LAW THROUGH U.S. LEGISLATION

ENFORCING INTERNATIONAL LAW THROUGH U.S. LEGISLATION

by
Elisabeth Zoller

Transnational Publishers, Inc.
Dobbs Ferry, New York

Library of Congress Cataloging-in-Publication Data
Zoller, Elisabeth.
Enforcing international law through U.S. legislation.

Bibliography: p.
Includes index.
1. Remedies (Law)—United States. 2. International obligations. I. Title. II. Title: Enforcing international law through United States legislation.
JX5486.U6Z65 1985 341.5′8 85-16470
ISBN 0-941320-32-2

Manufactured in the United States of America

CONTENTS

Table of Abbreviations

Adm. L. Rev.	Administrative Law Review
A.E.I.A.	Atomic Energy International Agency
A.J.I.L.	American Journal of International Law
A.S.I.L.	American Society of International Law
Atl. Comm'y. Q.	Atlantic Community Quarterly
Bus. Law.	Business Lawyer
CAB	Civil Aeronautics Board
C.F.R.	Code of Federal Regulations
C.M.R.	Common Market Reporter
Colum. H. Rts. L. Rev.	Columbia Human Rights Law Review
Colum. J. Trans. L.	Columbia Journal of Transnational Law
Colum. L. Rev.	Columbia Law Review
Cornell Int'l L.J.	Cornell International Law Journal
Duke L. J.	Duke Law Journal
EEC	European Economic Community
Exec. Ord.	Executive Order
F.2d	Federal Reporter (Second Series)
F. Supp.	Federal Supplement
F.R.	Federal Register
Ga. J. Int. & Comp. L.	Georgia Journal of International and Comparative Law
GATT	General Agreement on Tariffs and Trade
Geo. L. J.	Georgetown Law Journal
Harv. J. Int'l. L.	Harvard Journal of International Law

Harv. L. Rev.	Harvard Law Review
H. Rts. Q.	Human Rights Quarterly
I.C.J. Reports	Reports of Judgments, Advisory Opinions and Orders of the International Court of Justice
I.C.L.Q.	International and Comparative Law Quarterly
I.L.M.	International Legal Materials
Int'l. Law.	International Lawyer
Int'l. Stud. Q.	International Studies Quarterly
Iowa L. Rev.	Iowa Law Review
I.T.R.	International Trade Reporter
J.A.L.C.	Journal of Air Law and Commerce
J. Comp. Bus. & Cap. M.L.	Journal of Comparative Business and Capital Market Law
J. Mar. L. C.	Journal of Maritime Law and Commerce
J.W.T.L.	Journal of World Trade Law
Law & Pol'y. Int'l. Bus.	Law and Policy in International Business
Loy. L.A. Int'l. & Comp. L. J.	Loyola of Los Angeles International and Comparative Law Journal
Md. J. Int'l. L. T.	Maryland Journal of International Law and Trade
Mich. L. Rev.	Michigan Law Review
Minn. L. Rev.	Minnesota Law Review
N.C.J. Int'l. & Com. Reg.	North Carolina Journal of International and Commerce Regulations
N.Y.L. Sch. L. Rev.	New York Law School Law Review
N.Y. Univ. J. Int'l L. & Pol.	New York University Journal of International Law and Policy
O.J.E.C.	Official Journal of the European Community
P.C.I.J.	Permanent Court of International Justice
Pres. Procl.	Presidential Proclamation
R.C.A.D.I.	Recueil des Cours de l'Académie de Droit International de La Haye

R.G.D.I.P.	Revue Générale de Droit International Public
Rutgers L. Rev.	Rutgers Law Review
Stat.	United States Statutes at Large
Tex. Int'l. L. J.	Texas International Law Journal
T.I.A.S.	Treaties and Other International Acts Series
U.N.R.I.A.A.	United Nations, Reports of International Arbitral Awards
U.S.	United States Supreme Court Reports
U.S.C.	United States Code
U.S. Code Cong. & Adm. News	United States Code Congressional and Administrative News
U.S. Digest	United States Digest of International Law
U. of Pa. L. Rev.	University of Pennsylvania Law Review
U.S.T.	United States Treaties and Other International Agreements
Va. J. Int'l. L.	Virginia Journal of International Law
Yrbk. I.L.C.	Yearbook of the International Law Commission
Z.a.ö.R.V.	Zeitschrift fur ausländisches und öffentliches Recht und Völkerrecht.

Table of Cases

I. *INTERNATIONAL*

Introduction

Remedies in international law are in a striking state of neglect. Both the confidence placed after the First World War in the legal eradication of the so-called *guerre d'exécution* and the relative preeminence accorded the judicial and arbitral settlement of international disputes have played a major role in this jurisprudential oversight. The prohibition of armed reprisals by Article 2 (4) of the Charter of the United Nations has no doubt reinforced the conviction that the topic had in some ways become moot.

Nevertheless, the neglect of the subject of remedies due to the emphasis on prohibition against force should not have spilled over into the subject of peacetime unilateral nonforceful remedies. Peacetime unilateral remedies are actually the most common means of guaranteeing the effectiveness of international law in the international society.[1] Yet, the absence of a theory of remedies makes the unilateral application of international law unjustifiably suspect. Since it is clearly illusory to believe that states not only are free, but also feel free, to do whatever they want in resorting to nonforceful self-help, *i.e.* the so-called nonviolent sanctions of international law, the present study is designed to discover the rationale of unilateral remedies in international law. In short, my purpose is to propose a general theory of unilateral

[1] The *Second Restatement of the Law, Foreign Relations Law of the United States (revised)* contains no separate treatment of remedies but deals with some aspects of this subject in connection with responsibility of states (§ § 200, 204-4) and the effect of violations of international law (§ 3). Significantly the Tentative Draft for the Third Restatement now includes a whole part on the topic: Part IX, Remedies for Violations of International Law, § § 901-907 in Tentative Draft No. 5 (April 5, 1984).

remedies in peacetime, a goal that could not be within the scope of my previous study, *Peacetime Unilateral Remedies: An Analysis of Countermeasures*.[2]

The purpose of *Peacetime* was to discover (1) the rationale that led the Arbitral Tribunal in the 1978 *Air Service Award* (France/United States[3]) to coin the new word ''countermeasure'' in the field of unilateral remedies, (2) the conceptual usefulness of this new terminology, and (3) the legal framework that could be attached to it. I endeavored to demonstrate that countermeasures are in substance law enforcement measures that go beyond the principle of reciprocity that is embodied in the maxim *Inadimpleti non est adimplendum* without, however, reaching the severity of punishment, since no state is entitled under international law to impose a final harm upon another. Obviously, countermeasures do not cover the whole spectrum of unilateral remedies. Besides countermeasures, there are simple measures and genuine sanctions. The former differ from the latter in that they do not infringe on the rights of foreign countries, whereas the latter have such an effect and in addition entail a punitive component. Having located countermeasures in the spectrum of unilateral remedies, my purpose now is to go a step further: to grasp this spectrum as a whole and see whether it is possible to present an overall justifiable system of enforcement procedures in international law.

The problem is that in order to build such a theoretical model, one needs substantive materials, *i.e.* hard facts, as preconditions.[4] Just as there would be no such thing as a law of treaties if treaties were not available, so is a law of remedies inconceivable without factual examples of remedies in the practice of international intercourse. These remedies are difficult to describe since, on the one hand, many of them are not made public because of the confidentiality of diplomatic correspondence and, on the other, those that are made public, especially through various digests

[2] Transnational Publishers, Dobbs Ferry, N. Y., 1984 (hereinafter referred to as *Peacetime*).
[3] 18 *U.N.R.I.A.A.* 417-493.
[4] Claude Bernard, *Introduction à l'étude de la médecine expérimentale* (Transl. Henry Copley Green, 1927), esp. Chapter I: Observation and Experiment, at 5-26 and Chapter II: The *A Priori* Idea and Doubt in Experimental Reasoning, at 27-57.

of international law, are selected and as a result cannot be considered comprehensive. As a result, the first obstacle in the path to a theory of unilateral remedies is entirely methodological. Where may such remedies be found? Where is it possible to find these "empirically referential tests [which are] particularly necessary in the international system where law does not emerge from predetermined or easily recognizable institutions"?[5] In order to answer such questions, one must bear in mind that there is no comprehensive international legislation in the field of remedies. There is no such thing as a treaty on nonforceful reprisals. Although the final clauses of treaties may authorize some responses to certain breaches, these responses are not exclusive from others. This is so because treaty law does not usually preempt customary legal remedies, especially regarding "secondary norms," *i.e.* those obligations which are concerned with determining the legal consequences of failure to fulfill obligations established by "primary rules."[6] Moreover, the remedies to be found in treaty law are limited and sometimes inadequate. If treaty law cannot therefore be considered as a comprehensive source of unilateral remedies, then their only general source is bound to be customary international law.

The customary law to be found in state practice may take several forms, chief among which is state legislation. However, states' legislations rarely provide an overall approach to unilateral remedies for violations of international law by foreign nations. Because of the usually wide authority of executives in foreign affairs, such remedies are most of the time taken on a case-by-case basis. They are not predictable. A conspicuous exception to this general practice is to be found in the United States. The United States is, indeed, the only state in the world that has systematically made its unilateral peacetime remedies public by legislation, primarily by reason of the constitutional requirement of the separation of powers. These laws address a generality of cases. Each of them is a definite response to an indefinite number

[5] W. Michael Reisman, "Deterrence and International Law," in Arthur S. Miller & Martin Feinrider [Ed.], *Nuclear Weapons and Law* (1984), 129.
[6] *Yrbk. I.L.C.*, 1973, Vol. II, p. 169, § 40.

of possible violations of international obligations. Insofar as state legislation constitutes the state practice that shapes the content of customary international law, United States legislation represents in my opinion an exemplification of enforcement mechanism in international law. As a result, United States legislation provides international scholars with a unique experimental field and a first-hand opportunity to systematize these remedies in a theoretical model.

International remedies doubtless stand in sharp contrast to the legal remedies available in municipal legal orders. But it would be wrong to believe that their differences rule out any common features between them. The truth is that international remedies are still affected by the relatively undeveloped international legal order.

Unlike municipal law, international law barely leaves room for a distinction between preventive and repressive remedies. While the purpose of preventive relief is to avoid a forthcoming injury, repressive remedies seek redress for an injury already sustained. Preventive remedies are generally granted in municipal law by declaratory judgment, temporary restraining orders, and injunctions.[7] In the case concerning the Northern Cameroon *(Cameroon v. United Kingdom),* the International Court of Justice refused a declaratory judgment on the ground that the case did not fall within its judicial function.[8] But the other types of preventive relief, although quite common under United States law,[9] are still extremely controversial in international law. They

[7] See Arwed Blomeyer, Types of Relief Available (Judicial Remedies), Chap. 4, Vol. XVI: Civil Procedure, *International Encyclopedia of Comparative Law* (1982), § § 4-83, 4-110.

[8] I.C.J. *Reports* 1963, p. 64.

[9] Preventive measures are obviously not the same according to whether or not they affect international subjective rights of third states. As long as the measure does not affect an international obligation, a state has total discretion to decide the action it considers best to protect its national interests. Export controls, for instance, fall within this category, since a country is under no international obligation to allow its nationals the freedom to export goods, services or technologies to other countries. The problem, however, is completely different when outside a prior delegation embodied in an international instrument (*e.g.* an ''escape clause'' in a treaty), a state avails itself of the right not to comply with one or several international obligations whenever an injury is caused or even liable to be caused to its national interests. Several United States statutes provide for possible occasional dispensations from complying with, *e.g.*, the international customary rule

entail disputable and disputed concepts such as *force majeure* or state of necessity, fortuitous events in customary and treaty law, and supervening impossibility of performance or fundamental change of circumstances in treaty law. As a result preventive remedies raise entirely specific problems which are beyond the scope of this study.

Repressive remedies for international offenses are, however, more elaborate. They include distinction based on the author of the breach. International rules may be violated by individuals or corporations, *i.e.*, private parties, or by states. Remedies for the two kinds of offenses are not all internationally relevant. Within the political and legal system provided for by every domestic legal organization, breaches of international law may be sanctioned through a mechanism of individualized responsibility whenever the offense against the law of nations is not attributable to the state itself. In the United States, such is the case with anyone committing the crime of piracy,[10] conspiring to injure or destroy specific property situated within a foreign country and belonging to a foreign government,[11] starting a military or naval expedition against a friendly nation,[12] or abducting, torturing and murdering another individual within the boundaries of a foreign nation.[13] This is also true for less important offenses against international law; for instance, in the field of maritime law, for

of nondiscrimination in the absence of a clear prior unlawful act of a foreign state. For instance, in order to protect United States fishing rights, Section 205 of the 1976 Fishery Conservation and Management Act provides that whenever a foreign country has refused to begin negotiation or has failed to negotiate in good faith in order to conclude an international fishery agreement allowing U.S. fishing vessels equitable access to its fisheries, action will be taken to prohibit the importation into the United States of all fish and fish products of that foreign country (16 U.S.C. § 1825(b) (1982)). In order to protect U.S. air carriers rights, Pub. L. 96-192 (Feb. 15, 1980) provides that, whenever a foreign country engages in a practice which, without being necessarily "unlawful," results in "substantial adverse competitive impact" upon U.S. carriers, the Civil Aeronautics Board may suspend the permits of the foreign air carriers of such country (49 App. U.S.C. § 1372(f) (2) (1982)). Similarly, in order to protect U.S. national security, Section 203 of the International Emergency Economic Powers Act leaves the door open for possible discriminatory action in the regulation of financial transactions with foreign states (50 U.S.C. § 1702(a) (1) (1982)). These pieces of legislation raise legal problems which are obviously outside the law of international responsibility.

[10] 18 U.S.C. § 1651 (1982).

[11] 18 U.S.C. § 956 (1982).

[12] 18 U.S.C. § 960 (1982).

[13] See *Filartiga v. Peña-Irala,* Court of Appeals of New York 1980, 620 F.2d 876 and *U.S. Digest* 1979, 522-25.

engaging without a valid permit in fishing within the exclusive fishery conservation zone of the coastal state,[14] or for whaling in violation of the 1946 International Convention for the Regulation of Whaling;[15] or, in the field of international trade regulations, for resorting to unfair methods of competition and unfair acts in the importation of articles,[16] or for importing a class or kind of foreign merchandise to be sold at less than its fair value.[17] In all these situations the breach of the international rule is also a breach of a domestic rule as long as the relevant international obligation has become part of the supreme law of the land. But above all, the remedy provided for the breach is entirely domestic in nature since the individualization of the breach makes redress possible as a matter of domestic law. That is why the enforcement of international law is always fully efficient where the breach is attributable to private individuals.[18]

However, when the breach can be ascribed to a foreign state as opposed to a private person,[19] remedies cease to be simply a matter of domestic law and necessarily assume international relevance. This result seems to derive less from the potential infringement on the subjective right of the offending foreign state than from the fact that international remedies are in essence based upon a system of collective responsibility. Indeed, international law's recognition of collective responsibility constitutes an essential distinction between international and domestic remedies.

Collective responsibility derives from the organization of the state system itself in that it indirectly holds every national of a state responsible for any breach committed by the state. The concept is often viewed as an example of the "primitive savagery" that prevails in international society, since it gives states a right to harm innocent individuals in return for an injury in-

[14] 16 U.S.C. § 1824(a) (1982).
[15] 16 U.S.C. § 916c(a) (1982).
[16] 19 U.S.C. § 1337(a) (1982).
[17] 19 U.S.C. § 1673 (1982).
[18] See the classic Quincy Wright, *The Enforcement of International Law Through Municipal Law in the United States* (1916).
[19] See the curious situation raised by a person engaging in clandestine intelligence-gathering activities on behalf of a foreign power. That breach is sanctioned by domestic remedies (in the United States, cf. 50 U.S.C. §1801 seq., Pub. L. 95-511, Oct. 25, 1978, 22 Stat. 1783) and by international remedies (the most common form being in this case reciprocal action).

flicted by their leaders. However, collective responsibility is in some ways a highly rational institution in the absence of political institutions where responsibility, if individualized, could too easily be avoided. To that extent, collective responsibility serves a logical need where political anarchy prevails.[20]

In that respect, collective responsibility is to be viewed as more important than self-help as a distinguishing feature of international and domestic remedies. International legal scholars often assert that the major distinction between municipal and international remedies is that the latter still recognizes self-help. This is only partially true, since municipal orders still admit, although to a limited extent, the legitimacy of self-help. For example, self-help is allowed in many countries in the landlord-tenant relationship in that the landlord may, upon vacation of the premises by the tenant, take possession of the tenant's belongings on his own behalf and so strengthen his landlord's lien into a possessory lien.[21] Self-help is also recognized under the law of adjacent properties, when the trimming of overhanging branches or of roots originating on neighboring land is permitted. Last but not least, self-help is recognized under the law of contracts, when a breach of an agreement entitles the wronged party not to perform counterpart obligations *(Exceptio Non Adimpleti Contractus)*.

In municipal law, the *Exceptio Non Adimpleti Contractus* is a legacy of the principle of reciprocity which once was the norm in primitive societies. Its scope is limited to the field of contracts imposing mutual obligations (synallagmatic contracts). In international law, the principle of reciprocity itself has not yet been reduced to the *Exceptio Non Adimpleti Contractus*. Reciprocity applies to any international rule, whether treaty rule or custom, so long as the obligation is not fundamental in character (for instance, the prohibition of genocide). To some extent, it may be said that the true *Exceptio* in international law is an *Exceptio Non Adimpletae Normae,* a legal principle commonly known as retaliation. As a result, the temporary dispensation from a legal

[20] See William Seagle, *The Quest for Law* (1941), 43.
[21] See Blomeyer, *supra* n.4, at § 4.4.

rule made permissible under the *Exceptio Non Adimpleti Contractus* only as related to a symmetrical obligation, acquires in international law an apparently unlimited scope, *i.e.* covering reprisals. In the 1978 *Air Service* Award (France/United States), the arbitral tribunal coined a new word to designate all the possible infringements on the subjective rights of a foreign state as a reaction to prior unlawful conduct, namely the word "countermeasures."[22] In the following analysis, we will always refer to "countermeasures," as opposed to measures, to designate any response to a prior unlawful act of a foreign state, the effect of which is noncompliance with one or several international obligations. This should not be construed as prejudging the legitimacy of the response under international law.

There are many measures and countermeasures in United States law. In such different areas as trade law, human rights, air law, maritime law, and taxation, the United States has enacted legislation which gives warning of the measures which may be taken against foreign states that do not abide by the law.[23] These statutory provisions are very specific. They define (1) the wrongful acts which will be responded to, (2) the response which the United States government will direct to that foreign state and (3) the procedural safeguards which are attached to such actions. Whatever their legitimacy under international law, these measures and countermeasures at least give transparency to United States international remedies. The remedies have been made public; they are open to the knowledge of foreign countries. This openness deserves some consideration in that publicity is a crucial test of the legal recognition of custom. On the other hand, pub-

[22] 18 *U.N.R.I.A.A.* 417-493; see E. Zoller, *Peacetime*, at xvi-xvii.

[23] Federal legislation is sometimes preceded, completed, or reinforced by legislation of the member states. For instances, in the field of foreign trade, the Pennsylvania Trade Practices Act of July 23, 1968 (71 PS § 773.101) prohibits discrimination against the steel and aluminum industries of Pennsylvania. Practices of foreign countries in subsidizing manufacture of certain steel and aluminum products have been found discriminating against manufacture of similar items in Pennsylvania (see *Lucchino v. Brazil, et al.*, Commonwealth Court of Pennsylvania, No. 1 FRD, April 17, 1984, 5 ITRD 2532-37). In foreign boycott matters, the State of Maryland enacted on May 17, 1966, a law relative to foreign discrminatory boycotts, XV *I.L.M.* 662-668 (1976). Other states such as New York, Illinois (*U.S. Digest* 1975, p. 700) and California (*U.S. Digest* 1976, p. 576) passed anti-boycott laws. However despite the interesting problems that they raise, especially as constitutional law and relations between the federal government and other states are concerned, this study will not address state legislation.

licity deprives the remedy of its arbitrary character and subjects it to some kind of rule. Furthermore, the publicity of repressive remedies for internationally wrongful acts *mutatis mutandis* introduces into the international law society the postulate of classic criminal law *"nullum crimen, nulla poena sine lege,"* a principle which is a basic requirement of the Rule of Law *(Etat de Droit, Rechtstaat).*

The reason why United States law embodies a whole array of international remedies is to be found in the constitutional system. Under United States constitutional law, the authority for all powers exercised by organs of the federal government derives from the Constitution. While these powers are subject to a broader construction for foreign affairs than for domestic affairs,[24] the powers of the federal government in foreign affairs are shared by the President and Congress. In international intercourse, unilateral remedies are generally decided and exercised by the executive branch. But under the Constitution and outside the use of force,[25] the President has no general retaliatory authority.[26] He may act only under a delegation which, falling short of being

[24] In the leading case *U.S. v. Curtiss-Wright Export Corp. et al.* [299 U.S. 304 (1936)], the Supreme Court held: "The broad statement that the federal government can exercise no powers except those specifically enumerated in the Constitution, and such implied powers as are necessary and proper to carry into effect the enumerated powers, is categorically true only in respect of our internal affairs." (at 315-6) and "(T)he investment of the federal government with the powers of external sovereignty did not depend upon the affirmative grants of the Constitution." (at 318).

[25] Article II, § 2, of the Constitution provides that "[t]he President shall be Commander in Chief of the Army and Navy. . . ." In his classical *Foreign Affairs and the Constitution* (1972), Louis Henkin elaborates on "The Commander in Chief" as follows: ". . . Without a Congressional declaration of war, the power of the President to use the troops and do anything else necessary to repel invasion is beyond question. Wilson even claimed the right to strike deep in Mexico. The President has power not merely to take measures to meet the invasion, but to wage in full the war imposed upon the United States. In our day of instant war, all assume that the President would have the power to retaliate against a nuclear attack, if only on the theory that retaliation was a form of defense and might prevent or deter a second strike; probably, he has authority also to anticipate by a preemptive strike an attack he believes imminent." (at 52, footnotes omitted.)

[26] Nor does he seem to have a general authority to resort to preventive remedies in the case of circumstances liable to threaten to impair national security; see especially Lawrence H. Tribe, *American Constitutional Law* (1978), 165.

embodied in the Constitution, may be given only by the legislative branch.[27] This constitutional requirement is all the more necessary as the Constitution confers upon Congress, beyond the appropriations power, legislative powers directly relating to foreign affairs. These powers are laid down in Article I, Section 8. Those directly relevant to peacetime remedies are, to "lay and collect . . . duties, imports and excises;" to "regulate commerce with foreign nations;" to "define and punish . . . felonies committed on the high seas, and offenses against the law of nations."

International remedies are scattered throughout the United States Code without ever having been unified. The task of unifying needs to be undertaken because, whatever their diversity, there is unity of purpose among these measures. They all aim at providing redress for an injury *lato sensu, i.e.*, any disruption whether particular or general in the social order caused by the violation of an international obligation by a foreign nation. The injury is indeed the key component of a law of remedies, since remedies make sense only when intended to correct, counteract or remove an evil or a wrong. The word "injury" is more satisfactory than "damage," because the breach of an international obligation does not always result in a monetary loss. This is particularly true when the breach concerns an obligation of a fundamental character such as the prohibition of genocide or, more generally, when it affects more than one state. The number of states affected by the violation is a crucial test for outlining international remedies because these remedies are not on the

[27] The concept of delegation is under United States constitutional law very narrowly construed, even in foreign affairs. For example, Art. II, § 2 of the Constitution authorizes the President to make treaties with the advice and consent of the Senate. But since no constitutional provision *explicitly* confers upon the President the power to terminate treaties, it has been wondered whether or not the President has such an authority. In *Goldwater et al. v. Carter*, [444 U.S. 996 (1979)] the Supreme Court was at pains to justify President Carter's notice of termination of the Mutual Defense Treaty of 1954 with the Republic of China (Taiwan). While the court of appeals sitting *en banc* upheld the President's power, the Supreme Court refused to give plenary consideration to the problem and cautiously remanded the case with directions to dismiss the complaint.

same footing when the breach affects one state, a group of states or the entire international community. Accordingly, the aim of the present study is to review the remedies provided by United States law for particular, collective and universal injuries, in order to attempt a general theory of unilateral remedies for international offenses.

1

Remedies for Particular Injuries

A breach of an international obligation that affects one state in particular entitles it to claim "reparation in an adequate form."[1] This concise formula was developed by the Permanent Court of International Justice in the *Chorzów Factory* Case (Merits) as meaning to "as far as possible, wipe out all the consequences of the illegal act and reestablish the situation which would, in all probability, have existed if that act had not been committed."[2] Therefore, reparation is the *restitutio in integrum* and necessarily entails the return to the *status quo ante*.[3]

It is commonly acknowledged that the return to the rightful previous conditions may be achieved by acting in the same way or doing the same thing as the offender, *i.e.* by applying the principle of reciprocity. Should reciprocity prove inadequate or unfeasible, the wronged party may, under certain circumstances, resort to nonreciprocal measures.

From a historical point of view, a survey of the United States international remedies shows that unlike reciprocity, which was the remedy of common law in the 19th century, the practice of nonreciprocity is a recent one. This legislative trend is significant since reciprocity is indeed the primitive remedy known as retaliation.

[1] *Chorzów Factory Case (Jurisdiction),* P.C.I.J., Ser. A/8, 21.
[2] *Chorzów Factory Case (Merits),* P.C.I.J., Ser. A/13, 47.
[3] For details, see E. Zoller, *Peacetime,* at 47-51; 63-70.

I. Reciprocity

Because of its close connection with equality, reciprocity has always been very appealing to the United States, whose earliest foreign policy objective was to be recognized as an equal partner by the European states. The United States has always displayed great concern for reciprocity, especially in trade matters.[4] This quest for reciprocity goes back to the middle of the nineteenth century when the United States paved the way for the so-called reciprocity agreements by signing a treaty with Great Britain on June 5, 1854, providing for mutual concessions in trade between the United States and Canada. The essence of the special treaties of reciprocity was that the equivalence given for the privileges secured was exceptional—the like of which no other state could offer.[5] As a result the favors extended by these treaties could not be enjoyed under the most-favored-nation clause. The most-favored-nation clause was made conditional.[6] In the period between the two world wars, the 1934 Reciprocal Trade Agreement Act, which was passed "for the purpose of extending foreign markets for the products of the United States,"[7] strongly emphasized reciprocity by recognizing, for the first time in the United States, the basic link between exports and imports and by making equality of treatment the cornerstone of the new policy.[8] The claim for equality of treatment derived directly from the strong United States opposition to the privileged trade relations which existed at the time between the European powers and their colonies. At the end of World War II, the United States, as the major victorious state among the Allied powers, was in a position to make its views prevail. It is scarcely surprising, therefore, that the

[4] Quincy Wright, *The Control of American Foreign Relations,* 301-303 (1922). See also the countervailing measures against official export bounties that the United States adopted at the beginning of the century in Jacob Viner, *Dumping: A Problem in International Trade* (Reed 1966), 163-191.

[5] See Joseph Rogers Herod, *Favored Nation Treatment, An Analysis of the Most Favored Nation Clause With Commentaries On Its Uses in Treaties of Commerce and Navigation* (1901), 113.

[6] Baron Boris Nolde, "Droit et technique des traités de commerce", 3 *R.C.A.D.I.* 295, 427 (1924, II).

[7] Statutes of the United States of America, 73d Congress, 2d Session, Part I, Washington 1934, p. 943.

[8] Henry J. Tasca, *The Reciprocal Trade Policy of the United States, A Study in Trade Philosophy* (1938), 40.

Havana Charter made the most-favored-nation treatment and equality of treatment the basic tenets of the proposed new world trade organization. Today, colonies have dwindled, but privileged treatment is still widely granted in world trade either by states to their own nationals or by one state or several states, to another state or group of states. For the past few years, Congress has been greatly concerned with the inequities of foreign trade restrictions imposed on United States competitors, notably by the European Economic Community and Japan. This concern has become stronger following the disillusionment with the GATT's ability to ensure "an overall balance of legal reciprocity."[9] As a result, numerous bills have been introduced in Congress to achieve reciprocity in foreign trade by amending the present unfair trade practices laws.[10] Protectionist pressure has culminated in the adoption of the 1984 Trade and Tariff Reform Act.[11] But reciprocity in foreign trade is only the tip of the iceberg. The United States claims reciprocity in international exchanges as a whole,[12] with the curious result that unlike its stance in

[9] R.E. Hudec, *The GATT Legal System and World Trade Diplomacy* (1975), 267.
[10] See William R. Cline [Ed.], *Trade Policy in the 1980s,* Institute for International Economics (1983), 796 pp.; Paul Dymock and Donna Vogt, "Protectionist Pressures in the U.S. Congress, A Review of the 97th Congress in 1982," 17 *J.W.T.L.* 496-512 (1983); R. Michael Gadbaw, "Reciprocity and Its Implications for U.S. Trade Policy," 14 *Law & Pol't. Int'l Bus.* 691-746 (1982); Keith A.J. Hay & B. Andrei Sulzenko, "U.S. Trade Policy and Reciprocity," 16 *J.W.T.L.* 471-479 (1982); *Reciprocity in Foreign Trade,* C.R.S., Archived Issue Brief No. IB82043, 08/17/83, 15 pp; Leonard Weiss, "Reciprocity," in Seymour J. Rubin & Thomas R. Graham [Ed.], *Managing Trade Relations in the 1980's* (1983), 165-231.
[11] Pub. L. 98-573; Oct. 30, 1984; 98 Stat. 2948.
[12] In aviation matters, for instance, President Ford approved on September 8, 1976, a statement of international air transportation policy recommended by the Economic Policy Board Task Force on International Air Transportation Policy. In bilateral international negotiations, the statement recommended as the primary objective the achievement of an international environment in which privately owned and operated U.S. air carriers have a fair and equal opportunity to compete for benefits at least as great as those available to foreign carriers. See *U.S. Digest 1976,* pp. 410-413. On the "fair and equal opportunity" clause embodied in the Bermuda Agreement, see Bin Cheng, *The Law of International Air Transport* (1962), 429-30.

In striving for "fairness" in international relations, the United States often overlooks the distinction between equality, reciprocity and nondiscrimination. This confusion is unfortunate because there can be no such thing as a nonspecific discrimination. In other words, an undiscriminated discrimination is not discriminatory in character. In that sense a recent international trade case relating to the Canadian licensing policy of U.S. motor carriers has shed some light on the relation that should exist between equality, reciprocity and discrimination. The U.S. Interstate Commerce Commission has concluded that reciprocity (hence equality) still exists between two countries when the same regulations are applicable to both foreigners and nationals, whether or not the regulations of one country are more restrictive than the regulations of the

domestic affairs, it is favoring equality over freedom in foreign affairs.

Reciprocity is indeed inseparable from equality and the importance of reciprocity in international law derives from the principle of equality between states. This principle directs that no state can be "more equal than others," for all states have the same rights and no state shall have an advantage over others or be entitled to claim rights which, under corresponding circumstances, it would not be bound to grant. Reciprocity is so closely connected with equality that, in the United States, the Supreme Court has often associated the two terms when dealing with the interpretation of treaties and has emphasized the need to carry out "the apparent intention of the parties to secure equality and reciprocity between them."[13] However, just as there is a formal and a substantive equality, so reciprocity, like Janus, has two faces, looking one to the future and the other to the past.

When facing the future, reciprocity may be said to be positive. It is merely a suspensive condition attached to a certain legal status. States may grant each other some rights, but generally under a condition of reciprocity; State A will grant certain privileges to the nationals of State B only if the nationals of State A are given the same privileges by State B. The particular treatment that each state gives the other is made conditional. United States statutes have laid down many provisions under which a specific legal status is granted to another state or its nationals upon condition of reciprocity. For instance, foreign fishing shall not be authorized in United States waters if the foreign nation does not grant substantially the same fishing privileges to United

other. It turns out that, as a matter of fact, the only foreigners concerned in that particular case were United States nationals and, therefore, as long as the comparison was made between two indivisible or undifferentiable categories, the Commission's determination made some sense. See Note, "International-Trade-Canada-United States Motor Carriers Reciprocity," 13 *G.J. Int'l & Comp. L.*, 857 (1983). However, whenever foreigners of several different countries are concerned, the appraisal of reciprocity within a single category, encompassing these foreigners and the nationals, remains debatable. This results from the fact that in order to maintain a distinction between an unequal and a discriminatory treatment, it is necessary to assert discrimination between comparable elements, unless nondiscrimination is to be viewed as the other face of equality.

[13] *Geoffroy v. Riggs*, 133 U.S. 258, 271 (1889); *Factor v. Laubenheimer*, 290 U.S. 276, 293 (1933). See also Jean Hostie, "Contribution de la Cour Suprême des Etats-Unis au développement du droit des gens," 69 *R.C.A.D.I*, 237, 274-9 (1939, II).

States fishing vessels;[14] or citizens of any foreign country shall not have the right to sue the United States in the United States Claims Court if United States citizens cannot institute proceedings against that country in its courts;[15] or amateur station licenses shall not be issued to aliens if there is no bilateral agreement between the United States and the alien's country for such operation on a reciprocal basis for United States amateur radio operators.[16]

Facing the past, reciprocity may be said to be negative. Here lies retaliation, the only form of reciprocity that we are concerned with. Negative reciprocity is a device to respond to an internationally wrongful act by an act of the same kind. As such, reciprocity has been embodied in the primitive archaic codes such as the Code of Hammurabi or the Twelve Tables. Remnants of it are found in the Bible (Exodus 21:22)[17] and in the Koran (xx, 2, 175).[18]

Negative reciprocity may be carried out in two different manners. The simplest is reciprocity by identity or by similarity, which consists in acting the same way as another party. Reciprocity by identity implies exactly the same conditions, whereas reciprocity by similarity allows slightly adjusted conditions since it is goverend by the rule of *ejusdem generis*. This first form of reciprocity ensures a symmetry of conditions between the parties; the conditions are the same for both. However, this form of reciprocity is conceivable only when the parties are bound by

[14] Section 201(f) of the Fishery Conservation and Management Act of 1976 (90 Stat. 338) codified at 16 U.S.C. § 1821(f) (1982).

[15] Title 28, United States Code, Section 2502 (62 Stat. 976) as amended by P.L. 97-164 (96 Stat. 92) codified at 28 U.S.C. § 2502(a) (1982).

[16] Section 310 of the Communications Act of 1934, as amended by Sec. 2(c) of P.L. 93-505 (88 Stat. 1576) codified at 47 U.S.C. § 310(d) (1982).

[17] This deals with the case of a miscarriage caused by struggling men. It provides that if "no mischief follow," the punishment shall be at the discretion of the pregnant woman's husband. But "if any mischief follow, then *thou* shalt give life for life, eye for eye, tooth for tooth, burning for burning, wound for wound, stripe for stripe." On the debate raised by an apparently misplaced clause, see Seagle, *supra,* Introduction, n.17, at 121, 389.

[18] The Koran provides: "O ye who believe! Retaliation is prescribed for you in the matter of murdered; the freeman for the freeman and the slave for the slave, and the female for the female. And for him who is forgiven somewhat by his (injured) brother, prosecution according to usage and payment unto him in kindness. This an alleviation and a mercy from your Lord. He who transgresseth after this will have a painful doom." See Mian Rashid Ahmad Khan, *Islamic Jurisprudence* (n.d.), 238.

the same obligation. Whenever the parties are not bound by identical or symmetrical obligations, negative reciprocity can be implemented only through a mechanism of equivalence. The aggrieved party, unable to stop performing the same obligation, may refuse to fulfill a *quid pro quo* obligation of equal value or equal meaning. This form of reciprocity by equivalence is generally to be found in the municipal legal orders under the *Exceptio Non Adimpleti Contractus*.

Both forms of negative reciprocity can be found in the laws of the United States. But the statutes that provide for reciprocity by identity or by similarity are far more numerous than the laws that organize reciprocity by equivalence.

1. Reciprocity by Identity or by Similarity

Reciprocity by identity or by similarity seems to be historically the very first form of action taken by Congress to respond to internationally wrongful acts of foreign countries. This took place at the end of the last century and in what were then the two most frequent fields of international intercourse: shipping and fishing. Section 17 of the 1886 Shipping Act still in force provided that, should United States vessels be discriminated against in the ports of any foreign country, vessels of that foreign country in the ports of the United States would also be discriminated against, since all the commercial privileges that had been granted to them would be withdrawn.[19] In 1887, an act was passed to protect the rights of United States vessels in British North American waters. It provided that if American fishing vessels were denied their treaty rights, vessels of the British Dominions of North America would also be denied the same treaty rights. Their entrance into United States waters would be forbidden and, in addition, the President could prohibit the importation of fresh fish or salted fish or any other Dominion product.[20] In some ways, these statutes stand for a legal expression of the ''Big Stick'' policy. However, they remained isolated cases.

During the First World War, when Congress endeavored to

[19] 46 U.S.C. § 142 (1982).
[20] 46 U.S.C. § 143 (1982).

respond to unfair trade practices from foreign countries, a more refined content was given to the principle of reciprocity. An act of September 8, 1916, attempted to meet foreign prohibitions of United States products with import prohibitions of "similar articles," reserving the possibility to reach other products only when the United States did not import similar articles.[21] This act stands for the first step made toward substantially equalizing redress; i.e. compensatory remedies. Since then the same trend has been followed. All United States reciprocal steps against internationally wrongful acts have sought the reestablishment of equality and ruled out the measure in excess. In other words, a class of genuine reciprocal actions has emerged from retaliation.[22]

In 1966, the Foreign Investors Tax Act added to the Internal Revenue Code two amendments which were aimed at preventing foreign imposition of more burdensome or discriminatory taxes on United States citizens or domestic corporations.[23] In both cases, the foreign imposition is to be countered by equalizing reciprocity. The foreign taxes are matched by identical action insofar as similar foreign income within the United States is taxed without regard to the common law taxation applied to nonresident aliens and foreign corporations.[24] For such foreign taxes, the law is even more equalizing than in the case of discrimination, for United States taxation on foreign income is adjusted so as to bring the taxation rate substantially in line with that of the foreign country.[25]

A similar concern for the mere reestablishment of equality with the offender is also to be found in the action contemplated to counter excessive or discriminatory foreign charges on United States air carriers by equal compensating charges.[26] Similarly, foreign noncompetitive financing amounting to predatory prac-

[21] 15 U.S.C. § 75 (1982); see also 15 U.S.C. § 76 (1982).

[22] There is little doubt that the severability of retaliation and reciprocity was not immediate. Still in 1930, Section 350 of the Tariff Act responded to foreign import restrictions with modifications of existing duties that could be applied to "any article covered by foreign trade agreements" codified at 19 U.S.C. § 1351(a) (1) (B) (1982).

[23] See S. Rep. No. 1707, 89th Congress, 2nd Sess. (1966); [1966] *U.S. Code Cong. & Adm. News*, Vol. 3 (1966), at 4449, 4486-8.

[24] 26 U.S.C. § 896(a) (1982).

[25] 26 U.S.C. § 896(b) (1982).

[26] 49 App. U.S.C. § 1159a (1982).

tices is countered by equivalent financial arrangements that Eximbank may be authorized to grant competing United States sellers.[27] However, in 1979, in an apparently isolated case, Congress still resorted to retaliatory reciprocity in threatening restrictions on travel by foreigners within the United States when U.S. citizens are faced with similar restrictions in the foreigners' countries.[28]

Gradually, while the content of reciprocity has been reduced to a search for equality, reciprocal measures have been subject to preliminary procedural steps. This trend is significant insofar as customary international law regards negative reciprocity as a right of immediate action. It is not subject to preliminary procedures since the mere existence of the wrongful act gives the aggrieved party the right to react at once in kind.

All pre-World War II statutes have followed this pattern. For instance, the retaliatory suspension of commercial privileges to United States vessels is not subject to any preliminary procedure. The President may retaliate as soon as he is satisfied of the continuance of such discrmination.[29] Such is also the case with retaliation against any foreign country which prohibits the import of any United States article not injurious to health or morals. Retaliation can be immediate.[30]

However, since 1945 most of the relevant statutes have made United States reciprocal actions subject to preliminary procedural steps. Before taking such action, the government has to "request" the foreign country, for instance, to revise its taxes;[31] or to eliminate such rate of tax;[32] or to withdraw the noncompetitive financing.[33] Similarly, in the case of unreasonable charges imposed on United States carriers, the government shall promptly undertake negotiations with the foreign country before contem-

[27] 12 U.S.C. § 635a-3 (1982). See additional views of Hon. Mark W. Hannoford in H. Rep. No. 95-1115, at 27, 95th Congress, 2nd Sess. (1978); [1978] *U.S. Code Cong. & Adm. News*, Vol. 7 (1978), at 9399-9400.

[28] 22 U.S.C. § 2691 note (1982).

[29] 49 U.S.C. § 142 (1982).

[30] 15 U.S.C. § 75 (1982).

[31] 26 U.S.C. § 896(a) (1982).

[32] 26 U.S.C. § 896(b) (1982).

[33] 12 U.S.C. § 635a-3 (1982).

plating reciprocal action.[34] Once such steps have been taken, the government cannot act immediately. The foreign country must have a chance to mend its ways. Action can be taken only if the preliminary steps have failed to provide a solution within a reasonable period;[35] or if there is no immmediate response to the request.[36] These provisions have extended to reciprocal measures which are, theoretically, free from any preliminary procedures, something specific to reprisals; namely: "la représaille n'est licite que lorsqu' elle a été précédée d'une *sommation* restée infructueuse."[37] In other words, the foreign country must be informed of the reciprocal action contemplated by the aggrieved party. Moreover, even where immediate reciprocal action is still authorized, the government has to seek an agreement with the foreign country to eliminate the subject of the dispute.[38]

These diplomatic steps have to be seen in relation to the obligation to negotiate, which "merely constitutes a special obligation of a principle which underlies all international relations, and which is moreover recognized in Article 33 of the Charter of the United Nations as one of the methods for the peaceful settlement of international disputes."[39]

As to their adequacy, these remedies certainly fit their primary purpose, which is "to restore in a negative way the symmetry of the initial positions."[40] Conditions are made equal between the parties. The restored equality is to last as long as the original equality is in abeyance, *i.e.* as long as the foreign country does not mend its ways. It lasts exactly as long as the unlawful action.

This feature appeared as early as the end of the nineteenth century. Retaliation against a denial of commercial privileges to United States vessels is merely a suspension of similar privileges accorded to foreign vessels;[41] or retaliation against a foreign

[34] 49 App. § 1159a (1982).
[35] *Ibid.*
[36] 12 U.S.C. § 635a-3 (1982).
[37] *Naulilaa Incident,* Arbitral Award of July 31, 1928, 2 *U.N.R.I.A.A.*, 1027 (italics in the text).
[38] 22 U.S.C. § 2691 note (1982).
[39] *North Sea Continental Shelf* Case, I.C.J. *Reports* 1969, p. 47, para. 86.
[40] *Air Service Agreement (France/United States),* Arbitral Award of Dec. 9, 1978, 18 *U.N.R.I.A.A.* 445, § 90.
[41] 46 U.S.C. § 142 (1982).

prohibition of United States imports is set to last for as long as such prohibition is in force.[42] Contemporary statutes have in some ways improved the concordance between the reciprocal action and the foreign behavior. For instance, the adjustment of tax on foreigners has to be lifted in case of an alleviation of more burdensome or discriminatory taxes by the foreign country;[43] or Eximbank will provide matching noncompetitive financing only if the foreign country keeps doing the same thing;[44] or compensating charges will continue to be imposed on foreign air carriers unless the foreign state reduces its similar charges.[45]

To be sure, the equality restored by these measures is merely formal in character. It is to some extent an equality before the law; it is not a substantive equality. In other words, despite their compensatory purpose, few of the measures reestablish equivalence between the parties. This derives from the fact that reciprocal measures are fitted to identical or similar obligations which may not have the same substantive bearing on each party. As a result, these measures do not necessarily entail full reparation, *i.e.* the *restitutio in integrum* which any breach of law should theoretically direct. Reciprocal action is somewhat blind. The first reciprocal actions provided for by United States statutes give ample evidence of this fact. For instance, the President may contemplate retaliatory suspension of previously granted commercial privileges to foreign vessels on the sole basis of the denial to United States vessels of similar privileges by that foreign country, irrespective of the number of United States vessels affected or of the economic importance for the United States of maritime shipping with the other party.[46] Similarly, a ban on the importation into the United States of any articles similar to United States articles affected by an import ban in a foreign country is resorted to without taking into consideration the economic impact of the foreign ban on the industry of the United States.[47] Still

[42] 15 U.S.C. § 75 (1982).
[43] 26 U.S.C. § 896(c) (1982).
[44] 12 U.S.C. § 635a-3 (1982).
[45] 49 App. U.S.C. § 1159a (1982).
[46] 46 U.S.C. § 142 (1982).
[47] 15 U.S.C. § 75 (1982).

today, in more recent laws, the tax adjustment on foreigners, for instance, is decided without regard to the number of United States citizens or corporations in the foreign country and the number of nationals of that country within the United States.[48] If the two are out of proportion, equivalence is not restored between the parties.

Interestingly enough, Section 11 of the 1974 International Air Transportation Fair Competitive Practices Act endeavors to restore substantive equality by providing that the charges imposed on foreign air carriers will accrue to an account from which payments will be made to United States air carriers to compensate for charges paid by them to the foreign countries involved.[49] This provision can be viewed as an attempt to reestablish equivalence between the parties. However its efficiency still hinges on the number of air carriers involved on each side.

The inadequacy of these measures for compensatory purposes does not make them ineffective in other respects. Insofar as they are seldom applied,[50] they certainly act as a deterrent. They serve as threats or warnings against foreign nations. By contrast, when reciprocity is implemented through a mechanism of equivalence, things apparently run the other way. Reciprocity by equivalence does not necessarily deter wrongful acts of foreign nations, but does provide for true compensation.

2. Reciprocity by Equivalence

There is only one provision for reciprocity by equivalence in the entire United States Code. It is to be found in Section 125(d) of the 1974 Trade Act. This subsection expressly gives the Pres-

[48] 26 U.S.C. § 896(b) (1982).

[49] 49 App. U.S.C. § 1159a (1982).

[50] An exception however is to be found in foreign noncompetitive financing. For instance, on November 15, 1984, Eximbank announced that it was offering a U.S. telecommunications equipment supplier very low financing rates to compete against a French mixed credit offer for a project in Cyprus. The Eximbank loan to TIW Systems Inc. of Sunnyvale, California will cover 100 percent of the U.S. export contract with an interest rate of 4.957 percent and a repayment term of 10 years (1 I.T.R. 651, Nov. 28, 1984). In October 1984, Eximbank and the Agency for International Development announced their first mixed credit to offset a similar deal offered by Canada (1 I.T.R. 531, Oct. 31, 1984).

ident a "retaliatory authority,"[51] incidentally a wording which is not used in Section 301 of the same act.[52] Unlike Section 301, which does not refer to retaliation and which has never but once[53] given rise to positive action, Section 125, which expressly refers to retaliation, has in fact been applied on several occasions.[54] To that extent, it can be said that the true retaliation in trade matters is embodied in Section 125 and not in Section 301.

Section 125(d) (1) of the Trade Act of 1974 authorizes the President to withdraw, suspend, or modify the application of trade agreement obligations substantially equivalent to those which have been withdrawn, suspended, or modified by a foreign country, and to proclaim under Section 125(c) of the Trade Act such import restrictions as are appropriate to effect adequate compensation from that foreign country. No doubt the particular terminology of "substantially equivalent trade agreement obligations" as referred to in this section is directly taken from Article XXVIII of the General Agreement on Tariffs and Trade. Article XXVIII on modification of schedules is aimed at maintaining "a general level of reciprocal and mutually advantageous concessions" between the parties. The article provides in substance that whenever a contracting party proposes to modify or withdraw a trade concession initially negotiated, the aggrieved party is free to reciprocate by equivalence within six months, *i.e.* to modify or withdraw substantially equivalent concessions.

The legislative history of Section 125(d) shows that it was

[51] 19 U.S.C. § 2135(d) (1982). This specific wording makes sense insofar as, *stricto sensu*, retaliation is indeed always a form of reciprocal action. The word comes from the Latin *talis:* alike, of the same kind. The Oxford English Dictionary defines retaliation as "a punishment or a penalty similar to the injury done" while, similarly, Webster defines "to retaliate" as "to return like for like."

[52] 19 U.S.C. § 2411 (1982). The difference is in every respect justified since Section 301 makes reciprocal as well as nonreciprocal actions possible. However the distinction is in practice scarcely made by legal scholars who curiously see retaliation as only implied by Section 301. See *e.g.* Robert E. Hudec, Retaliation Against "Unreasonable" Foreign Trade Practices: The New Section 301 and GATT Nullification and Impairment," 59 *Minn. L. Rev.*, 461-539 (1975) or John H. Jackson, *Legal Problems of International Economic Relations* (1977), who does not include Section 125 of the Trade Act in the subject heading "Retaliation in Trade Policy: Focus on United States Law" (Section 12.4, at 832-847).

[53] See *infra*, Chap. 4, p. 140.

[54] Between 1980 and 1984, see *e.g.* 45 F.R. 62409 (1980), 45 F.R. 84188 (1980); 46 F.R. 1249 (1981); 46 F.R. 5851 (1981); 46 F.R. 46857 (1981); 46 F.R. 51707 (1981); 47 F.R. 49625 (1982); 47 F.R. 49005 (1982); 47 F.R. 52258 (1982).

adopted to ensure that the President would "obtain adequate and equivalent compensation when a foreign country withdraws trade agreement obligations of benefit to the United States. Such compensation could be offered by the foreign country itself or could be obtained through unilateral action by the United States."[55] To be sure, the novelty of the provision is indisputable with respect to the former retaliatory authority under Section 252(b) (c) of the 1962 Trade Expansion Act.[56] Section 252 did not provide for the reestablishment of equivalence between the offender and the United States. The retaliatory authority was not limited in nature, for it could reach any products of the foreign country, regardless of their similarity to the products involved by the concession concerned, nor was it limited in intensity since it was not merely compensatory in purpose. In practice, it proved impossible to resort to this sweeping authority, for the United States was at that time bound by the provisions of the GATT, and especially by the obligation to seek compensation within the limits of equivalence as set forth by Article XXVIII. That is why in the "Chicken War," the United States could retaliate against the EEC only by withdrawing substantially equivalent concessions.[57] As a result, the former retaliatory authority set forth in Section 252 of the Trade Expansion Act has actually been split into two different sections of the Trade Act: Section 125(d) which provides for reciprocity by equivalence and Section 301 which covers reciprocity by identity or by similarity, as well as nonreciprocal action.[58]

Reciprocity by equivalence gives substance in international law to the *Exceptio Non Adimpleti Contractus,* which is widely recognized in every municipal legal order as a general principle of the law of contracts. But just as the *Exceptio* is limited in domestic law to a contract, reciprocity by equivalence can apply

[55] S. Rep. No. 93-1298, 93rd Congress, 2nd sess. (1974); [1974] *U.S. Code Cong. and Adm. News,* Vol. 4 (1974) at 7242.

[56] Pub. L. 87-794, Oct. 11, 1962, 76 Stat. 872, 879. Section 252 was repealed by Section 602(d) of Pub. L. 93-618, January 3, 1975, 88 Stat. 2072.

[57] Proclamation 3564 was enacted, "having due regard for the international obligations of the United States, particularly paragraph 3 of Article XXVIII of the General Agreement on Tariffs and Trade," 77 Stat. 1035.

[58] See *infra,* Chap. 1, p. 42.

in international law only to a treaty. The bilateral or multilateral character of such a treaty is irrelevant as to the right of action, but it has some significance with respect to the scope of the action that may be resorted to by the aggrieved party. This may be illustrated by several examples from multilateral and bilateral trade agreements.

Whenever the treaty is multilateral in character and covers a wide variety of products, the aggrieved party may take measures against other products than those affected. That is precisely what the United States did when it increased tariffs on brandy, potato starch, dextrine and modified starches, and trucks valued at $1,000 or more,[59] although the dispute between the United States and the EEC concerned frozen poultry. In that respect, it is doubtful that in the "Cattle War"—a dispute between the United States and Canada which took place within the scope of the GATT—the United States was under an obligation to restrict its action to Canadian meat exports (cattle, beef, veal, swine and pork),[60] following Canadian import quotas on beef and cattle. However, the United States action made some sense for compensatory purposes because of the existence of two-way trade in the North American cattle market.[61]

By contrast, whenever the breach of equality takes place within a bilateral trade agreement of limited scope, the aggrieved party may seek the reestablishment of equivalence only by taking action against the products covered by the agreement. Such was the case, for instance, when the United States increased from one percent to five percent its duty on bovine leather following Argentina's failure to phase out its tax on cattle hides[62] as it agreed to do in the bilateral agreement concerning hide exports and other trade matters;[63] or when the United States suspended its tariff concessions on litharge and red lead as a way to reestablish equivalence with Mexico, which had failed to abide by a bilateral trade agreement on certain lead products.[64]

[59] 28 F.R. 8066 (1963).
[60] 39 F.R. 36518 (1974); 39 F.R. 40741 (1974).
[61] See Hudec, *supra* n.52, at 536 (n.201).
[62] Compare 46 F.R. 51707 (1981) and 47 F.R. 49625 (1982).
[63] T.I.A.S. 9976.
[64] 46 F.R. 5851 (1981).

Reciprocity by equivalence is therefore very different from reciprocity in kind. Unlike reciprocity by identity or similarity, reciprocity by equivalence allows an aggrieved party to seek compensation on *different* items from those originally under dispute. The best example in that respect is the Chicken War.[65] But it is not certain that the United States has always rightly exploited the possibilities under Section 125(d) especially with respect to the differences between identity and equivalence. In that sense, two particular applications of Section 125 shed some light on the distinction between compensation and retaliation. The President specifically invoked Section 125(d) of the Trade Act in Proclamation 4793 of September 17, 1980.[66] By that proclamation, the President threatened to increase the tariffs on a number of textile products from the European Community in response to the EEC announcement of quotas on certain textile articles imported into the United Kingdom. Like the Community, the President remained within the field of textile articles. Should the Community impose quotas on polyester filament yarn and polyamide (nylon) carpet yarn, the United States would increase the rate of duty for yarns of man-made fibers and for certain woolen coats, jackets and knitwears. It so happens that these last products are made primarily in the United Kingdom. Therefore, a search for equivalence may not in practice be completely devoid of retaliatory character, whereas in theory equivalence and retaliation are mutually exclusive. Another disputable application of Section 125 is to be found in Proclamation 4991 of October 27, 1982, which suspended the most-favored-nation treatment for Polish products.[67] Such an action was taken *inter alia* because Poland failed to meet certain import requirements under its Protocol of Accession to the General Agreement on Tariffs and Trade. The protocol governing Poland's accession to the GATT provided for a given annual increase in Polish imports from Western countries, which the United States claimed was not being complied with. Whether

[65] See H. Walker, "Dispute Settlement: The Chicken War," 58 *A.J.L.L.* 671-685 (1964); Andreas F. Lowenfeld, " 'Doing Unto Others. . . .'—The Chicken War Ten Years After," 4 *J. Mar. L.C.*, 599-617 (1973).

[66] 45 F.R. 62409 (1980).

[67] 47 F.R. 49005 (1982).

United States action reestablished equivalence with Poland is certainly debatable, especially with respect to its unlimited scope. But the most controversial aspect is to be found in its duration, for the measure was still in force in April 1985, whereas in 1983 Poland increased its imports from Western nations by 9.8 percent, and the figures for 1984 show the final increase to be a further 10 percent.[68] Here again the search for equivalence is tainted with retaliatory concern. A legal remedy has in some ways been turned into a political instrument.

With respect to procedures, Section 125 is in complete contrast to reciprocity by identity or by similarity. The reestablishment of equivalence is a right of immediate action, which is not subject to any preliminary diplomatic steps. Article XXVIII of the GATT actually provides only for a period of six months, during which the aggrieved party must reciprocate if it so desires. But the absence of international procedures is in some ways counterbalanced by domestic procedural requirements.

On the one hand, any action taken under Section 125 must be preceded by a public hearing, during the course of which interested persons shall be given a reasonable opportunity to be present, to produce evidence and to be heard.[69] The hearing process is governed by regulations of the Trade Policy Staff Committee.[70] Written and rebuttal briefs may be submitted pursuant to a public notice of public hearing published in the Federal Register. Oral testimonies may also be presented by any interested parties. These procedural safeguards are primarily aimed at safeguarding the rights of United States nationals. Although nothing in the text itself or in the Trade Act seems to preclude their availability to the nationals of the foreign state concerned, these persons are usually defended by their own government. In the Cattle War, for instance, the view of the United States cattle producers was presented in the hearings conducted by the Trade Information Committee,[71] while the Canadian view was put forward in a press

[68] See 1 I.T.R. 587, Nov. 14, 1984.
[69] 19 U.S.C. § 2135(f) (1982). In case of a need for expeditious action, the President may immediately reciprocate; but a public hearing must take place promptly after such action.
[70] Codified at 15 C.F.R. § 2003 (1984).
[71] Office of the Special Representative for Trade Negotiations, Docket No. 741-1 (Oct. 25, 1974).

release of October 25, 1974, issued by the Canadian Department of External Affairs.

On the other hand, any executive determination taken under Section 125 may be challenged in United States courts. In *United States v. Star Industries, Inc.* (1972), the Court of Customs and Patent Appeals challenged Presidential Proclamation 3564, which effected compensatory withdrawal of previously proclaimed tariff concessions as a response to EEC import duties on poultry.[72]

The technique of reciprocity by equivalence is the perfect adequate remedy for compensatory purposes. Unlike reciprocity by identity or by similarity, it provides the aggrieved party with a substitute for what that party has lost or suffered.

The problem, however, is that the availability of such a remedy appears restricted to the possibility of evaluating the missing equivalent, *i.e.* the *quid pro quo*. In other words, the major problem raised by reciprocity by equivalence is to be found in the measurement of the injury sustained by the aggrieved party. In the Chicken War, the United States originally valued its claims at $46 million, whereas the panel appointed by the GATT valued United States poultry exports at $26 million (c.i.f.).[73] When the losses are not estimated by an impartial panel, the wronged party must act on its own. In that respect the above-mentioned domestic procedures give the importer of the products affected by the reciprocal move an opportunity to challenge disproportionate and exaggerated evaluations. To some extent, the procedural requirement of a public debate is an indirect safeguard. However, generally speaking it is difficult to assess the loss suffered by the withdrawal or the alteration of a trade concession. To what extent, for instance, should the elasticity of demand or the possibility of substitution be taken into account?[74] In any event,

[72] 462 F.2d 557 (1972); see also 320 F. Supp. 1018 (1970) and L. Thomas Galloway, "*Star Industries, Inc. v. United States:* Sequel to the Chicken War," 6 *Int'l. Law.*, 48-63 (1972). Whenever equivalence is reestablished with a particular defaulting party by the temporary non-performance of a trade concession, such a reciprocal move need not to be taken on a most-favored-nation basis, See E. Zoller, *Peacetime*, at 25-26.

[73] See Walker, *supra* n.65, at 678-9.

[74] See Lowenfeld, *supra* n.65, at 602 (n.12).

reciprocity by equivalence is a more adequate remedy for compensatory purposes than reciprocity by identity or by similarity.

Whatever its form, reciprocity is only compensatory. Like reciprocity by identity, reciprocity by equivalence provides for a compensation that has to last as long as the offending party does not mend its ways.[75] On December 11, 1979, as a result of the reciprocal concessions obtained at Geneva (1979), Presidential Proclamation 4707 alleviated some of the measures taken during the Chicken War, but "following unsatisfactory negotiation with the European Economic Community" with respect to imports of poultry from the United States, the suspension of tariff concessions on automobile trucks valued at $1,000 or more was maintained.[76] In short, even when implemented through a mechanism of equivalence, reciprocal actions do not always succeed in making the foreign state revert to the *status quo ante*. Therefore one may wonder whether in certain circumstances the aggrieved party may take steps going beyond reciprocity.

II. Nonreciprocal Actions

Although reciprocity is said to be "the norm" in international law,[77] the United States statutory provisions that address reciprocity are a small minority compared to those calling for nonreciprocal action. This is hardly surprising, since reciprocity is seldom adequate. First, it is not always efficient; it does not necessarily reestablish the *status quo ante*. It "freezes" rather than "thaws" the behavior of the offending state. As long as the harm inflicted on it does not become unbearable, the foreign state has no incentive to revert to a law-abiding attitude. Secondly, reciprocity is not always possible either because the obligations are not symmetrical in character, or because the condition of reciprocity is not attached to the nonfulfilled obli-

[75] For the temporary duration of any retaliatory action taken in pursuance of Section 125(d) of the Trade Act, see Section 125(b) and 604 of the same act codified at 19 U.S.C. § 2135(b) (1982) and 19 U.S.C. § 2483 (1982).

[76] 44 F.R. 72348 (1979), as amended by Exec. Ord. No. 12204, Mar. 27, 1980, 45 F.R. 20704 (1980). See also *U.S. Digest* 1976, p. 469.

[77] See Stephen M. Schwebel, "The Compliance Process and the Future of International Law," 75 *A.S.I.L. Proceedings*, 178, 181 (1981).

gation, such as an obligation related to the protection of human rights.[78]

Any move beyond reciprocity may have two different purposes. On the one hand, it may be a means of obtaining, beyond reciprocity, the compensation that reciprocal action does not necessarily achieve. On the other hand, it may be a means of obtaining more than compensation. In other words, nonreciprocal actions may seek the *restitutio in integrum* and the return to the *status quo ante*. The striking feature of all United States nonreciprocal actions is that they seldom seek compensation alone. All of them aim at *restitutio in integrum*.[79] This derives from the fact that they are never tailored to the injury actually sustained. For instance, the Hickenlooper Amendment provides for the suspension of all financial aid to a foreign country which nationalizes United States property without compensation,[80] and not for the suspension of an amount equal to the losses suffered; or the Trading With the Enemy Act, superseded today in peacetime by the International Emergency Economic Powers Act, authorizes the freeze of all the foreign assets within the country,[81] and not merely what would be needed to compensate the injury actually sustained by the United States; or in the case of a foreign state's action inconsistent with a trade agreement, Section 301 of the Trade Act does not limit the presidential authority to compen-

[78] For instance, an unjust imprisonment of a United States citizen abroad cannot be compensated by reciprocal action. The President is authorized only to demand the release of such citizen, and if the release is unreasonably delayed or refused, he "shall use such means, not amounting to acts of war, as he may think necessary and proper to obtain or effectuate the release." 22 U.S.C. § 1732 (1982).

[79] The only possible exception to this general statement is to be found in the provisions of the Fishermen's Protective Act [22 U.S.C. § § 1971-1975 (1982)], which compensate United States vessels for losses arising out of certain seizures in foreign waters. In particular, the Secretary of State is authorized in certain circumstances to withdraw from the funds appropriated for assistance to a foreign country an amount equal to the claims that remain unpaid by such country. However the inclusion of these provisions within our analysis is disputable insofar as the foreign "seizures" are not internationally wrongful acts, especially since the United States has created its own exclusive economic zone. It must be borne in mind that these provisions were enacted to counter the policy of certain Latin American countries that claimed jurisdiction over fishing in territorial waters or fishery zones in excess of the 12 miles recognized by the United States at that time as the maximum for fishery zones. See Theodor Meron, "The Fishermen's Protective Act: A Case Study in Contemporary Legal Strategy of the United States," 69 *A.J.I.L.*, 290-309 (1975) and Richard B. Lillich, "Requiem for Hickenlooper," 69 *A.J.I.L.*, 97, n. 17 (1975).

[80] 22 U.S.C. § 2370(e) (1) (1982).

[81] 50 U.S.C. § § 1701-1702 (Suppl. V, 1981).

sation, but authorizes him to take all appropriate and feasible action within his power.[82]

However, if all these provisions are devices to obtain the *restitutio in integrum,* they do not, except for one, effectuate by themselves the return to the *status quo ante*. This is because they are temporary in duration; they are to last as long as the foreign state has not reverted to a law-abiding conduct. For instance, assistance is generally only suspended;[83] or foreign assets are frozen and not vested;[84] or foreign air carrier permits are only suspended.[85] To some extent, they pave the way to *restitutio in integrum,* and they are lifted if such a result is attained; they coerce the foreign state to revert to law compliance. In short, they are actions for performance. By contrast, in the only case when the nonreciprocal action leads to a final solution, that action is a genuine action for restitution.

1. Action for Restitution

Insofar as the Trading With the Enemy Act of 1917 has never in peacetime given rise to a final seizure of foreign property or funds, this statute has obviously never been considered as a restitutionary remedy in peacetime.[86] The sole genuine restitu-

[82] 19 U.S.C. § 2411(a) (1982).

[83] See, for example, 22 U.S.C. § § 2370(a) (1), 2370(c), 2370(e) (1), 2370(j), 2370(o), 2370(q) (1982).

[84] 50 U.S.C. § 1702 (Suppl. V, 1981).

[85] 49 App. U.S.C. § 1372(f) (1982).

[86] Before the enactment of the 1977 International Emergency Economic Powers Act [91 Stat. 1625, codified at 50 U.S.C. § § 1701-1706 (Suppl. V, 1981)] and under the authority of Section 5(b) of the 1917 Trading With the Enemy Act (50 App. U.S.C. § 5(b) (1976) and Suppl. V 1981), the President was authorized "during the time of war or during any other period of national emergency" to issue regulations which could provide, *e.g.*, the power to vest foreign property. As a consequence of the 1977 reform, this power now applies only "during the time of war" [50 App. U.S.C. § 5(b) (1) (Suppl. V, 1981)], without specific reference to "declared or nondeclared" war, an omission which has some significance since most of the wars fought by the United States since World War II, in particular the Vietnam War, were never declared.

There is no doubt that in wartime, enemy property may be vested and not merely blocked because war always entails the right of the victorious state to claim reparation for the losses sustained. See *Propper v. Clark* (337 U.S. 472, 484); *United States v. Chemical Foundation* (272 U.S. 1, 11); *Silesian-American Corp. v. Clark* (332 U.S. 469, 476). In *Clark v. Ubersee Finan. Corp.* (332 U.S. 480), the Supreme Court held that the 1941 Amendment to the Trading With the Enemy Act (First War Powers Act of 1941, 55 Stat. 839) authorized the Alien Property Custodian to seize and vest in himself all property of any foreign country or national, even that of friendly or neutral nations. However, at the same time, the Supreme Court refused to hold that the 1941 amendment deprived friendly or neutral nations or nationals of the right to have

tionary remedy to be found in peacetime derives from the Foreign Sovereign Immunities Act of 1977.[87] Whenever property rights are the subject of a violation of international law in the foreign state, the property of that state in the United States may under certain circumstances, be subject to attachment or execution.[88]

As international remedies, dispensations from granting sovereign immunity to foreign states for acts *jure imperii*[89] within their territories have completely different meanings according to whether they apply to jurisdiction or to execution. Whenever a plaintiff succeeds in obtaining a court's ruling on the validity of an act *jure imperii* by a foreign state, that person has merely in his hands a declaratory judgment if the judgment cannot be enforced. Therefore, a provision such as the Sabbatino Amendment, which bars United States courts from applying the act of state doctrine to defeat a claim based upon confiscation in violation of international law,[90] cannot be viewed as a restitutionary remedy if restitution cannot be obtained because the property of the foreign state is completely immune. By contrast, there is a true restitutionary remedy whenever a court can allow execution against the property of a foreign state; *i.e.*, whenever a court may restore the victim to the situation which would have existed

their assets returned if they could prove that they were free of any open or concealed enemy taint. The Supreme Court went on to find that the purpose of the amendment was "*not to appropriate friendly or neutral assets*" (at 485, emphasis added). As a result there is indeed a difference in the treatment of foreign property between enemy and friendly or neutral nations. In *Kaufman et al. v. Société Internationale pour participations industrielles et commerciales S.A. et al.* (343 U.S. 156) the Supreme Court was even more specific: "While Congress has clearly provided for forfeiture of enemy assets, it has used no language requiring us to hold that innocent interests must be confiscated . . . nor does any legislative history pointed out persuade us that Congress intended to inflict such harsh consequences upon the innocent" (at 159).

[87] Pub. L. 94-583, Oct. 21, 1976, 90 Stat. 2892.

[88] 28 U.S.C. § 1610(a) (3) (1982).

[89] The restrictive theory of sovereign immunity as applied to acts *jure gestionis* is not within our concern because the intention is not to provide a remedy for an internationally wrongful act. This theory essentially consists in not granting immunity to foreign states when they engage in commercial activities and business. Its codification has been one of the central goals of the Foreign Sovereign Immunities Act. This theory, which has become nowadays a rule of customary international law, was actually already embodied in the *Schooner Exchange v. McFadden & Others* (1812) when Chief Justice Marshall declared: "Should a sovereign *enter* the territory of another without the consent of that other, expressed or implied, it would present a question which does not appear to be perfectly settled. . . . If he did not thereby expose himself to the territorial jurisdiction of the sovereign, whose dominions he had *entered*, it would seem to be because all sovereign impliedly engage not to avail themselves of a power of their equal, which a romantic confidence in their magnanimity has placed in their hands." (11 U.S. (7 Cranch) 116, 138; emphasis added).

[90] 22 U.S.C. § 2370(e) (2) (1982).

if the unlawful act had not been committed. The *restitutio in integrum* may be accorded either in kind or, when such a result is not attainable, by equivalence. For instance, in case of expropriation, restitution in kind theoretically authorizes the court to order the transfer to the victim of the unlawfully seized property whenever that property or the products thereof are within its territorial jurisdiction. Should such a possibility be unfeasible, restitution by equivalence would direct a substitutionary, monetary restitution which could be obtained with the seizure of foreign government property and could theoretically involve compensatory damages based upon the losses of the plaintiff and an amount (restitution *stricto sensu*) based upon the gains of the nationalizing state.

The final character of such actions makes them different in substance from the prejudgment attachments which are aimed at securing satisfaction of a judgment that may ultimately be given against a foreign state.[91] However, insofar as such seizures operate a dispensation from the foreign state's immunity from execution, they are not comparable to the setoffs that banks may realize in implementing a syndicated loan made to a foreign country in order to cover their proportionate share of loans in default. These setoffs do not respond to internationally wrongful acts, and, moreover, the loans are governed by municipal laws.[92] Both these preliminary remarks show that the numerous litigations that followed United States freezing of Iranian assets in 1980 are of little assistance in solving the problems raised by the seizure of any foreign government property as a restitutionary remedy for a prior internationally wrongful act. Things would, of course, be different if all the judicial proceedings introduced in United States courts by potential creditors in order to attach every Iranian government asset available had not been terminated

[91] 28 U.S.C. § 1610(d) (1982). See Jeremiah D. Lambert & William D. Coston, ''Friendly Foes in the Iranian Assets Litigation,'' 7 *The Yale Journal of World Public Order,* 88, 100 (1980). See also the difference made by French law between the ''saisie-éxécution'' and the ''saisie-conservatoire'' in Roger Perrot, *Cours de voies d'éxécution,* at 62 and 204 (1965-1966).

[92] For instance New York law applies to Eurodollar loans, see Edward Gordon, ''The Blocking of Iranian Assets,'' 14 *Int'l. Law.*, 659, 678 (1980).

by Executive Order No. 12283[93] as a consequence of the Agreements of Algiers (Jan. 19, 1981).

Before the enactment of the Foreign Sovereign Immunities Act, the United States adhered to the theory of absolute foreign sovereign immunity from execution. Execution against foreign state property by attachment or seizure was not permissible.[94] That strict prohibition was, however, mitigated by the general compliance of foreign states at least with international awards rendered against them.[95] Meanwhile, continental systems of law had already departed from the absolute immunity from execution when the property of the state was connected with its private acts. Such a move was perfectly logical, for it was the only way to give meaning to the restrictive theory of immunity from jurisdiction applied to commercial activities of foreign states outside their territory. When the United States endeavored to codify the restrictive theory of sovereign immunity, it went much further than some European states. Not only did it subject commercial activities of foreign states to the restrictive theory of immunity from jurisdiction and execution, but it also extended the restrictive theory of immunity from jurisdiction to acts *jure imperii*, when such acts impaired property rights in violation of international law. However, the United States did not dare draw all the consequences of such a move, *i.e.*, provide that the property of a foreign country which seizes United States property in violation of international law will not be immune within United States territory. Hence the extraordinarily complicated tangle which basically makes execution possible only against commercial property, as if the Congress had been unable to strike a balance between the Sabbatino Amendment and the theory of sovereign immunity.

One point is sure: Restitutionary international remedies are not widely open under United States law. The Foreign Sovereign Immunities Act makes execution against foreign government

[93] 46 F.R. 7927 (1981).

[94] See *Restatement of the Law* (Second), Foreign Relations of the United States (1962), § 69, Reporters' Notes (2) at 215.8.

[95] See Oscar Schachter, "The Enforcement of International Judicial and Arbitral Decisions," 54 *A.J.I.L.*, 1-24 (1960).

property possible, but in a very narrow manner.[96] The principle is that the property of a foreign state in the United States is immune from execution, attachment or seizure.[97] To that extent, United States law remains faithful to a principle of customary international law. It provides, however, for an exception to that principle, the only relevant exception for our concern, when the execution relates to a judgment establishing rights regarding property which has been taken in violation of international law or which has been exchanged for property taken in violation of international law.[98] From a methodological point of view, this exception, which involves a dispensation from an international obligation, is a genuine countermeasure;[99] it is a statutory reprisal.

This exception, however, mostly applies to property used for a commercial activity because other types of property enjoy absolute immunity; such is the case for funds of a foreign central bank or monetary authority, deposited with an American bank and "held for its own account,"[100] unless the central bank has waived immunity from execution, and for all property used in connection with a military activity when it is of a military character or under the control of a military authority or defense agency.[101] However, execution is not allowed against all commercial property. The commercial property of a foreign state is liable to execution only if that state has waived its immunity explicitly or by implication,[102] or if the property is or was used for the commercial activity on which the claim is based.[103] Under

[96] See Mark C. Del Bianco, "Execution and Attachment Under the Foreign Sovereign Immunities Act of 1976," 5 *Yale Studies in World Public Order*, 109-146 (1979).
[97] 28 U.S.C. § 1609 (1982).
[98] 28 U.S.C. § 1610(a) (3) (1982). As to international violations of rights other than rights in property, it must be borne in mind that United States courts have construed the Act of State Doctrine as having survived the enactment of the Foreign Sovereign Immunity Act (*Frolova v. Union of Soviet Socialist Republics* (1983) N.D. Ill. 558 F. Supp. 358). This means that whenever the unlawful act is an act of sovereignty *(jure imperii)* not related to rights in property, the claim should be dismissed. This is hardly surprising, since the Foreign Sovereign Immunities Act apparently circumscribes the scope of the exception to the principle *par in parem* to rights in property.
[99] See E. Zoller, *Peacetime,* at 75.
[100] 28 U.S.C. § 1611(b) (1) (1982).
[101] 28 U.S.C. § 1611 (b) (2) (1982).
[102] 28 U.S.C. § 1610(a) (1) (1982).
[103] 28 U.S.C. § 1610(a) (2) (1982).

such stringent requirements, the victim of discriminatory or confiscatory expropriation is not likely to get restitution from United States courts unless, for instance, the nationalized property is movable and is used by the nationalizing state for a commercial purpose in the United States.[104]

In theory, there is an international restitutionary remedy in United States law. But in effect this remedy merely gives alms to the victims of internationally wrongful acts. This illusory remedy provided by the Foreign Sovereign Immunities Act is hardly surprising insofar as the United States has always afforded foreign sovereigns greater protection against execution of judgments than against suits.[105] Victims of international offenses are generously allowed to start a full-fledged legal battle in United States courts against violators of international rules. To that extent, they are granted "a day in court;"[106] but they will very seldom get "something" from the court,[107] except a declaratory judgment which they can perhaps have enforced abroad, provided they meet the *exequatur* requirement. To that extent, one may wonder whether this unique restitutionary remedy is not in fact meant to deter foreign states from seizing United States property and whether it is not primarily aimed at securing performance with international rules.

2. Actions for Performance

Falling short of unilaterally granting the country and its citizens complete *restitutio in integrum*, most United States nonreciprocal actions are aimed at bringing "pressure" on the offender to

[104] See Robert B. von Mehren, "The Foreign Sovereign Immunities Act of 1976," 17 *Colum. J. Trans. L.*, 33, 64 (1978).

[105] *Ibid.* at 65. When Congress passed the Sabbatino Amendment, the Johnson administration was opposed to the amendment and some members of Congress insisted that the amendment not be viewed as allowing seizure of any foreign government property as reparation for the expropriation of unexported property. See Brett R. Turner, "The Harvest of *Sabbatino: Vishipco Line v. Chase Manhattan Bank*," 8 *N.C.J. Int'l & Com. Reg.*, 87, 97 (n.57) (1982).

[106] See Michael H. Cardozo, "Sovereign Immunity: The Plaintiff Deserves a Day in Court," 67 *Harv. L. Rev.* 608 (1954).

[107] In his thorough analysis (*supra* n.96 at 111) Mark C. Del Bianco has recorded only one United States court that has permitted execution against the property of a foreign state. *Harris & Co. Advertising Inc. v. Republic of Cuba,* 127 So.2d 687 (Fla. Dist. Ct. app. 1961). The case, however, concerned a commercial activity of the Republic of Cuba (promotion of Cuba's tourist business).

restore compliance with the law. These measures are never punitive in character, for they can always be lifted when such a result is attained. They are not, therefore, true "sanctions."[108]

The pressure exercised by the United States on foreign countries is manifold. From a legal point of view, it is to be divided into two classes of actions. The first group includes actions that are neutral with respect to international law. They are acceptable under the international legal order as inimical measures of retorsion. The second group is that of countermeasures, *i.e.*, actions that may infringe on specific obligations of international law, regardless of their treaty or customary character. They consist in the nonfulfillment of an international obligation different from the breached obligation.

A. Measures

The power of the purse is doubtless as important in foreign affairs as in domestic concerns. The vast majority of measures of retorsion against those states that have infringed the international rights of the United States are carried out by financial coercion, notably by suspension of economic assistance. The Hickenlooper Amendment, "the result of considerable effort,"[109] prohibits assistance to any country that has nationalized United States property without compensation.[110] Assistance is also prohibited to any country which permits the damage of United States property and fails to provide compensation;[111] any country which seizes United States fishing vessels in international waters;[112] any country which is in default of payment to the United States of any loan made under assistance.[113] Similarly, the power of the purse is still resorted to, but in a more subtle way, in the policy with respect to aid in financing United States exports. Section 2(d) of the 1945 Export-Import Bank Act as amended, requires

[108] The terms "pressure" and "sanction" are used here in the sense given to them by the Arbitral Tribunal in the *Air Service Agreement* (France/United States) 18 *U.N.R.I.A.A.* 442, § 78. See also E. Zoller, *Peacetime,* at 46-47.

[109] Senate Report No. 1535, 87th Congress, 2nd Sess. (1962); [1962] *U.S. Code Cong. & Adm. News,* Vol. 1 (1962), at 2062.

[110] 22 U.S.C. § 2370(e) (1) (1982).

[111] 22 U.S.C. § 2370(j) (1982).

[112] 22 U.S.C. § 2370(o) (1982).

[113] 22 U.S.C. § 2370(q) (1982).

the bank not to approve credit in support of United States exports to any country which has violated an agreement for cooperation concerning the civil use of nuclear energy with the United States.[114] The harm inflicted may not directly be financial in character, but it still bears on economic matters. Section 502(b) of the 1974 Trade Act, for instance, rules out the designation as a beneficiary of duty-free treatment of any developing country which nationalizes United States property without discharging its obligations under international law.[115] The harm is also economic in substance when nondiscriminatory treatment is denied to nonmarket economy countries which fail to cooperate in efforts to repatriate United States personnel missing in action in Southeast Asia.[116] Finally, and in the absence of a bilateral tax treaty providing for equal treatment, one must include among nonreciprocal measures Section 48(7) (D) of the Internal Revenue Code, which states that if a foreign country maintains nontariff trade restrictions or engages in discriminatory acts, the articles (or class of articles) of that foreign country will not be considered as property eligible for tax credit for investment purposes.[117]

Most of these measures are designed to put pressure on the offender, to induce it to comply with the law, and, especially, to compel it to provide reparation in an adequate form for the injury sustained by the United States. The foreign state is always given a chance to mend its ways, and more often than not in a manner that is not exacting. For instance, to avoid the effects of the apparently formidable Hickenlooper Amendment, the foreign state does not have to ensure immediate compensation of United States nationalized property, but it must at least ''take

[114] 12 U.S.C. § 635(b) (4) (1982).

[115] 19 U.S.C. § 2462(b) (4) (1982).

[116] 19 U.S.C. § 2433(a) (1982).

[117] 26 U.S.C. § 48(f) (D) (1982). That section was not applicable in case of trade restrictions or discriminatory acts that foreign countries resorted to when Proclamation 4074 was in force. Proclamation 4074 withdrew certain prior trade concessions and imposed a supplemental duty amounting to 10 percent *ad valorem* on all dutiable articles imported into the customs territory of the United States [36 F.R. 15724 (1971)]. This proclamation, which was enacted for balance of payments purposes, was repealed by Proclamation 4098 [36 F.R. 24201 (1971)]. But it nevertheless lasted more than four months, and during that period foreign countries were entitled by way of reciprocity to resort to trade restrictions or to discriminatory acts against the United States as a device to restore the balance of comparative advantage. As a result, their moves, if any, during that period could not be viewed as infringements of international obligations.

appropriate steps'' to discharge its international obligation.[118] Similarly, a developing country will not be denied the benefit of the United States generalized system of preferences for having nationalized a United States property without compensation if good faith negotiations are in progress.[119] The same good faith test is to be applied for the same purposes with respect to any foreign country which refuses to be bound by, or to enforce, arbitral awards in favor of United States citizens or corporations.[120] In the past 15 years, the United States has considerably mellowed the potential pressure on violators of international obligations, especially with respect to suspension of economic assistance. Humanitarian assistance is not subject to the provisions of the Foreign Assistance Act. As a result, when the United States applied the Hickenlooper Amendment against Ethiopia in 1979, two-thirds of the program was unaffected.[121] The origin of the Hickenlooper Amendment was in the 1962 expropriation by the Brazilian State of Rio Grande do Sul of assets of a local subsidiary of ITT. The amendment was easily adopted by Congress because the expropriation shortly preceded a visit by the Brazilian President to the United States to obtain further financial assistance.[122] The amendment was applied to Ceylon in 1963 and was threatened against a number of other countries without actually being used very often. The record of the Hickenlooper Amendment is indeed rather poor.[123]

However, it must be borne in mind that all these measures are subject to a presidential waiver whenever the ''interest of the United States'' is at stake.[124] As a result, some of them have

[118] 22 U.S.C. § 2370(e) (1) (1982).
[119] 19 U.S.C. § 2462(b) (4) (D) (ii) (1982).
[120] 19 U.S.C. § 2462(b) (6) (1982).
[121] See *U.S. Digest* 1979, pp. 1388-9.
[122] See Richard B. Lillich, ''The Protection of Foreign Investment and the Foreign Assistance Act of 1962,'' 17 *Rutgers L. Rev.*, 405 (1963); Henry J. Steiner & Detlev F. Vagts, *Transnational Legal Problems,* (1976), 482-3; Don Wallace, Jr., ''The President's Exclusive Foreign Affairs Power Over Foreign Aid,'' 1970 *Duke L. J.*, 293-328, 454-494, esp. 478.
[123] See Lillich, ''Requiem for Hickenlooper,'' *supra* n. 79, at 98.
[124] See, for example, 12 U.S.C. § 635(b) (4) (1982); 22 U.S.C. § 2370(c) (1982); 22 U.S.C. § 2370(e) (1) (1982); 22 U.S.C. § 2370 (q) (1982). In *Aerotrade, Inc. v. Agency for International Development* (October 17, 1974), the United States District Court for the District of Columbia granted the defendant's motion for summary judgment against the plaintiff's suit for an order from the court directing that all foreign aid to Haiti be terminated in accordance with the provisions of the Hickenlooper Amendment. The court said, in the relevant part of the judgment: ''The statute on its face places substantial discretion in the President.'' See *U.S. Digest* 1974, pp. 511-513.

never been resorted to. This is especially the case of the denial of tax credit to foreign property for investment purposes although, with respect to the United States claim for reciprocity in trade, it is hard to believe that the investors' governments have never maintained nontariff restrictions or engaged in discriminatory acts.

The adequacy of these measures for performance purposes is difficult to assess. The scarcity of the record seems to imply that they are to some extent paper tigers, although this scarcity could also be construed as evidence of their efficient deterrent effect.[125] In any event, there is little doubt that in order to compel the offender to comply once again with the law, the United States is doing, or threatening to do, more than would be necessary to restore the symmetry of the initial position. To that extent, these measures are not equivalent to the breach, although their ultimate purpose is the reestablishment of equivalence between the parties. Theoretically, as long as such nonreciprocal actions do not infringe on international obligations, they are not subject to the proportionality test. As a matter of fact, a distinction could be made with respect to the suspension of assistance between the states which are parties to the Charter of the Organization of American States and those which are not. Article 19 of the OAS Charter prohibits "the use of coercive measures of an economic or political character in order to force the sovereign will of another state and obtain from it advantages of any kind." As to the states entitled to claim compliance with this provision, the United States measures are not simple measures, but genuine countermeasures, *i.e.* legitimate reprisals taken in response to an unlawful act. These countermeasures have to stand the proportionality test, although there is no doubt that Article 19 does not imply that either the furnishing or the acceptance of assistance

[125] In that respect, it is worth noting that on March 24, 1975, President Ford issued a determination under Section 502(b) (4) (D) (ii) of the 1974 Trade Act, that in the case of 18 countries with which the United States had investment disputes, good faith negotiations to provide prompt, adequate, and effective compensation were in progress. As a result, the countries concerned—Afghanistan, Argentina, Bangladesh, Bolivia, Central African Republic, Congo (Brazzaville), Dahomey, Egypt, El Salvador, Ethiopia, India, Morocco, Pakistan, Sri Lanka, Sudan, Syria, Tanzania and Zaire—were designated as beneficiary developing countries for the purposes of the United States system of generalized tariff preferences. See *U.S. Digest* 1975, p. 486.

or other special benefits is obligatory.[126] As a result, the difference, if any, between the two groups of states is very small in substance.

B. Countermeasures

Whenever a breach of an international obligation cannot be redressed by reciprocal action, the wronged party is entitled under customary international law to resort, vis-à-vis the offender, to nonperformance of an international obligation different in substance from the breached obligation. Several provisions in the United States Code provide for such countermeasures. For instance, the Sabbatino Amendment provides that United States courts will not respect a foreign state's immunity from jurisdiction for sovereign public acts *(jure imperii)* when such state nationalizes United States property without discharging its obligation under international law;[127] or, in order to respond to the same internationally wrongful act, the United States representatives of several international financial obligations will systematically vote against any loan in favor of such countries, whatever the constitutional provisions of those organizations which subject voting rights to developmental priorities;[128] or Section 301 of the Trade Act authorizes the President "to take all appropriate and feasible action within his power" to respond to any foreign state's action inconsistent with treaty and customary rules related to international trade;[129] or section 5(b) of the Trading With the Enemy Act, superseded today in peacetime by Section 203 of the International Emergency Economic Powers Act, gives the

[126] See *U.S. Digest* 1973, p. 380.

[127] 22 U.S.C. § 2370(e) (2) (1982).

[128] 22 U.S.C. § 284j (1982). In the case of the *Admission of a State to the United Nations (Charter, Art. 4),* the International Court of Justice was of the opinion that: "To ascertain whether an organ has freedom of choice for its decisions, reference must be made to the terms of its constitution" I.C.J. *Reports* 1948, p. 57, especially p. 64. In that respect, Article III(1) (a) of the Agreement of the International Bank for Reconstruction and Development (60 Stat. 1440; T.I.A.S. 1502) provides: "The resources and the facilities of the Bank shall be used exclusively for the benefit of members with equitable consideration to projects for development and projects for reconstruction alike." Similarly, Article V(1) (b) of the Agreement of the International Development Association (11 U.S.T. 2284; T.I.A.S. 4607) reads as follows: "Financing provided by the Association shall be for purposes which in the opinion of the Association are of high developmental priority in the light of the needs of the area or areas concerned and, except in special circumstances, shall be for specific projects."

[129] 19 U.S.C. § 2411(a) (1982).

President the power "to block" or "to freeze" foreign property within the United States;[130] or Section 402(f) of the Federal Aviation Act entitles the Department of Transportation to summarily suspend the permits of foreign air carriers whose government impairs the operating rights of United States air carriers.[131] These actions may infringe on treaty rules or customary rules as well. However, insofar as all of them result in treating a single country in a less favorable manner than the United States treats other nations, they all are to be viewed as dispensations from the principle of nondiscrimination, which implies that states have to be treated equally.[132]

With few exceptions,[133] most of these countermeasures affect individuals whose only crime is to have been born in another country and to have strong attachment to it. They are based upon the assumption that every national of the offending state is to be indirectly held responsible for the breach committed by that state. In short, they are based upon a system of collective responsibility. Moreover, some of these countermeasures may be triggered by United States citizens themselves as a way of obtaining redress for the injury they have sustained or are sustaining because of the unlawful conduct of the foreign government. Such possibil-

[130] 50 App. U.S.C. § 5(b) (Suppl. V, 1981); 50 U.S.C. 1702 (Suppl. V, 1981).

[131] 49 App. U.S.C. § 1372(f) (2) (1982). As of January 1, 1985, and with respect to foreign transportation, the authority of the Civil Aeronautics Board was terminated and transferred to the Department of Transportation, which shall exercise such authority in consultation with the Department of State [49 App. U.S.C. § 1551(b) (1) (B) (1982)]

[132] The customary rule of nondiscrimination does not imply that a state is under the obligation of treating every other state in the same manner; nondiscrimination does not imply identity. But the rule of nondiscrimination requires every state not to treat one foreign state and its nationals in a less favorable manner than it treats other foreign countries. That is why nondiscrimination does not rule out differences between states as long as they are in favor of some states with respect to the standard treatment accorded to the majority. In short, nondiscrimination is not the other side of the most-favored-nation treatment (*Yrbk. I.L.C.* 1978, II(2), at 11-12). As a result, whenever a state is not required by treaty to grant another country the most-favored-nation treatment for the products covered by the agreement (Article I of the GATT), that country cannot on the ground of nondiscrimination claim the same rights as those bestowed upon the most-favored-nation. The point is not purely academic. The United States has often viewed the rule of nondiscrimination as having the same meaning as the rule of the most-favored-nation treatment. This trend culminates today with Section 304(f) (5) of the 1984 Trade and Tariff Act which provides: "The term 'discriminatory' includes, where appropriate, any act, policy, or practice which denies national or most-favored-nation treatment to United States goods, services, or investments," 98 Stat. 3006 to be codified at 19 U.S.C. § 2411(3) (5).

[133] Such as a suit against a foreign government or the freezing of assets that concern only the property of the foreign government (Iran) and not the property of the foreign government and its nationals (Cuba).

ities are provided by Section 302(a) of the Trade Act, which gives any interested person the right to file a petition,[134] and by Section 2 of the 1974 International Air Transportation Fair Competitive Practices Act, which grants any United States air carrier the right to file a complaint.[135] In both cases, the redress obtained by a trade remedy (increase in duties, withdrawal of commercial privileges, penalty of any sort)[136] or by a suspension of foreign air carrier permits usually affects innocent foreign individuals or corporations. This feature deserves some consideration because it emphasizes the essence of reprisals: Reprisals were historically private rights and especially the right of private persons to "take back" from foreign individuals what the latter had unlawfully stolen or seized from the former.[137] Reprisals were devices to force the lawbreaker to disgorge the gains it would be unjust for him to retain.

In that respect, a conspicuous feature of United States countermeasures is to be found in the legal safeguards that the legal system has attached to such actions. To some extent, these safeguards entail mitigating effects on the system of collective responsibility and at the same time shed some light on the adequacy of these countermeasures in relation to their goals.

(a) Safeguards

The substantive and procedural safeguards attached to countermeasures provide ample evidence that the United States does not consider itself as vested with rights across the board when responding to internationally wrongful acts. Most of these safeguards derive from its own legal system and not from international legal norms.

Nevertheless, several United States provisions relating to countermeasures take into account the humanitarian considerations, imposed by international norms. Recently, such humani-

[134] Under the Tariff and Trade Reform Act (98 Stat. 2348), to be codified at 19 U.S.C. § 2412(a) (1).

[135] 49 App. U.S.C. § 1159(b) (2) (1982).

[136] Section 301 authorizes the President to take "all appropriate and feasible action." Such language may cover anything: Custom duties may be doubled, imported products may be excluded.

[137] See E. Zoller, *Peacetime,* at 36-38.

tarian considerations have been made mandatory when the President decides to resort to emergency powers. Section 203(b) of the 1977 International Emergency Economic Powers Act precludes the President from prohibiting any postal, telegraphic, telephonic or other personal communication or donations of articles, such as good, clothing, and medicine, for the purpose of relieving human suffering.[138] In a different manner, but with a similar purpose, the Cuban Assets Control Regulations permit remittances for necessary living expenses, not to exceed $100 per month, when the blocked account is in the name of, or in which the beneficial interest is held by, the payee or members of his household.[139] On December 22, 1977, an amendment to these regulations authorized a person in the United States to send a maximum of $500 in any 3-month period to close relatives in Cuba.[140]

These humanitarian provisions are obviously limited in scope; but they show that the ban on the use of force is not the only constraint on states resorting to reprisals and ultimately that the traditional system of collective responsibility has to be assigned certain safeguards. There is little doubt that these limits have been inspired by the laws of warfare. However, peacetime limits in the United States go beyond wartime constraints, for they rule out certain regulations which, in wartime, would be perfectly lawful, such as the interruption of all communications between the belligerents.

However, by far the most interesting safeguards provided by United States law are the domestic procedures which either precede or follow the implementation of United States countermeasures. These procedural guarantees directly derive from the Constitution, and especially from the Fifth and Fourteenth Amendments. The Fifth Amendment provides that ''No person shall be . . . deprived of life, liberty, or property without due process of law; nor shall private property be taken for public use, without just compensation,'' and the Fourteenth Amendment

[138] 50 U.S.C. § 1702(b) (1982). See Executive Order 12205 prohibiting certain transactions with Iran, 45 F.R. 24099 (April 7, 1980), 45 F.R. 26685 (April 17, 1980).
[139] 31 C.F.R. § 515.521 (1983).
[140] 31 C.F.R. § 515.563 (1983). See also *U.S. Digest* 1978, pp. 1361-2.

guarantees "to any person . . . the equal protection of the laws." The United States courts have always construed the term "person" as applying to aliens and have thus extended the mandate of due process of law and the equal protection clause to all persons within the territorial jurisdiction of the United States without regard to race, creed, color, or nationality. These provisions obviously do not rule out the system of collective responsibility. They have nevertheless clothed it in a definite framework of procedural and substantive safeguards. To that extent, aliens are entitled under United States law to rights that are far above international standards, especially since they are generally granted without a condition of reciprocity.[141]

The impact of domestic procedures on the implementation of United States countermeasures does not have the same meaning, however, when they benefit United States citizens as when they benefit nationals of the errant foreign state. In that respect, it must be borne in mind that the collective responsibility which underlines the essence of reprisals, is in some ways counterbalanced by a system of collective solidarity.

The organization of human association on the European model of the state system makes it inevitable for the national collectivity of the injured state to respond as a whole. Countermeasures may, therefore, have adverse effects not only on nationals of the for-

[141] See Hostie, "Contribution. . . .," *supra* n. 13, at 321. An exception, however, is to be found in the right to sue the United States in the United States Claim Court in 28 U.S.C. § 2502(s) (1982). With respect to the right to sue the United States for the injurious consequences of a reprisal, it goes without saying that under any municipal legal order, there could be no such thing as a foreign government suing the responding state in its courts. Such issues have to be addressed through diplomatic channels. In *Swiss Confederation v. United States* (1947) (70 F. Supp. 235, 108 Ct. Cl. 388, certiorari denied 332 U.S. 815), the claims court held: "A foreign government might be unwilling to submit itself to the jurisdiction of the courts of the United States, but if it is willing to do so, we can conceive of no reason why Congress should have intended to prohibit a court established by it from giving to the foreign government the same redress which would be accorded to any other litigant." This rather puzzling statement has apparently never had any further consequences since the court considerably toned down its possible effects in admitting "whether or not we are correct in the foregoing, we are clearly of the opinion that the Swiss government is entitled to sue under the provisions of the Act of October 10, 1940, ... (54 Stat. 1090, 1091)." This statute provides that the owner of property requisitioned by the government shall be entitled to sue the United States for such additional sum as, when added to the sum already received by such owner, such owner may consider fair and just compensation for such article or material. The claims court added: "No limitation whatever is placed upon the character or status of the owner authorized to sue." See also 17 Wright, Miller & Cooper, *Federal Practice and Procedure: Jurisdiction 2d,* § 4101, pp. 203-204 (n. 15).

eign country, but also on nationals of the responding state. As a result, the availability of judicial review, for instance, does not make the same sense for both categories of persons. Whenever foreigners are entitled to bring a suit against the responding state to challenge the adverse effects of a countermeasure affecting them, they always seek to alleviate such effects. For them there is no question that their claim is necessarily aimed at lifting or reversing the reprisal. Whenever nationals of the responding state seek judicial review of governmental determinations related to countermeasures against a foreign country, the object of their suits may be similar to those initiated by foreigners. For instance, nationals, like foreigners, may try to have the reprisals lifted because of adverse effects on their own patrimonial interests. However and in any case, the legal grounds of their suits are very different from those of foreigners since they never derive from international entitlements. The problem they actually raise pertains exclusively to the constitutional rights of citizens with respect to foreign affairs, and its solution depends, in the United States, on federal law and not on international law. This does not mean that citizens are never entitled to claim rights bestowed upon them by international law which would be invocable against the federal government, especially when international law is part of the law of the land. This means only that the rights of citizens as to the conditions under which reprisals are carried out are not international rights.[142]

By contrast, the procedural safeguards that may be accorded to foreigners directly affected by the countermeasures are doubt-

[142] United States authors have devoted scrupulous attention to the constitutional rights of citizens when foreign affairs are involved. See Monroe Leigh & Timothy Atkeson, "Due Process in the Emerging Foreign Relations Law of the United States," 21 *Bus. Law*. 853-878 (1966) and 22 *Bus. Law*. 3-28 (1966); Sigmund Timberg, "Wanted: Administrative Safeguards for the Protection of the Individual in International Economic Regulation," 17 *Admin. L. R.*, 159-172 (1965). The principle of due process is so well enshrined in constitutional law that recently, the Supreme Court has to some extent made the claims court the court of appeals for private litigants with claims against Iran. The Supreme Court held that after the forced international arbitration process had run its course, such litigants could bring a takings claim against the United States in the claims court. In other words, the claims court will have jurisdiction to review the fairness of the arbitral awards of the United States/Iran Tribunal and to decide whether the tribunal's decisions amounted or not to a taking of United States property without payment of just compensation as required by the Fifth Amendment. To some extent, the due process principle prevailed over the statutory exception to claims court jurisdiction for claims "growing out of or dependent upon" a treaty; *Dames & Moore v. Regan,* 453 U.S. 654, 688-690 (1981).

less internationally relevant by reason of their possible mitigating effects on the system of collective responsibility. In that respect, the requirements of the Constitution, and above all the due process clause, obviously apply to legal aliens, but also to aliens who came and remained in the country in violation of the express law thereof,[143] and even to aliens who are not resident or doing business in the United States, provided that they meet other judicial requirements.[144]

As to countermeasures, these domestic procedures do not have the same significance when they precede as when they follow the United States responses against internationally wrongful acts.

(1) Preliminary Procedures

Under customary international law, the only preliminary procedures before countermeasures are international in character. Before contemplating the possible use of an act of reprisal, whether foreceful or not, the responding state is under an obligation to make representation to the offending state. This requirement derives from the statement made by the Arbitral Tribunal in the *Naulilaa Incident*.[145] It has been reinforced by Article 33 of the United Nations Charter, which imposes upon the parties to an international dispute an obligation to negotiate.[146] Such an obligation does not require formal discussions with the offender, should it make it clear that it would have no direct contact with the representatives of the aggrieved party.[147] But this obligation, at least, requires the victim state to file a formal protest with the foreign government. The protest is implicitly to be construed by the offender as a warning of possible "responses." Admittedly, the question whether the victim state must at the same time make its possible response public is debatable.

[143] *United States v. Wong Dep Ken,* D.C. Cal. 1893, 57 F. 206. See also *Choy Gum v. Backus,* CCA Cal. 1915, 223 F. 487, certiorari denied 239 U.S. 649.

[144] See *Restatement 2nd, Foreign Relations Law of the United States,* § 167, comment b; and *Restatement, Foreign Relations Law of the United States,* Tentative Draft No. 3, § 722.

[145] "La repésaille n'est licite que lorsqu'elle a été précédée d'une *sommation* restée infructueuse" (italics in the text), 2 *U.N.R.I.A.A.* 1027.

[146] See *North Sea Continental Shelf,* Judgment, I.C.J. *Reports* 1969, p. 47, § 86.

[147] In the *Hostages* case, the International Court of Justice expressly referred to the fact that "despite the efforts of the United States Government to open negotiations, it became clear that the Iranian authorities would have no direct contact with representatives of the United States Government concerning the holding of the hostages." I.C.J. *Reports* 1980, p. 15, § 26.

There is a case in which such a prerequisite is unfulfillable as a matter of fact, especially when the victim state is contemplating a freeze of the assets of the foreign government and its nationals. Obviously prior warning in that case would only lead to immediate withdrawal of the foreign funds.[148]

In any event, the legislative evolution in the United States is meaningful in that respect. Previously, in contemplating the use of reprisals, the President was not required to make representation to the wrongful foreign state. Countermeasures were then rights of immediate action. For instance, Section 338 of the 1930 Tariff Act authorized the President to exclude from importation into the United States the products of any foreign country found to be imposing upon United States articles any unreasonable charge or discrminating against the commerce of the United States.[149] This, however, remains the only provision relating to countermeasures that does not subject the United States response to preliminary diplomatic steps in one way or another. Sometimes the government is under the obligation to request consultations with the foreign country,[150] or to act only when that country persists over the objections of the government of the United States.[151] Sometimes the duty to negotiate is implied by linking the countermeasure contemplated and the progress of good faith negotiations.[152] In the only case where negotiations are unfeasible because the process is beyond its control as a matter of fact, the government is still required to notify the foreign state of the procedure under way.[153]

[148] See E. Zoller, ''Quelques réflexions sur les contremesures,'' *Mélanges Colliard,* 361, 379 (1984). In that connection, it is interesting to note that Section 203 of the 1977 International Emergency Economic Powers Act [50 U.S.C. § 1702 (Suppl. V, 1981)] did not depart from Section 5(b) of the 1917 Trading with the Enemy Act [50 App. U.S.C. §5(b) (Suppl. V, 1981)]. No international preliminary procedural move is imposed upon the President; emergency actions are, by nature, to be taken immediately.

[149] 19 U.S.C. § 1338 (1982). Although still in force, Section 338 is, to a large extent, superseded by Section 301 of the 1974 Trade Act as amended [19 U.S.C. § 2411(a) (1982)].

[150] 19 U.S.C. § 2413 (1982).

[151] 49 App. U.S.C. § 1372(f) (2) (1982).

[152] 22 U.S.C. § 284j(c) (1982).

[153] The 1976 Foreign Sovereign Immunities Act and the regulations adopted in pursuance thereof have put muscle into the obligation to inform the foreign state of the existence of a legal proceeding. Section 1608 of the statute requires that adequate notice of suit be given to the foreign state, especially by the service of judicial documents (a summons and complaint). Regulations were issued by the Department of State [42 F.R. 6367 (1977)] prescribing the form of services through the diplomatic channel and the form of a ''Notice of Suit'' [22 C.F.R. Part 93 (1984)].

Apart from these preliminary steps, the most conspicuous feature of the United States countermeasures is to be found in the domestic procedures that have been set forth in two particular fields: international trade law and international air transport. Section 301 of the Trade Act and the regulations adopted in pursuance thereof,[154] as well as Section 213 of the Economic Regulations relating to foreign air carriers permits,[155] organize a genuine contradictory debate over the countermeasure contemplated at the domestic level. In both cases, the effect of these provisions is to give the foreigners liable to be affected by the United States response fair warning of the limits of possible countermeasures and to provide them a reasonable opportunity to know and challenge the decision before it becomes final. At the outset, it must be borne in mind that these procedures have been mostly provided in the interest of United States individuals and corporations. Such is doubtless the case of Section 304 of the Trade Act, which calls for a public hearing in the case where the investigation follows a petition for action (*i.e.*, by a private party).[156] But opportunities to present views are also provided when the President or the United States Trade Representative acts on his own motion.[157] Any interested party may request the United States Trade Representative to provide for such debates. Of course, the term ''interested party'' includes first and foremost a United States producer or a United States commercial importer or exporter whose economic interests are likely to be affected by possible United States retaliatory action. But the regulations have never been construed as excluding foreigners or even foreign governments from participating in the proceedings. Both may appear at a public hearing provided they have submitted a written

[154] See Procedures for Complaint filed under Section 301 of the 1974 Trade Act as amended, 15 C.F.R. § 2006 (1984).

[155] See Terms, Conditions and Limitations of Foreign Air Carriers Permits, 14 C.F.R. § 213 (1984).

[156] 19 U.S.C. § 2414(b) (1) (1982).

[157] When the President determines that expeditious action is required, he ''shall provide an opportunity for the presentation of views concerning the taking of such action'' [19 U.S.C. § 2411(c) (1) (1982)]. Since the enactment of the 1984 Tariff and Trade Reform Act, the Trade Representative may initiate an investigation on his own motion. Such a determination is to be treated as an affirmative determination under Subsection (b) (2) of Section 2412 of the statute and therefore is subject to a hearing if requested by an interested party.

brief before the close of the period of submission announced in the public notice.[158] Foreign governments and their nationals may therefore defend a Section 301 case. In the vast majority of cases, governments will make representation through diplomatic channels. But they may choose to make representation to the United States Trade Representative by counsel and even to take part in a public hearing.[159]

As far as foreign air carrier permits are concerned, things are different. The purpose of the procedures does not have the same significance as in a Section 301 case. Initially, the Civil Aeronautics Board delivered and withdrew foreign carrier permits without giving United States airlines an opportunity to present their views. In 1955, a particular foreign airline carrier was granted, without prior warning to other foreign airline carriers, rights they had sought for years. This action, which had serious effects on domestic and foreign competing air carriers, elicited strong protests from the governments of the foreign airlines. As a result, informal procedures were adopted in order to provide foreign governments and airlines with information of pending negotiations and opportunities to present their views.[160] Under present regulations, whenever a foreign government impairs operating rights of, or denies fair and equal opportunity to, United States air carriers, the board may "with or without hearing" initiate a procedure to be held within ten days that could lead, subject to stay or disapproval of the President, to the suspension of the air carrier permits of the foreign country concerned.[161] With respect to the latitude granted to the board, it may be said that the question whether a foreign air carrier permit can be revoked without a hearing is still unresolved.[162] In the United

[158] 15 C.F.R. § 2006.8(a) (1984).

[159] See Shirley A. Coffield, "Using Section 301 of the Trade Act of 1974 as a Response to Foreign Government Trade Actions: When, Why and How," 6 *N.C.J. Int'l. & Com. Reg.*, 381, 401-2 (1981).

[160] See Timberg, *supra* n. 142, at 162. See also the Air Transport Agreement Between the United States and the Federal Republic of Germany signed at Washington, July 7, 1955 (T.I.A.S. 3536, 7 U.S.T. 527).

[161] 14 C.F.R. § 213.3(c) (d) (1984).

[162] See Andreas F. Lowenfeld, "CAB v. KLM; Bermuda at Bay," 1 *Air Law* 2, 9 (1975). Section 402(f) of the Federal Aviation Act expressly provides that the suspension of a foreign air carrier permit may be initiated through a summary procedure "without hearing but subject to approval of the President," 49 App. U.S.C. § 1372(f) (2) (1982).

States/France dispute of 1978, it is worth noting that the Civil Aeronautics Board specifically invited Air France to submit any matters which might have justified other or different schedule limitations. The board even noted that it was prepared to modify its order upon an appropriate showing. Air France, however, did not avail itself of this opportunity.[163] In any event, there is no doubt that neither Section 301 of the Trade Act, nor Section 402(f) of the Federal Aviation Act is subject to the procedural requirements to be found in the Administrative Procedure Act, which does not apply when a foreign affairs function of the United States is at stake.[164] To be sure, these preliminary procedures are rather limited in scope. But, especially with respect to Section 301, their existence often makes up for the fact that the legality of the countermeasure cannot be challenged by judicial review.

(2) Subsequent procedures

Few legal systems have placed in their courts the long-standing confidence that the United States legal system has placed in the judicial branch. Few municipal judges outside the United States are so unanimously praised as being the best custodians of individual rights. This unfailing trust is, most of the time, put in relation to fundamental civil rights. Its possible international relevance is very often overlooked. However, insofar as the constitutional system allows the ultimate victims of United States countermeasures to challenge the validity of such actions in court, that particular legal feature is internationally relevant in every respect.

There is no question that the United States forum is generously open to foreigners affected by the countermeasures taken against them. Private remedies are liberally available to them, and the constitutional system will always provide them with a day in court, whether or not they are resident in the United States. In that sense, a nonresident alien owning property within the United States is entitled to the protection of the Fifth Amendment and

[163] See *U.S. Digest* 1978, p. 776.
[164] 5 U.S.C. § 553(a) (1) (rulemaking) and § 554(a) (4) (adjudication).

may file a complaint challenging the regulations issued by the Secretary of Treasury freezing bank deposits of Cuban nationals *(Sardino v. Federal Reserve Bank of New York)*.[165] Similarly a resident alien is entitled to the same protection and may seek declaratory and injunctive relief against the Attorney General, challenging the constitutionality of the regulations directed at Iranian students *(Narenji et al. v. Civiletti)*.[166] So far, so good. But what can the innocent victims of United States countermeasures actually expect from the courts? What are the chances that United States courts will uphold their challenge of executive determinations implemented against them?

A first attempt to tackle this problem could start with a common sense observation. Among all the decisions that the executive branch may take in foreign affairs, countermeasures are doubtless an interesting example of what a "political question" may be.[167] In *First National City Bank v. Banco National de Cuba* (1972), Mr. Justice Brennan (dissenting) precisely considered "the power of the Executive alone to effect a fair remedy for all United States citizens who have been harmed" as a point toward the existence of a 'political question.' "[168] Indeed, the extent to which an affected state should or should not take reprisals against the offending state, the amount of harm to be inflicted, as well as the scope of such actions, definitely raise political issues. Therefore one could presume that in theory innocent foreign victims of United States countermeasures should always be unable to leap over the "passive virtues of U.S. courts."[169] The

[165] 361 F.2d 106.

[166] 481 F. Supp. 1132; 617 F.2d 745.

[167] In *Baker v. Carr* (1962), Mr. Justice Brennan found six elements, at least one of which had to be present for an issue to be political: "[A] textually demonstrable constitutional commitment of the issue to a coordinate political department; or a lack of judicially discoverable and manageable standards for resolving it; or the impossibility of deciding without an initial policy determination of a kind clearly for nonjudicial discretion; or the impossibility of a court's undertaking independent resolution without expressing lack of the respect due coordinate branches of government; or an unusual need for unquestioning adherence to a political decision already made; or the potentiality of embarrassment from multifarious pronouncements by various departments on one question," 369 U.S. 186, 217.

[168] 406 U.S. 759, 788.

[169] See Alexander Bickel, "The Supreme Court, 1960—Forward: The Passive Virtues," 75 *Harv. L. Rev.*, 40 (1961). The term has been used to describe various devices used by United States courts to avoid "on-the-merits" adjudication of certain types of "cases confessedly within [their] jurisdiction," *Ashwander v. Tennessee Valley Authority*, 297 U.S. 288, 346 (1935). See also Note, *"IAM V. OPEC:* 'Acts of States' and 'Passive Virtues,' " 5 *Loy. L.A. Int'l & Comp. L.J.*, 159 (1982).

truth is that the political question doctrine[170] does not apply to foreigners challenging the validity of countermeasures carried out by the executive branch when those executive acts violate the constitutional rights of aliens or are beyond the President's authority under the Constitution or act of Congress. No foreign individual or corporation has ever had his "day in court" nullified on the ground that the challenged countermeasure was not within the scope of judicial review because it lay within the exclusive executive power "beyond the competence of the courts to adjudicate."[171] Neither Sardino, a Cuban plaintiff residing in Havana, who was challenging the validity of the regulations issued by the Secretary of Treasury freezing bank deposits of Cuban Nationals,[172] nor the Cuban refugees who brought similar actions before the United States District Court (D.C.),[173] nor Narenji *et alii,* the Iranian students who sought relief against Regulation 214.5, which required all nonimmigrant Iranian post-secondary school students to provide information as to their residence,[174] ever had their claims dismissed on the ground that the question was political. In those three cases, not only did United States courts find that they had jurisdiction *ratione materiae;* but they also assessed the "reasonableness" of the countermeasure resorted to.[175] To some extent, the domestic content of the due process principle coincides in such cases with the international prohibition of the denial of justice, according to which a state is required to administer justice with respect to foreigners and to guarantee them court access to defend their rights.[176] In that sense, it seems doubtful that the *Waterman* doctrine is fully consistent with customary international law. In *Chicago & Southern Airlines v. Waterman Steamship Corp.*, the Supreme Court

[170] See Edwin D. Dickinson, "The Law of Nations as National Law: 'Political Questions,' " 104 *U. of Pa. L. Rev.*, 451 (1956).

[171] See *Chicago & Southern Air Lines v. Waterman Steamship Corp.* 333 U.S. 103, 114 (1948).

[172] *Sardino v. Federal Reserve Bank of New York,* 361 F.2d 106 (1966).

[173] *Nielsen v. Secretary of Treasury,* 424 F.2d 833 (1970).

[174] *Narenji v. Civiletti,* 617 F.2d 745 (1979).

[175] The *Sardino* Court referred to the "reasonable response" by the affected state (361 F.2d 111[9]), the *Nielsen* Court verified the "reasonableness of the position of the United States (424 F.2d 843[8]) and the *Narenji* Court did not hesitate to verify that Regulation 214.5 had "a rational basis" (617 F.2d 748[5]).

[176] Alwyn V. Freeman, *The International Responsibility of States for Denial of Justice,* 67-68 (1938).

addressed a controversy between two United States corporations on routes involving overseas air transporation. The Court held in a general statement:

> We conclude that orders of the Board as to certificates for overseas or foreign air transportation are not mature and are therefore not susceptible of judicial review at any time before they are finalized by Presidential approval. After such approval had been given, the final orders embody Presidential discretion as to political matters beyond the competence of the courts of adjudicate.[177]

Insofar as this doctrine precludes judicial review of a CAB order suspending an air permit after such order has been approved by the President, it runs counter to the international prohibition of the denial of justice, especially when the rights of foreign air carriers derive from a bilateral air service agreement with another country.[178] However, even if international law is part of United States law, the chances that U.S. courts will abandon the *Waterman* doctrine are very slim. The reason is that the doctrine is today enshrined in Section 1006(a) of the Federal Aviation Act, which explicitly excepts from judicial review "any order in respect of any foreign air carrier subject to the approval of the President."[179]

Indeed the true obstacle faced by innocent foreigners who challenge the validity of countermeasures implemented against them is to be found in the place of international obligations in the municipal legal order of the United States.[180] No doubt innocent foreigners may invoke the rights stemming from fundamental international obligations, *i.e.* obligations not subject to

[177] 333 U.S. 103, 114 (1948). See the doubts cast by Lowenfeld, *supra* n. 162, at 14. See also William E. Miller, "The *Waterman* Doctrine Revisited," 54 *Geo. L.J.*, 5, 18 (1965).

[178] See O.J. Lissitzyn, "The Legal Status of Executive Agreements on Air Transportation—Part II," 18 *J.A.L.C.*, 12, 32 (1951).

[179] 49 App. U.S.C. § 1486(a) (1982). In *Dan-Air Services, Ltd. v. Civil Aeronautics Board* (1973), the Court of Appeals (DCC) explicitly held: "Review of such orders in respect of foreign air carriers is clearly precluded by statute." But the court implicitly referred to the *Waterman* doctrine when it stated: "Moreover, under traditional equity principles, review is inappropriate," 475 F.2d 408. See also *Diggs v. CAB*, 516 F.2nd 1248 (D.C. Cir. 1975), *cert. denied* 424 U.S. 910 (1976).

[180] See Pitman B. Potter, "Relative Authority of International Law and National Law in the United States," 19 *A.J.I.L.*, 315 (1923) and for a recent analysis, Louis Henkin, "International Law as Law in the United States," 82 *Mich. L. Rev.*, 1555 (1984).

any dispensation whatsoever. No doubt United States courts will make these fundmental rights prevail over any executive or even legislative determinations. However, such is the case less because these rights are internationally recognized as fundamental than because they are constitutional entitlements of foreigners in the United States.[181] This derives from the fact that United States courts will not entertain an objection that a countermeasure violates international law because it is not necessary or because it is excessive, where Congress directed or clearly allowed such action.[182] But in any event the courts may challenge the constitutionality of statutory countermeasures.[183]

As a result, the best protection granted to innocent foreigners against United States countermeasures mainly derives from the Constitution itself, whose most relevant provisions are to be found in the Bill of Rights, as well as in the constitutional separation of powers.[184] To be sure, this protection does not eliminate the effects of the principle of collective responsibility; but it alleviates them substantially as long as the Constitution embodies substantive guarantees which represent a considerable step forward from standards of international law, especially in the field of economic rights, where customary international law has not yet reached a very advanced level. It is worth noting in this connection that it is the Fifth Amendment and not a fundamental customary obligation that has restricted the United States countermeasures against confiscatory expropriation, to the freezing rather than seizing of foreign assets.[185] Although the *Sardino*

[181] For a survey, see, for example, *Restatement of the Law, Foreign Relations of the United States* (revised), Tentative Draft No. 3, (March 15, 1982), § 722 at 238-257.

[182] See *ibid.*, Tentative Draft No. 1, (April 1, 1980) § 135, Comment d, at 67.

[183] See, for instance, the judicial control of constitutionality as applied to the Sabbatino Amendment in *Banco National de Cuba v. Farr,* 383 F.2d 166, 178-185.

[184] See, for example, *Yoshida International Inc. v. United States,* 378 F. Supp. 1155 (Cust. Ct. 1974), *rev'd* 526 F.2d 560 (C.C.P.A. 1975) in which a presidential proclamation imposing a 10 percent surcharge on most imports into the United States was ruled unconstitutional by the customs court as infringing on Congress's authority to set import duties and regulate foreign trade under Article I, section 8. However, the court of appeals specifically held that the President had such an authority under Section 5(b) of the Trading With the Enemy Act (at 576).

[185] In *Russian Volunteer Fleet v. United States,* 282 U.S. 481, 489, 491-2 (1931), the court held that an alien friend is entitled to the protection of the Fifth Amendment's prohibition against taking without just compensation—even when his government was no longer recognized by the United States. In *United States v. Pink,* 315 U.S. 203, 228 (1942), the court declared, with respect to nonresident aliens owning property within the United States, that they "as well as citizens are entitled to the protection of the Fifth Amendment." See also *Guessefeldt v. McGrath,* 342 U.S. 308, 317-319 (1952).

Court rightly pointed out that "the unquestioned right of a state to protect its nationals in their persons and property while in a foreign country . . . must permit initial seizure and ultimate expropriation of assets of nationals of that country in its own territory if other methods of securing compensation for its nationals should fail," it also noted that Congress had not yet chosen to invoke the ultimate sanction and that "such *commendable forbearance* should not be understood as connoting lack of power."[186] The *Nielsen* Court went a step further in that direction in stating: "Even aliens not resident have the right to reasonable compensation for property taken by the State. In effect the burden is on the government to put forward the special reasonableness of and justification for any measure discriminating against aliens."[187] Ultimately, one may wonder whether in *Dames & Moore v. Regan,* the Supreme Court did not implictly expand the legal consequences of the Fifth Amendment in reducing the frozen assets to "a 'bargaining chip' to be used by the President when dealing with a hostile country,"[188] although the Iranian freeze concerned exclusively governmental assets. To some extent, *Dames & Moore v. Regan* meets the suggestion made by Louis Henkin that "perhaps in new situations, . . . might the Constitution yet be read to require that the (United States) plaintiff . . . be compensated by the United States."[189]

(b) Adequacy

Although the United States countermeasures affect the violator of an international obligation and its nationals in very different ways, there is no question that they are not genuine measures of compensation. Insofar as reparation encompasses compensation and restitution, they pave the way to full reparation, *i.e. restitutio in integrum* and to the return to law compliance. But they are not compensatory in character. This distinctive feature is not always perceived for two reasons.

[186] 361 F. 2d 106, 113[11] (1966) (emphasis added).
[187] 424 F. 2d 833, 846[12] (1970).
[188] 453 U.S. 654, 673 (1980).
[189] Henkin, *Foreign Affairs and the Constitution, supra,* Chap. 1, n.21, at 265-6 (1972) and compare with Stanley L. Sommerfield, "Treasury Regulations Affecting Trade With the Sino-Soviet Bloc and Cuba," 19 *Bus. Law.,* 861, 862, 867 (1964).

First, there is one countermeasure that until recently carried with it the legacy of its compensatory purpose in wartime, namely the freezing of the assets of a foreign state and of its nationals.[190] In wartime, a belligerent state may avail itself of the right to freeze foreign funds whether they are enemy property or not. This was the practice followed by the United States during World War II.[191] At the end of the hostilities, the freeze of non-enemy assets should cease, since the purpose for which they had been frozen has vanished. However, as far as enemy funds are concerned, things are different because they may be used for compensatory purposes to settle war reparations. That is why, in principle, enemy property in wartime may be "vested" and not merely "blocked".[192] However, it must be borne in mind that this is so because war always entails the right of the victor to claim compensation for the losses sustained. But the vesting of enemy property or funds and the freezing of foreign funds in peacetime are not to be put on the same footing, since they do not exactly serve the same purpose.[193] Indeed such is the difference between them that Congress saw fit in 1965 to repeal a rule that originally provided for the vesting and sale of assets owned by the Cuban government.[194] However, in the case of Iran, President Carter said in his message to Congress that as far as blocking Iranian government property was concerned,[195] the freeze had been ordered to "enable the United States to assure that these resources will be available to satisfy lawful claims of citizens

[190] See *supra*, n. 86.

[191] See Exec. Ord. No. 8389 as amended, set as a note under 12 U.S.C. § 95a (1982).

[192] In *Nielsen v. Secretary of Treasury,* the court of appeals (DDC) rightly pointed out: "The blocking of accounts is generally recognized different from taking," 424 F.2d 833, 843[9] (1970).

[193] In wartime, as the Supreme Court held in *Propper v. Clark:* "If transactions are blocked, vesting may or may not follow. When the custodian vests blocked property, title passes to the custodian and his authority to vest and hold canot be questioned except as provided in the Trading With the Enemy Act. The freezing order of June 14, 1941, immobilized the assets covered by its terms so that title to them might not shift from person to person, except by license, until the government could determine whether those assets were needed for prosecution of the threatened war or to compensate our citizens or ourselves for the damages done by the governments of the nationals affected," 337 U.S. 472 (1948).

[194] Pub. L. 89-262, 79 Stat. 988, Oct. 19, 1965.

[195] See Exec. Ord. No. 12170, 44 F.R. 65729 (Nov. 14, 1979).

and entities of the United States against the Government.''[196] This careless statement naturally led private litigants to believe that the freeze order was a preliminary step to seizure and vesting exactly as in wartime where vesting amounts as it were to the ''withholding of spoils of war.''[197] As a result numerous suits were introduced in United States courts by potential creditors in order to attach every Iranian government asset available. All these judicial proceedings were terminated by Executive Order No. 12283,[198] following the agreements between the United States and the government of Iran, as reflected in declarations of the government of the Democratic and Popular Republic of Algeria (Jan. 19, 1981). Following the executive order, *Dames & Moore v. Regan* dealt a death-blow to the purported compensatory purpose of a freeze in peacetime. In turning frozen assets into ''bargaining chips,''[199] the Supreme Court made it clear that the vesting and the seizure of such assets are not within the scope of a freeze in peacetime, *i.e.* are not valid. Therefore, a freeze of assets in peacetime is a measure paving the way to reparation, *i.e.* a genuine action for performance.

Secondly, the apparent compensatory character of certain countermeasures derives from their substance. Several United States countermeasures remain confined within the same substantive field that is covered by the violation. For instance, a ban on imports of fish or fish products is ordered in response to an illegal seizure of United States fishing vessels,[200] or a suspension of a foreign air carrier permit counters any adverse effects on United States air carriers of a foreign state's air policy.[201] In such situations, the countermeasure is tainted by reciprocity in kind, *i.e.* retaliation, although it is doubtful that the logic of countermeasures imposes on the responding state a duty to resort to an action substantially connected with the offense. In any case, this

[196] 15 *Weekly Compilation of Presidential Documents* 2118 (Nov. 14, 1979). Five months later the justifications of the U.S. government were more elaborate. See the statement made by Roberts B. Owen, Legal Adviser to the Department of State, oral argument to the International Court of Justice on March 20, 1980, *Department of State Bulletin*, 56 (1980).

[197] *Guessefeldt v. McGrath*, 342 U.S. 308, 313-4 (1952).

[198] 46 F.R. 7927 (1981).

[199] 453 U.S. 654, 673 (1980).

[200] 16 U.S.C. § 1825 (1982).

[201] 49 App. U.S.C. § 1372(f) (1982).

particular characteristic makes such actions resemble "compensation" for the breach even though the compensation at stake stems from the traditional retaliatory character of any reciprocal action in kind. But these countermeasures are never fitted to the damage; they remain tailored to the breach. To that extent, it is disputable that they are adequate to achieve their ultimate purpose, which is to ensure a return to law compliance.

There is no question that the adequacy of an action for performance is difficult to assess. But such an action is adequate first and foremost if it affects the offender and not, at the same time, other subjects of international law. In that respect, Section 12 of the International Development Association Act,[202] which requires United States representatives to vote against any loan in favor of a foreign country that has nationalized American property without compensation, affects not only the foreign state, but the international financial institution as well. Such an action is totally inadequate insofar as it represents in some ways a "measure" against the offender and a "countermeasure" against the organizations, the constitutive charters of which are put in abeyance.

Insofar as countermeasures are actions for performance, they are necessarily not tailored to the injury sustained by the United States. This is inevitable, since the return to law compliance, *i.e.* to the *status quo ante,* can be achieved only by adding something more than would be necessary to reestablish equivalance between the parties. This additional step may take various forms, but in any event it must be subject to the rule of proportionality.[203] Here lies one means to test the "legitimacy" of the countermeasure under international law.[204] Proportionality does not call for a response matching the breach, but for a response fulfilling its purpose, which is to revert to the *status quo ante*. In other words, the response must not entail disproportionate effects with respect to its goal. In that sense, some United States countermeasures appear quite controversial. For

[202] 22 U.S.C. § 284(j) (1982).
[203] See E. Zoller, *Peacetime,* at 131-137.
[204] See *Yrbk. I.L.C.*, 1979, II(2), at 119 and 121.

instance, proportionality becomes meaningless when the freeze of Cuban assets is compared to the freeze of Iranian governmental funds.

The Foreign Claims Settlement Commission has certified claims against Cuba in excess of $1.8 billion. In addition to these private claims, the federal government has claims of approximately $200 million. Cuban assets frozen in the United States amount to only $33 million, or about 1.65 percent of the United States claims against Cuba.[205] By contrast, the freezing of $13 billion of governmental Iranian assets more than covered the total of United States claims.[206] Nevertheless the freezing of the Iranian assets resulted in the safe delivery of the hostages and the establishment of an Arbitral Tribunal for the settlement of private claims. To that extent the freeze was a successful action for performance.

Among all the United States statutory countermeasures, Section 301 of the Trade Act is indeed the most successful action for performance, although it is impossible to verify the proportionality test since, apart from the Border Broadcasting dispute between the United States and Canada,[207] the mere threat of action has been always sufficient to obtain satisfaction. Section 301 is no doubt a spurious form of statutory countermeasure, since it was not designed to always result in an infringement of an international obligation. But Section 301 is quite meaningful with respect to performance, since its primary purpose is "to enforce" United States rights. Since 1976, Section 301 has been used more than 40 times and in every case upon a private complaint.[208] On some occasions the investigation was discontinued on the ground that there was not sufficient justification to the claims; on others the investigation was terminated following a bilateral settlement of the dispute, in which case actions for performance were successful. But the reasons for success are

[205] See *U.S. Digest* 1979, p. 119.

[206] See Anthony D'Amato, "The Concept of Human Rights in International Law," 82 *Colum. L. Rev.*, 1110, 1154 (1982).

[207] See *infra*, Chap. 4, pp. 140-141.

[208] Section 301 Table of Cases, Office of the United States Trade Representative, 11/26/84. See also Bart S. Fischer & Ralph G. Steinhardt, III, "Section 301 of the Trade Act of 1974: Protection for U.S. Exporters of Goods, Services, and Capital," 14 *Law & Pol'y. Int'l. Bus.*, 569 (1982).

difficult to pinpoint, as negotiations between the United States and foreign countries are not made public. The reasons which justify the full achievement of the action for performance have to be guessed at, although there is no question that the threat may be brandished under various forms.[209] A conspicuous feature of Section 301 is to be found in the decisive role bestowed upon private individuals, since the threat proposals are expressly to be developed by the petitioner at a very early stage in the proceedings.[210] To some extent Section 301 represents a modern version of private reprisals. Moreover it has the invaluable advantage at the international level of making it appear that the United States government is not responsible for the possible disproportionate effects of the action contemplated. Nevertheless, the efficiency of Section 301 with respect to enforcement problems casts doubts on the possibility of subjecting proportionality to a measure of rule.

If proportionality calls for an action tailored to the goal of the responding state, there is no doubt that in order to match the proportionality test, the response has to remain purposive in character. In other words, the countermeasure must give the offender a chance to mend its ways. In that respect, all United States countermeasures are temporary in duration insofar as they are to be lifted when the offender reverts to law compliance. An apparent exception, however, seems to derive from the Sabbatino Amendment,[211] since the legal suit initiated thereby may put the offender before a *fait accompli, i.e.,* a condemnation of the foreign sovereign public act. Regarding the practice followed by

[209] See, for example, the interesting suggestions made by Jeanne S. Archibald, Chairman of the Section 301 Committee at the U.S.T.R.: "One approach is to target the retaliation to the sector which is the focus of the unfair trade practice. An example of this approach would be the imposition of import restrictions on finished leather goods from a country which restricts access for United States leather exports. Another approach is to target the trade interests of those individuals or businesses in the foreign country which benefit from the unfair practice. For example, assume foreign insurance firms are restricted in the areas in which they can compete with domestic firms. Assume further that the parent companies of these domestic insurance firms engage in shipping to the United States. Retaliation may be directed to those shipping activities. A third approach calls for the imposition of restrictions on the products or services of greatest value to the economy of the foreign country generally. Such retaliation is unlikely to be related to the offending act, policy or practice," in *Manual for the Practice of International Trade Law,* VII-17 (1984).

[210] *Ibid.*

[211] 22 U.S.C. § 2370(e) (2) (1982).

the Carter administration after the Agreements of Algiers with Iran (Jan. 19, 1981), upheld as constitutional by the Supreme Court in *Dames & Moore v. Regan,*[212] the President has authority to terminate preliminary and even final rulings of United States courts following an agreement between the United States and the offending state.

However, United States countermeasures show that there are two ways to give the offender a chance. The adequacy of the remedy provided does not have the same significance in both cases. These two ways depend on the presence or the absence of preliminary procedures. When action is taken immediately without prior consultation such as a freeze on foreign assets or a court action taken by a private plaintiff under the Foreign Sovereign Immunities Act, the foreign state is called to revert to the *status quo ante* at once under United States pressures. By contrast, when action works as a sword of Damocles as in the case of Section 301, the foreign state knows in advance what measure it will be exposed to should it refuse to revert to law compliance. It is submitted that the two situations are not on the same footing, especially with due respect to the *United States/France Air Service* Award (1978), in which the tribunal clearly limited the response of the affected state, before and during negotiations, to the right "to restore the symmetry of the initial positions,"[213] *i.e.*, to reciprocal action. But countermeasures are by nature nonreciprocal actions. It is doubtful that such considerations were not taken into account when in 1974, the CAB proposed an amendment to Part 213 of the Economic Regulations,[214] the purpose of which was to clarify the regulation so that its provisions could be invoked under various circumstances, in particular in case of failure by foreign governments to maintain a "fair and equal opportunity for United States carriers to exercise their bilateral rights."[215] The foreign air carriers argued that bilateral air services agreements precluded any restrictive action against them until such time as either the agreement was ter-

[212] 453 U.S. 654.

[213] 18 *U.N.R.I.A.A.*, 445, § 90.

[214] 14 C.F.R. Part 213.3(c) (1984).

[215] 39 F.R. 30842 (1974).

minated, or the dispute had been submitted to arbitration. The board dismissed this interpretation since, assuming compliance with the obligations of prior consultations, ''there would be no basis for concluding that the proposed amendment would be inconsistent with the bilateral provisions. . . . This is particularly true since the vast majority of U.S. bilaterals in terms provide that arbitration procedures will be invoked only at the option of either party''.[216] Such considerations provide ample evidence that the international procedures attached to the response are an important element of its general adequacy and that ultimately, as to particular injuries, the choice between reciprocity and nonreciprocity is not just linked to the identical or nonidentical character of the violated obligation. In other words, a step beyond reciprocity is to be taken only after prior warning. The foreign state's response to such a warning is indeed a prerequisite to going beyond reciprocity.

[216] The Board's interpretation has not been invalidated by the Arbitral Tribunal in the *Air Service* Award between the United States and France (Dec. 7, 1978), but based on broader grounds, 18 *U.N.R.I.A.A.* 446, § 98.

2

Remedies for Collective Injuries

A collective injury in international law may be defined as an injury affecting a group of states as a whole. It is the injury that jeopardizes a solidarity established between several members of the international community. Theoretically that solidarity is twofold: It may be *de facto* solidarity, the collective interests which unify states of a same continent or geographical area; usually however, it is a *de jure* solidarity, *i.e.* a solidarity clothed in a legal instrument. Indeed the development of regional solidarities has not been prevalent enough to give rise to other forms of solidarity than those resulting from a multilateral agreement.[1] Consequently a collective injury is the injury deriving from the breach of a multilateral convention.

Breaches of multilateral agreements raise intricate problems because they do not always entail the same consequences for each contracting party. They may affect one state in particular, or the group of states as a whole, or both. Whenever the rights and interests of one state are ''specifically affected'' (Article 60(2) (b) of the Vienna Convention on the Law of Treaties), that state suffers a particular injury which under the law of international responsibility ought to be treated exactly as any other particular injury. The specially affected state is an ''injured state;'' the remedies available to it to make up for the wrong are similar in substance or in nature to those available in the case of a particular injury. This is inevitable, since the Permanent

[1] Bruno Paradisi, ''L'amitié internationale; les phases critiques de son ancienne histoire,'' 78 *R.C.A.D.I.*, 329-378 (1951, I).

Court of International Justice in the *Chorzów Factory* case made no distinction between bilateral treaties and multilateral agreements when it stated: "It is a principle of international law that the breach of an engagement involves an obligation to make reparation in an adequate form."[2] As a matter of fact, all United States statutory provisions seeking redress for nationalization without compensation, discriminatory trade practices, or restrictions on United States commerce do not depend on the bilateral or multilateral character of the violated agreement; nor for that matter do they take into account the customary origin of the violated form. That is a sound position, since any particular injury has to be treated in the same way, regardless of the origin of the breach.[3]

The problem becomes more complicated when the breach of the multilateral agreement does not affect one state in particular, but the contracting parties as a whole. In such a situation, where the breach affects each contracting party, there is little doubt that the collectivity of contracting parties as a whole suffers an injury and is entitled to claim reparation in an adequate form. As to the form that such a reparation may take, a distinction must be made between the situations in which the consequences of the violation are organized by the treaty itself and those in which they are not.

Sometimes the treaty provides remedies against the offender. These remedies may be collective or unilateral. Collective reparation under the form of a joint action is to be found, for example, in the provisions of the constitutive charters of international organizations which provide for remedies against a defaulting party. For instance, Article 19 of the United Nations Charter provides for a collective remedy insofar as the General Assembly may suspend the voting rights of a state in default of payment. Unilateral remedies may also be bestowed upon one contracting party, either for the benefit of the entire contracting parties as a whole (*e.g.*, a contracting party to an international labor convention may file a complaint with the International Labor Office if it is dissatisfied with another contracting party's

[2] P.C.I.J., *Chorzów Factory (Jurisdiction)* Ser. A/8, 21.
[3] See E. Zoller, *Peacetime,* at 81-93, and *supra* p. 13.

compliance with the convention), or for its own benefit (*e.g.* a contracting party to the Agreement on Subsidies and Countervailing Measures of Article VI, XVI, XXIII of the GATT is entitled to levy countervailing duties on the products of a contracting party that subsidizes its exports, but only in the case of a "material injury" caused to its own industry).

Whenever the treaty fails to set forth provisions regarding the consequences of its violation, the situation is more intricate. To what extent may one contracting party which is no more affected than the others take unilateral steps against the offender? This problem may be dealt with in two different manners.

The first approach links the lawfulness of these unilateral steps with an injury sustained by the acting state. This approach is to be found partially in the proposals by the Special Rapporteur on State Responsibility, Willem Riphagen, in his fifth report to the International Law Commission.[4] Under Article 60(2) of the Vienna Convention on the Law of Treaties, a contracting party to a multilateral agreement can take unilateral steps only if "injured" following a breach of that agreement. However, an approach based only upon treaty law has a major flaw: The concept of "injured State" is elusive to grasp because it is connected with the unsettled notion of "moral damage" in international law. Eventually this approach ends up by considering any breach of a multilateral agreement as invariably injurious to the contracting parties, a result which does not advance international legal reasoning very far.

The second approach is to be found in the laws of the United States. It disconnects the right to take unilateral steps from a possible injury sustained by the responding state. Many United States statutory provisions in the case of a collective injury call

[4] According to the Special Rapporteur, a state which is a contracting party to a multilateral agreement could claim to be "injured" following a breach of that multilateral agreement only if it is established that,

(i) the obligation was stipulated in its favour, or

(ii) the breach of the obligation by one State party necessarily affects the exercise of the rights or the performance of the obligations of all other States parties, or

(iii) the obligation was stipulated for the protection of collective interests of the States parties, or

(iv) the obligation was stipulated for the protection of individual persons, irrespective of their nationality, Report of the International Law Commission, 39 G.A.O.R., Supplement No. 10 (A/39/10), p. 237.

for measures and countermeasures against the offending state without ever taking into account a possible injury suffered by the country. This approach puts the United States in the position of a sheriff for the benefit of the contracting parties as a whole, a result which *a priori* is quite troublesome inasmuch as these steps are taken across the board, *i.e.*, against any foreign country that violates the agreement, regardless of whether or not it is a party thereto.

The two approaches address the same problem under completely different perspectives. The injury approach addresses the problem as a matter of international responsibility, whereas the United States approach deals with it as a matter of enforcement. The injury approach stems directly from the solutions provided by the Vienna Convention on the Law of Treaties. Under Article 60 of that convention, violations of multilateral agreements entail different consequences on the treaty law remedies available to the contracting parties. In particular, a contracting party that is not specially affected by the breach of the multilateral agreement can suspend the operation of the treaty for itself only insofar as the breach radically changes the position of every party with respect to the further performance of the treaty, *i.e.,* insofar as the breach concerns a treaty of an ''integral character.'' *Mutatis mutandis* the treaty oriented approach proposes the same solution in the law of international responsibility. Just as under treaty law a contracting party may take steps unilaterally only when ''specially affected'' by the breach, the same solution should prevail under the law of international responsibility: The contracting party may take steps only when ''injured'' by the breach. The correctness of this approach lies in the assumption that the law of international responsibility is the counterpart of the law of treaties. But that is very doubtful, at least as far as multilateral agreements are concerned. The reason is that unlike bilateral commitments, reciprocal action is not and never has been contemplated as a redress following collective injuries. In particular, no United States statute providing for measures in case of collective injuries ever regards reciprocity as a possible response to such an injury.

By contrast, one may wonder whether the United States approach is not in some ways a response to a problem which was carefully avoided by the Vienna Convention on the Law of Treaties; namely whether general international law compels states not to hinder the execution of valid treaties concluded by other states.[5] The Vienna Convention makes such an obligation binding upon third states only when the rules embodied in the treaty have turned into customary rules of international law recognized as such. The problem is that the United States literally enforces against all states some rules which are not truly customary in nature. Such is the case of an international fishery program whose noncompliance by any state exposes the wrongdoer to a total ban of fish and fish product imports into the United States.[6] One may, of course, consider that the many treaties relating to the conservation of resources and to the protection of environment and endagered species have, as it were, created a general customary rule that precludes a noncontracting party from jeopardizing the objectives set forth in such treaties. But this would move the problem little further because an international fishery program may change each year, is to be applied immediately on its enactment, and is usually limited in scope to a definite geographical area. Assuming that the concept of regional customary rule would support the customary approach, it would still be necessary to explain as a matter of law the emergence of a customary rule at once, without state practice, and the concept of a yearly adjustable customary obligation.[7] Such straightforward observations already cast doubt on the possible customary entitlement that could justify an all-embracing enforcement of these conventions by the United States. In other words, the United States seems to enforce these conventions less because they have given rise to customary rules that are binding upon all

[5] See Sir Ian Sinclair, *The Vienna Convention on the Law of Treaties* (1984), 99.

[6] 22 U.S.C. § 1978(a) (1982).

[7] State practice is indeed a crucial test in the emergence of a customary rule because as Anthony D'Amato explains: "[S]tate practice reflects a consensus with respect to the secondary rule of custom-formation. When a rule is alleged to be a rule of 'custom,' the person asserting the rule must adduce a qualitative articulation of the rule *and* a quantitative element as well. Without the latter, one could not tell which of the numerous and often contradictory articulated norms were actually embodied in customary law," *The Concept of Custom in International Law* (1971), 87 [italics in the text].

states whether party to these multilateral conventions or not, than because these conventions may be invoked against any foreign country.

There is no question that a treaty does not create either obligations or rights for a third state without its consent. But the minimum requirement that can be expected from third parties or objecting states is to be found in their general duty "to respect, recognize, and in the legal sense, accept, the consequences of lawful and valid international acts entered into between other states."[8] Such a general duty does not confer any rights, nor does it impose any obligations on third states. It merely calls on them to acknowledge the lawfulness and the validity of treaties concluded between other subjects of law. As a matter of common sense, the acknowledgement of lawful legal titles is required by any legal orders insofar as, in order to avoid anarchy, legal entitlements have to be invocable against third parties.[9] Such a situation could be referred to as "invocability," whereas the concept of enforcement could designate the devices by which this legal situation is made effective.[10] It must be noted on the one hand that invocability is not necessarily linked to rights *in rem, i.e.*, to treaties providing for objective regimes, insofar as a loan agreement between an international financial institution and a foreign country, for instance, may be invoked against a third state that would also have debtor rights against such country.[11] On the other hand, third parties to bilateral or multilateral conventions may indeed invoke such legal instruments to

[8] Sir G. Fitzmaurice, Fifth Report on the Law of Treaties, *Yrbk. I.L.C.* 1960, Vol. II, p. 98, § 71. See also Paul Reuter, *Introduction au droit des traités* p. 114, § 159.

[9] That is why among other reasons the registration of treaties with subsequent publication thereof is an essential procedural requirement in order to enable a party to any such treaty to invoke it against any state before the organs of the United Nations (Article 102 of the United Nations Charter).

[10] The international vocabulary is not well settled in the field. In the *Fisheries case, Judgment of December 18th, 1951,* the International Court of Justice referred in the authoritative French text to "un titre historique qui lui (le Royaume- Uni) soit *opposable*" and in the English text to "an historic title *enforceable* against it," I.C.J. *Reports* 1951, p. 139 (emphasis added).

[11] As a result, in 1964 the International Law Commission was right to delete an article proposed by Sir Humphrey Waldock, which in substance would have limited the scope of "invocability" only to treaties providing for objective regimes. See *Yrbk. I.L.C.* 1964, Vol. I, pp. 96-109; Vol. II, pp. 26-34 and, for an insight in municipal law, J. Limpens, "De l'opposabilité des contrats à l'égard des tiers, Contribution à l'étude de la distinction entre les droits réels et personnels", *Mélanges Roubier,* Vol. II, pp. 89-104.

their own benefit. Such is the case of any state that invokes a bilateral or multilateral agreement to which it is not a contracting party in order to produce evidence of the emergence of a customary rule. In short, the principle of relativity of treaties *(pacta tertiis nec nocent nec prosunt)* is relevant in every respect as far as rights and obligations are concerned and irrelevant with regard to the legal existence of the treaty.

There is little doubt that the unilateral steps taken by the United States to compel every state to respect the legal consequences deriving from certain multilateral conventions have to be explained by the absence of collective mechanisms that would insure their enforcement. Indeed most international agreements do not provide for such organs (*e.g.*, the 1958 Geneva Conventions on the Law of the Sea; the 1982 Convention on the Law of the Sea), or if they do provide for international organs of control and management, these bodies are usually powerless to provide redress for collective injury (*e.g.*, the International Whaling Commission). Moreover, even if they had such powers, it is not certain that contracting parties would be precluded from taking unilateral steps unless the multilateral agreement had vested the international bodies with an exclusive responsibility to ensure compliance with the rights of contracting parties, as is the case for the European Economic Community Treaty (1957) for certain fields of jurisdiction.

In such circumstances, the United States Congress was right to imply in its legislation that collective injuries warrant a concern for each party to a mulilateral agreement and to adopt a number of statutes providing for unilateral action against countries that fail to abide by the provisions of international instruments. Those statutes, however, cannot be compared to the pieces of legislation surveyed so far. First, they usually refer to the relevant multilateral convention *expressis verbis*. For instance, the Marine Mammal Protection Act of 1972 formally refers to the International Convention for the Regulation of Whaling (1946);[12] or the Endangered Species Act of 1973 to the Convention of International Trade in Endangered Species of Wild Fauna and Flora

[12] 16 U.S.C. § 1402(a) (1) (1982).

(1973);[13] or the Nuclear Non-Proliferation Act of 1978 to the Treaty on the Non-Proliferation of Nuclear Weapons 1968;[14] or the Federal Aviation Act of 1958, as amended, to the Convention for the Suppression of Unlawful Seizure of Aircraft (1971).[15] Secondly, the violations of those conventions by foreign states do not affect specially the interests of the United States. Its interests, of course, are affected, but no more than those of the other contracting parties. That is why one should avoid including in remedies for collective injuries the statutory provisions which apparently provide for such remedies following the breach of a multilateral convention, but which actually tie such remedies to the positive evidence of a "material injury" caused to an industry of the United States such as, for example, the Trade Agreements Act of 1979, which expressly refers to the Agreements on Subsidies and Countervailing Measures of Articles VI, XVI, XXIII of the GATT.[16] Thirdly, as already noted, the remedies for collective injuries are usually invoked against any foreign country whether party to the multilateral conventions or not. This is obviously a very significant point. But its effect may vary according to the nature of the remedy provided for, which may be a simple measure or a countermeasure.

[13] 16 U.S.C. § 1532(4) (1982).

[14] 22 U.S.C. § 3201(c) (1982).

[15] 49 App. U.S.C. § 1514(a) (1982).

[16] 19 U.S.C. § 1671(b) (1) (1982); 19 U.S.C. § 2503(b) (1982). Similar examples could also be found in the Controlled Substances Act of 1970 which refers to the 1960 Single Convention on Narcotic Drugs [21 U.S.C. § 801(7) (1982)] or in the Psychotropic Substances Act of 1978 which implements the 1971 Convention on Psychotropic Substances [21 U.S.C. § 801a(2) (1982)]. Both consider illegal drug trafficking as a collective injury, but measures are provided only insofar as such substances as imported into the country. The particular injury supersedes as it were the collective injury. *Mutatis mutandis,* the situation is the same where a countervailing duty is levied upon the products of a foreign state that bestows bounties or grants upon the manufacture of its products without, however, being internationally bound not to do so [19 U.S.C. § 1303(a) (1) (1982)]. Admittedly Section 303 of the Tariff Act of June 17, 1930, could be construed nowadays as providing a remedy for a collective injury insofar as, with respect to the number of countries bound by the GATT obligations, the domestic or exports subsidies granted by any noncontracting party jeopardize the collective interests of the contracting parties to the GATT or the Subsidies Code and turn their own international obligation into inequitable commitments. However, the countervailing duty is always levied only insofar as the products are imported into the United States. In other words, the United States takes action only when its own interests are concerned without this effect always amounting to an injury (absence of "injury test" in this case). The particular effect, therefore, always takes precedence over the collective injury.

I. Measures

1. Subject Matter

In various fields such as non-proliferation, environment, conservation, fisheries and aviation, the United States has taken steps to induce foreign countries to respect certain international agreements which it regards as essential to the community of contracting parties. That community may be very small, such as the nuclear weapons states as defined in Article IX(e) of the Treaty on the Non-Proliferation of Nuclear Weapons; but it may also be very large, as in the case of the 1970 Hague Convention (Convention for the Suppression of Unlawful Seizure of Aircrafts). Most of the time, such steps are not inconsistent with international obligations.

Such is obviously the case first when the measure contemplated is nothing but the application of an act expressly authorized, if not required, by the treaty itself and implemented among the contracting parties. For instance, no international rule is infringed as to any contracting party to the Convention on International Trade in Endangered Species of Fauna and Flora (1973),[17] by a United States import ban on any such species from those countries.[18] In a more elaborate manner, although the International Convention for the Regulation of Whaling (1946)[19] does not authorize the contracting parties to prohibit the importation of marine mammals into their territory, Section 101 of the Marine Mammal Protection Act of 1972[20] which precisely provides for such action, does not violate an international obligation as to any foreign country which, although not a party to the Convention for the Regulation of Whaling, is nevertheless bound by the Convention on International Trade in Endangered Species, provided the prohibition applies to Cetacea listed in Annex I of that convention. The convention signatories have moreover recognized the right of each contracting party to implement ''stricter

[17] T.I.A.S. § 8249.

[18] Compare Section 9 of the Endangered Species Act of 1973 (Publ. L. 93-205, 87 Stat. 893 codified at 16 U.S.C. § 1538 (1982)), with Articles II, VIII(1) of the convention.

[19] T.I.A.S. § 1849.

[20] 16 U.S.C. § 1371(a) (3) (A) (1982).

domestic measures'' including ''complete prohibition'' of trade in a species (Article XIV, paragraph 1). Such measures may therefore supersede the minimum trade standards set forth in the convention. In *Cayman Turtle Farm, Ltd. v. Andrews et al.* (DDC., 1979)[21] the United States District Court upheld the validity of regulations issued by the secretaries of the Interior and Commerce under the authority of both the Endangered Species Act of 1973 and the convention which prohibited the importation and trade in the United States of all green sea turtle products produced in commercial mariculture activities, although such regulations eliminated the mariculture exemption for sea turtles bred in captivity as set forth in Appendix I of the convention.[22] In some cases steps have been taken to avoid any possible conflict between the domestic regulations and the international obligations of the United States. The regulations implementing the Marine Mammal Protection Act of 1972 expressly provide that the act and the regulations adopted in pursuance thereof shall not apply to the extent that they are inconsistent with the provisions of any international treaty, convention or agreement which was existent and in force prior to the passing of the act, and especially to the extent that they may run counter to activities carried out pursuant to the Interim Convention on the Conservation of North Pacific Fur Seals signed in Washington on February 9, 1957.[23]

Similar enforcement procedures have also been adopted in the field of narcotic drugs law enforcement. Section 1002 of the 1970 Controlled Substances Act[24] prohibits the importation of controlled substances from foreign states bound by the Convention on Psychotropic Substances (1971)[25] as well as from any state that is a party only to the Single Convention on Narcotic Drugs (1961).[26] This all-embracing enforcement is interesting with respect to the differences in import regulations between Article 31 of that convention and Article 13 of the Convention

[21] 478 F. Supp. 125.
[22] 42 F.R. 10452 (Feb. 22, 1977).
[23] 50 C.F.R. § 18.21 (1983).
[24] 21 U.S.C. § 952 (1982).
[25] T.I.A.S. § 9725.
[26] T.I.A.S. § 6298.

on Psychotropic Substances. In the latter, imports may be prohibited, whereas in the former they can only be controlled.

However, the most common means of exerting pressure on foreign countries in order to ensure compliance with the provisions of a multilateral agreement is still to be found in the boundless field of inimical measures. Just as many United States statutes sought economic hardship for the offender in case of particular injuries, so the aim of several statutory provisions is to inflict economic harm on foreign states whose behavior is viewed incompatible (and not necessarily inconsistent) with the provisions of a multilateral convention. Such a result is generally achieved by suspending an advantage granted to foreign countries by United States law. For instance, the Packwood-Magnuson Amendment to the Fishery Conservation and Management Act of 1976 provides for reductions in fishing allocations within the 200-mile U.S. fishery conservation and management zone to nations which the Secretary of Commerce certifies are diminishing the effectiveness of the International Convention for the Regulation of Whaling.[27] The Board of Directors of Eximbank shall not give approval to guarantee, insure, or extend credit in support of exports to any country violating the nuclear safeguards laid down in any trilateral agreement between the I.A.E.A., the United States, and that country.[28] The same measure is also applied to any country—except a nuclear-weapons state as defined in Article IX(3) of the Treaty on the Non-Proliferation of Nuclear Weapons—which detonates a nuclear explosive device.[29] Similarly, the benefit of assistance may be discontinued to any country failing in its obligations to the United Nations, especially if that country is in arrears in the payment of its financial contributions to that organization,[30] a measure which obviously can relate only to foreign countries in need of U.S. economic assistance.

In actual fact, the pressure is easily exerted when the foreign country is dependent on the United States. To some extent, the

[27] 16 U.S.C. § 1821 (e) (2) (A), (B) (1982).
[28] 12 U.S.C. § 635(b) (4) (1982).
[29] *Ibid.*
[30] 22 U.S.C. 2370(u) (1982).

well-known aphorism "beggars cannot be choosers" applies in foreign policy. One of the most striking examples is the position of the great majority of foreign countries regarding nuclear energy and technology. Ever since "the demon of nuclear warfare [was] unleashed at the end of the Second World War,"[31] the basic concern of the United States has been to avoid exports of nuclear materials enhancing the proliferation of nuclear weapons. As a result several statutes have been passed to control the spread of nuclear technology. Interestingly enough, such legislation has been enacted at two different levels, a particularly relevant fact, as it shows that the United States is fully aware of the limits on unilateral enforcement powers under international law. Provisions aimed at preventing nuclear proliferation are actually to be found in two different Titles of the United States Code. The first is Title 42 on Public Health and Welfare, which lays down all the provisions relating to nuclear cooperation with other nations. This title, which includes the Atomic Energy Act of 1954 as amended by the Nuclear Non-Proliferation Act of 1978,[32] is essentially devoted to export criteria and licensing procedures, a distinctive feature which proves that export controls are viewed as domestically relevant questions. The second is Title 22 on Foreign Relations and Intercourse, which includes the Nuclear Non-Proliferation Act of 1978.[33] This title squarely addresses the issue of nuclear non-proliferation, *i.e.*, the internationally sensitive question.[34] However, it carefully avoids any provisions that could be construed as an infringement on the right of other nations to use the benefits of atomic energy. Unlike the provisions related to export controls, which are unilaterally imposed on any recipient country, Chapter 47 of Title 22 emphasizes "discussions with other nations," "international approaches," "negotiating binding international undertakings" to prevent proliferation.[35] The truth is that export procedures for nuclear material are in fact an indirect approach to non-proliferation.

[31] Paul Szasz, "Sanctions and International Nuclear Controls," 11 *Conn. L. Rev.* 545 (1979).
[32] 42 U.S.C. § 2151-2168 (1982).
[33] 92 Stat. 120.
[34] 22 U.S.C. § 3201-3282 (1982).
[35] 22 U.S.C. 3223 (1982).

Such procedures put foreign nations under intensive pressure to ensure that exports are used solely for peaceful purposes, following an agreement for cooperation, and are not diverted to unauthorized uses.[36] A surprisingly ingenious legal mechanism has been set up which relentlessly ties any recipient state to the interests of the United States, as India was to realize in its operation of the Tarapur Atomic Power Station.[37] Any nuclear cooperation between the United States and a foreign country involves a twofold procedure which includes an agreement for cooperation and a contract. The agreement is a treaty to which incidentally the International Atomic Energy Agency may or may not be a party. Under the agreement, the United States pledges itself to supply nuclear technology to the recipient state provided it abides by a series of safeguards, chief among which are the I.A.E.A. safeguards. The agreement is followed by a contract which in practice turns out to be the key component of the transaction for the recipient state, since the contract actually implements the provisions of the agreement, *i.e.*, provides the state with the nuclear materials. But the most important legal aspect is its legal nature: it is a contract and not a treaty. As a result, the contract is subject to United States law, especially to the hierarchy of norms and to the principle that a contract shall not run counter to a public policy provision. Therefore, any change in U.S. regulations on nuclear export procedures automatically applies to the contract, and the treaty commitments cannot be relied upon to block any adverse effects of the new statutory regulations. In that respect the Tarapur Atomic Power Station case is quite significant. On August 8, 1963, the United States and India entered into a thirty-year agreement for nuclear cooperation for civil uses.[38] Article II(A) of the agreement provides: "During the period of the agreement the United States Commission will sell to the Government of India . . ., as

[36] 42 U.S.C. 2155 (1982).
[37] See Note, "Nuclear Non-Proliferation: Export of Nuclear Fuel to India," 22 *Harv. Int'l. L.J.* 227 (1981); Note, "Testing Statutory Criteria for Foreign Policy: The Nuclear Non-Proliferation Act of 1978 and the Export of Nuclear Fuel to India," 14 *N.Y. Univ. J. Int'l. L. & Pol.* 419 (1982).
[38] T.I.A.S. § 5446.

needed, all requirements of the Government of India for enriched uranium for use as fuel at the Tarapur Atomic Power Station," whereas Article VI established a series of safeguards the maintenance of which the Government of India guaranteed in Article VII. The contract of sale, however, expressly provided that the applicable law was the law of the United States (Article XVII) and under a 1971 amendment to that contract, India agreed to "comply with all applicable laws, regulations and ordinances of the United States"[39] concerning the supply of nuclear material. As a result, any interruption of supplies of nuclear fuel under United States export regulations could not have constituted a breach of the agreement and congressional committees could easily argue that such a rule would not have been inconsistent with the latter.[40]

2. Procedures

One of the most interesting aspects of these enforcing legislative measures is to be found in the procedures attached to them. However, it must be borne in mind that when these measures give effect to international obligations in domestic law, they necessarily introduce into the municipal legal order the procedural safeguards laid down in the international agreement. Such procedural safeguards are rather uncommon in international agreements insofar as they are mostly a matter of purely domestic concern. An attractive feature of United States law is that the domestic implementation of many international conventions is clothed in the procedural safeguards which derive from its longstanding commitment to the principles of due process. For instance, Section 4 of the Endangered Species Act, which relates to the determination by the Secretary of Commerce or the Secretary of the Interior of the lists of all species that are to be treated as endangered species within the jurisdiction of the United States, gives effect in domestic law to a unilateral step expressly

[39] The Contract of Sale of Enriched Uranium Between the United States and India (May 17, 1966) and the Amendment (Nov. 26, 1971) are reprinted in S. Rep. No. 96-939, 96th Cong. 2d Sess. (1980) at respectively 51-66 and 67-68.

[40] S. Rep. No. 96-939, *supra* n.38, at 20; H.R. Rep. No. 96-1318 and 96-1319, 96th Cong., 2d Sess. (1980), at 7-8.

authorized by Article XIV(1) of the Convention on International Trade in Endangered Species. However, following the constitutional tradition, Congress subjected such determinations to strong protective proceedings.[41]

In particular, any interested person may file a petition to add a species to, or remove it from, any of the lists of endangered or threatened species. If the secretary does not warrant the petitioned action, he shall promptly publish in the Federal Register his negative finding, which is subject to judicial review. If the secretary proposes to implement a positive determination, he shall publish a general notice and the complete text of the proposed regulation in the Federal Register and promptly hold a public hearing if any person files a request for such a hearing within 45 days after the date of general notice.[42] Those provisions are quite significant, bearing in mind that the term "person" means "an individual, corporation, partnership, trust, association, or any other private party, or any officer, employee, agent, department, or instrumentality of the federal government, of any state or political subdivision thereof, or of *any foreign government*."[43] At the administrative level, a whole set of regulations has been enacted to implement the Convention on International Trade in Endangered Species of Wild Fauna and Flora.[44] Export permits, re-export certificates, and certificates of origin are requirements which may be invoked not only against party countries, but also against countries that are not parties.[45] Participation of the public as well as different consultations with federal agencies are provided for in developing negotiating positions to be used by the representative of the United States at meetings of the conference of the parties to the convention. Notices of meetings of the conference must be published in the Federal Register and the public is invited to comment and provide further information. Public meetings are to be held, during which participants will be given an opportunity to speak.[46] A domestic and inter-

[41] 16 U.S.C. § 1533 (1982).
[42] 16 U.S.C. § 1533(b) (1982).
[43] 16 U.S.C. § 1532(13) (1982) (emphasis added).
[44] 50 C.F.R. § 23 (1983).
[45] 50 C.F.R. § 23.14 (1983).
[46] 50 C.F.R. § § 23.31-23.34 (1983).

national public debate is therefore organized. That debate is open to foreign nations as well as to private entities; it is transparent. For example, by a final rule issued May 8, 1978, the Director of Fish and Wildlife Service announced his determination that the African elephant was a threatened species under the Endangered Species Act of 1973. The decision was based in part upon the result of a survey by a scientist. But eight foreign governments sent responses to the service's official notification of rule-making, which had been transmitted to nearly all African nations and several of the major ivory reexporting countries.[47]

Similar procedures are also provided for the regulations governing the taking of marine mammals incidental to commercial fishing operations. The regulations must be established after opportunity for an agency hearing.[48] Such hearings are governed by the provisions of Sections 556 and 557 of the Administrative Procedure Act.[49] Any person wishing to participate as a party shall notify the director (U.S. Fish and Wildlife Service) by certified mail on or before the date specified in the notice of hearing.[50] The definition of the term "person" is similar to that provided in the Endangered Species Act.[51] However, expedited procedures are provided for consideration of proposed quotas and amended regulations as to the taking of marine mammals incidental to commercial fishing operations.[52] Still, foreigners and foreign countries may participate in the hearing proceedings.

In certain circumstances, the regulations may be subject to judicial review. However, the exact scope of judicial control of administrative action in that field must be the subject of close scrutiny. In *Jensen v. National Marine Fisheries Service* (9th Cir. 1975),[53] the Ninth Circuit Court of Appeals was presented with a case that challenged the validity of regulations approved under the Northern Pacific Halibut Act of 1973.[54] In keeping

[47] *U.S. Digest* 1979, pp. 1483-1485.
[48] 16 U.S.C. § 1373(d) (1982).
[49] 50 C.F.R. § 18.72 (1983) and 50 C.F.R. § 216.72 (1983).
[50] 50 C.F.R. § 18.75 and § 18.84(b) (1983); 50 C.F.R. § 216.74 (1983).
[51] 16 U.S.C. § 1362(a) (1982).
[52] 50 C.F.R. § 216 Appendix (1983).
[53] 512 F.2d 1189.
[54] 16 U.S.C. § § 772-772(j) (1976).

with the "political question" doctrine as enshrined in *Baker v. Carr,*[55] the *Jensen* Court found that the approval of the regulations was agency action in the field of foreign affairs that was committed to executive discretion and therefore nonreviewable. In *United States v. Decker, United States v. Marriott* (9th Cir. 1979),[56] the defendants, who had been convicted in a criminal proceeding for violation of fisheries regulations, challenged the validity of the regulations issued by the International Pacific Salmon Fisheries Commission established under Article II of the 1937 Convention between the United States and Canada. They alleged, *inter alia,* that United States partial approval of the commission regulations, as to non-Indian fishermen only, but not as to Indians, was no approval at all, and hence no valid regulations had been violated. Contrary to the contention of the United States, the court held that validity of the regulations was subject to judicial review, because (1) the authority of a convention party to make only partial approval of commission regulations was not expressly conferred by the convention, thus raising an issue of interpretation, and (2) the validity of the regulations was a prerequisite for the validity of the convictions. In *Hopson et alia v. Kreps et alia* (9th Cir. 1980),[57] the court of appeals reversed the district court's dismissal of an action challenging the validity of whaling regulations as presenting a nonjusticiable political question.[58] Although unlike the *Decker* case individual liberty was not at stake here, the court refused "(to) read *Decker* as holding that justiciability turns on the slender need that distinguishes the seeking of declaratory relief from the threat of prosecution and appellate review of a criminal conviction."[59] Instead, the court held that

> the analysis in *Baker* makes it clear that the criteria enunciated there generally do not apply to claims that the executive has exceeded specific limitations on delegated authority. . . . Questions of statutory authority are clearly

[55] 370 U.S. 186, 217.
[56] 600 F.2d 733, *cert. den.* 444 U.S. 855 (1979).
[57] 622 F.2d 1375.
[58] 462 F. Supp. 1374.
[59] 622 F.2d 1375, at 1379.

> susceptible of judicial handling and involve the classic judicial function of construing statutes to determine whether agencies have acted outside their jurisdiction.[60]

This judicial statement may be construed as calling the judicial branch to address indirectly treaty questions concerning the validity of the regulations issued by international commissions.

Turning to the procedures which accompany nuclear exports to foreign nations, things run the other way. The general policy of insisting upon full-scale safeguards as a condition for any nuclear shipment does in some ways associate foreign nations to the procedures insofar as the nuclear cooperation must be at the outset laid down in an international agreement. But the negotiation is doubtless limited, since the I.A.E.A. safeguards are not by definition "negotiable." Section 128 of the Non-Proliferation Act specified that no export of nuclear material or technology should be made "unless I.A.E.A. safeguards are maintained with respect to all peaceful nuclear activities" in the country of destination. The regulations relating to the export and import of nuclear equipment and material are essentially to be applied "to all persons in the United States,"[61] *i.e.*, mainly any corporation that has applied for a license for the export of any nuclear equipment. Hearings on export license applications are provided for,[62] but only to the extent that the person requesting the hearing may explain why a hearing or an intervention would be in the public interest, and how a hearing or intervention would assist the Nuclear Regulatory Commission in making the determinations required by the Atomic Energy Act.[63] Although the term "person" may include "any foreign government or political entity of such government; and any authorized representative of the foregoing,"[64] it is entirely a matter for the commission's discretion to grant or deny a hearing or intervention.[65] A negative determination is not subject to judicial review. Moreover, the

[60] *Ibid.*, at 1378-1379.
[61] 10 C.F.R. § 110.1(b) (1984).
[62] 10 C.F.R. § 110.80 (1984).
[63] 10 C.F.R. § 110.82(3) (1984).
[64] 10 C.F.R. § 110.2(ee) (1984).
[65] 10 C.F.R. § 110.84(g) (1984).

transparency of any hearing relating to export license applications is subject to stringent limitations which derive from security clearances and access to classified information.[66]

Any country importing U.S. nuclear technology or materials must have ''non-proliferation credentials.''[67] Even when such credentials are met, export licenses are not necessarily granted. Significantly, the regulations on Special Nuclear Controls provide:

> In view of the numerous considerations to be weighted in the case-by-case review process and changing circumstances, *it is not feasible to specify countries' status* for the purpose of implementing these controls.[68]

All those restrictions are scarcely surprising, given the sensitive political character of nuclear exports. But bringing them together with the open procedures prevailing in conservation matters is meaningful. There are indeed many different ways to organize the management of limited solidarities among members of the international community. An interesting aspect of that difference is that the more democratic the management, the less controversial the collective interests, whereas the more authoritative the procedures, the more disputable and disputed the collective solidarity. To some extent the procedures enlighten the substance.

Although the common purpose of these measures is to exert a pressure on foreign nations to abide by specific multilateral agreements, there is little doubt that other considerations can also be involved. In other words, these measures are not always

[66] 10 C.F.R. § 110.121 (1984).

[67] These credentials are based ''on consideration of factors'' such as:

> (1) A country's status as a party to the Treaty on the Non-Proliferation of Nuclear Weapons or the Treaty for the Prohibition of Nuclear Weapons in Latin America. . . .;
> (2) Whether the country has all its nuclear activities under International Atomic Energy Agency safeguards or equivalent full scope safeguards;
> (3) Whether there is an agreement for cooperation in the civil uses of atomic energy between the United States and the country concerned;
> (4) The country's public statements and policies concerning nuclear developments and non-proliferation;
> (5) The extent of cooperation in non-proliferation policy generally (indications such as willingness to consult on international non-proliferation issues); and
> (6) Intelligence data on a country's nuclear intentions and activities, 15 C.F.R. § 378.4(e) (1984).

[68] *Ibid.*, (emphasis added).

resorted to for the exclusive benefit of a community. Export controls on nuclear materials and technology provide the best example. One may wonder whether that is not precisely the reason why in the field of nuclear non-proliferation, as opposed to environmental and conservation issues, the United States has never dared to resort to countermeasures, *i.e.*, to infringe on international obligations toward states which refuse to abide by the 1968 Treaty on Non-Proliferation, although the logic pervading the defense of genuine collective interests would enable them to do so.

II. Countermeasures

1. Subject-Matter

In 1971, conservation of the Atlantic salmon appeared seriously jeopardized by the refusal of Denmark, the Federal Republic of Germany, and Norway to abide by the total ban on salmon fishing decided by the International Commission for the Northwest Atlantic Fisheries for the entire convention area outside national fisheries limits. In contrast to the 11 other members of the commission, the three members objected to the ban which, as a result, did not take effect for them.[69]

On February 2, 1971, Congressman Pelly introduced an amendment to the Fisherman's Protective Act, the purpose of which was to authorize the President to prohibit the importation of fishery products from nations whose fishing operations diminished the effectiveness of international fishery conservation programs. The Pelly Amendment was adopted by Congress and became Public Law 92-219 (Dec. 23, 1971).[70]

The novelty of the amendment was in its scope rather than its substance, for a similar approach had already been followed in the Tuna Conventions Act of 1950, which was amended in 1962 to authorize an embargo on imports of certain species of tuna from countries whose vessels acted "in such manner or in such circumstances as would tend to diminish the effectiveness of the

[69] See H.R. Rep. 92-468, 92d Congress 1st sess. (1971); [1971] *U.S. Code Cong. & Adm. News*, Vol. 2 (1972), p. 2409.

[70] 85 Stat. 786.

conservation recommendations'' of the Inter-American Tropical Tuna Commission.[71] Similarly, an identical approach had been followed to give effect to the International Convention for the Conservation of Atlantic Tunas, signed at Rio de Janeiro on May 14, 1966. Section 6(c) of the Atlantic Tunas Convention Act of 1977 authorizes the Secretary of Commerce to promulgate regulations to prohibit the entry into the United States from any nation of fish or fish products taken in violation of the conservation recommendations.[72]

The Pelly Amendment follows an ''oblique approach''[73] to the problem of remedies for collective injuries. It has proved so successful that it has been extended beyond the field of fisheries conservation.[74] In particular it was used to give effect to the 1973 Convention on International Trade in Endangered Species of Wild Fauna & Flora. Today, Section 8 of the Fisherman's Protective Act authorizes the President to prohibit the importation of fish products or wildlife products from any foreign country whose nationals are acting in a manner which diminishes the effectiveness of any international conservation program for fisheries and endangered or threatened species.[75] The same approach has also been adopted to give effect to the Convention for the Suppression of Unlawful Seizure of Aircraft (Hague Convention of 1971). In 1974, an amendment was added to Title XI of the 1958 Federal Aviation Act to authorize the President to suspend air services to any foreign nation which he sees as encouraging aircraft hijacking or permitting the use of its territory as a sanctuary for terrorist organizations.[76]

Although these provisions have been enacted in different fields, all of them aim at providing redress for the breach of a multilateral agreement to which the United States is a contracting party. But such legal status is never required in relation to other states. All provisions are directed at any foreign nation, whether

[71] 16 U.S.C. § 955(c) (1982).
[72] 16 U.S.C. § 971d(c) (4) (1982).
[73] H.R. Rept. 92-468, *supra* n. 69, at 2410.
[74] H.R. 95-1029, 95th Cong., 2d sess. (1978), pp. 8-11; [1978] *U.S. Code Cong. & Adm. News*, Vol. 3 (1979), pp. 1772-1775.
[75] 22 U.S.C. § 1978(a) (1982).
[76] 49 App. U.S.C. § 1514(a) (1982).

it is a contracting party to the multilateral conventions or not. As a result, questions have been raised as to the legal entitlement that may justify the adoption by a contracting party of measures to be applied against nonparties to a convention. Such was the problem submitted by Senator Cranston to Monroe Leigh, Legal Adviser of the Department of State, when the United States extended its fishery conservation jurisdiction to 200 miles from the coast line. With reference to the Fishery Conservation and Management Act of 1976 under discussion at the time, Senator Cranston asked whether, pursuant to Article 7 of the 1958 Geneva Convention on Fishing and Conservation of the Living Resources of the High Seas, the United States would be justified in adopting conservation measures which would be applied against nonparties to the convention. Mr. Leigh wrote in part:

> While the treaty may not be applied against non-parties as such, and article 7 did not represent a codification of international law at the time it was drafted, there is growing recognition in international law that coastal States may under certain circumstances take conservation measures of the kind prescribed in article 7. In the 1974 *Fisheries Jurisdiction* Case the International Court of Justice recognized a broad duty on all States to take conservation measures with respect to high seas fisheries adjacent to their coast. The Court also recognized the special interests that coastal States have in conservation and management of high seas fisheries adjacent to their coasts. And, the Court held that States are under a mutual obligation to undertake negotiations in good faith for the equitable solution of their differences concerning their respective fishery rights. Thus, a strong case can be made that where, for instance, a coastal State has a substantial economic interest in a particular coastal fishery and that particular stock is being depleted by fishing in excess of the maximum sustainable yield, the coastal State may legally initiate negotiations and other measures as prescribed in article 7 to protect that species pending agreement among the affected States.''[77]

Mr. Leigh's arguments are quite convincing as far as conservation measures relating to fisheries are concerned. But they

[77] *U.S. Digest* 1976, p. 355.

obviously cannot be extended to cover countermeasures following violations of the 1971 Hague Convention or the 1973 Convention on Endangered Species.

On the other hand, all these provisions entitle the executive branch to take stringent action against any foreign state which is flouting a multilateral agreement, for in each case the United States avails itself of the right not to perform vis-à-vis such state an international commitment, *i.e.* to resort to genuine countermeasures. Moreover, the obligations which may be put in abeyance are treaty obligations as well as customary rules. When Congress discussed the Pelly Amendment, reference was made only to Article XX of the GATT. The State Department was unable, at that time, even to provide the Committee on Merchant Marine and Fisheries with a straight interpretation of that article. Article XX amounts to an escape clause insofar as it authorizes a contracting party to take measures inconsistent with the agreement, provided such measures are taken on a nondiscriminatory basis and relate to the conservation of exhaustible natural resources. As such, Article XX is not relevant to the issue raised by the Pelly Amendment because the amendment allows by definition measures taken on a discriminatory basis, since a single state is affected (Such is indeed its very purpose: to affect an offender.), and also because the natural resources contemplated in Article XX are resources in the territory of each contracting party and not the international resources referred to in the Pelly Amendment.[78]

The truth of the matter is that the Pelly Amendment and all related provisions affect not only the rule of nondiscrimination but all kinds of international commitments. First, they affect customary law insofar as they all result in discrimination against a foreign state which is less well treated than other states. The

[78] As to the problem of knowing whether a unilateral prohibition of imports directed at one particular state would be consistent or not with the rule of nondiscrimination, there is no doubt that such a step is completely at variance with that rule. The lipservice paid by the Pelly Amendment to the General Agreement on Tariffs and Trade [22 U.S.C. § 1978(a) (4) (1982)] does not clear this vivid inconsistency. But as already mentioned, the rule of nondiscrimination implies equality and therefore only applies to comparable situations. Since a non-complying state is obviously not in the same situation as law-abiding states, there is no need to apply to it a rule whose implementation only makes sense if it applied in similar situations.

antihijacking provision even affects the foreign territorial jurisdiction which enables such sovereign country "to establish for itself its legal situation vis-à-vis other states"[79] and to grant asylum to a hijacker regarded by that country as a persecuted refugee. Secondly, all these provisions authorize actions inconsistent with any multilateral convention that requires each contracting party to grant any other contracting party the most-favored-nation treatment, such as the GATT. Thirdly, all these provisions run counter to any bilateral treaty of friendship, commerce, and navigation granting freedom of commerce and navigation between contracting parties on a reciprocal basis. The antihijacking provision authorizes measures inconsistent with any bilateral air services agreement. Indeed, when the provision was under discussion, the Committee on Interstate and Foreign Commerce emphasized the need for a subsection to the effect that, notwithstanding Section 1102 of the existing law, "the President's suspension authority shall be deemed to be a condition to any certificate of public convenience, or to any permit, or to any operating certificate to any foreign air carrier." The committee explained that "the notwithstanding clause is necessary because section 1102 of existing law requires the Secretary of Transportation and the Civil Aeronautics Board to exercise their powers and duties consistently with any treaty obligations of the United States."[80]

There are, therefore, strong reasons to hold that the legal effects of both these provisions on international norms go well beyond what was asserted when the bills were under discussion. They certainly allow the President to infringe several international obligations regardless of their customary or treaty nature. They do not, however, authorize noncompliance by the United States with an obligation of a fundamental character.

2. Procedures

Section 8 of the Fishermen's Protective Act of 1967 as amended and the other related provisions have given broad au-

[79] 18 *U.N.R.I.A.A.* 443, § 81 (1978).
[80] H.R. 93-885, 93rd Congress, 2d Sess. (1971); [1974] *U.S. Code Cong. & Adm. News*, Vol. 3 (1974), p. 3984.

thority to the executive branch. Subsection 8(3) requires the Secretary of Commerce and the Secretary of the Interior to "(A) periodically monitor the activities of foreign nationals that may affect the international programs. . . .; (B) promptly investigate any activity by foreign national[s]. . . .; (C) promptly conclude and reach a decision."[81] Such operations are not conducted at random. They follow a very specific pattern, especially as far as evidence of the violation is concerned. The offending foreign country must be "certified." Such certification is established by the Secretary of Commerce on the basis of the information furnished by the foreign country itself. For instance, no fish can be imported into the United States if it was caught in a manner prohibited by the regulations governing the taking of marine mammals.[82] Salmon, halibut, yellow fin tuna under any form cannot be imported if a responsible official of the country of origin is unable to certify that it was not caught in a manner prohibited for United States fishermen by these regulations, or in a manner that imperils the marine mammals' conservation.[83]

It should be borne in mind that such prohibitions apply well beyond the jurisdiction of the United States. In order to enforce the regulations enacted by the International Whaling Commission, Subchapter B of Chapter III (International Regulatory Agencies) has provided for a complete regulation on seasons and capture of whales which applies to any waters south of 40° south latitude, the Indian Ocean sanctuary including the Red and Arabian seas and the Gulf of Oman, the Atlantic Ocean, the Pacific Ocean, and their dependent waters north of 40° south latitude. In some of these waters, the use of factory ships or attached whale catchers is simply forbidden[84] and contracting governments must report to the commission all whale catchers operating in conjunction with factory ships and land stations, as well as detailed information on the methods used to kill each whale and the number of whales struck but lost.[85]

[81] 22 U.S.C. § 1978(a) (3) (1982).
[82] 50 C.F.R. § 216-24(e) (1) (1983).
[83] 50 C.F.R. § 216-24(e) (2-4) (1983).
[84] 50 C.F.R. § 351.32 (1983).
[85] 50 C.F.R. § 351.71 (1983).

These regulations are of the utmost interest becaue they make the implementation of international rules transparent. They give substance and meaning to the requirement that the Secretary of Commerce must investigate any activity by foreign nationals liable to diminish the effectiveness of an international program. Insofar as they associate foreigners and foreign countries to the rule-making process, they set up procedural safeguards in the municipal legal order with respect to due process. Such a policy is not so common regarding remedies for internationally wrongful acts. It may well be, however, that such practices are feasible only for conservation problems. Investigations into foreign policy relating to terrorism obviously cannot be transparent, which is why hearings are not required in the case of the suspension of foreign air carrier permits as a response to noncompliance with the 1970 Hague Convention. But to the extent that a state is legally entitled to avail itself of a right to protect norms of mulilateral agreements, which in the absence of such an initiative would be within the sole discretion of each contracting party, the United States practice proves that there are some possibilities of tailoring such implementation to certain democratic standards.

Because of these regulations, there is little doubt that in international law foreign states, whether they are parties to multilateral agreements or not, cannot pretend to be unaware of the common interests of the community of member states. The precision which characterizes the regulations makes it easier to establish the evidence of a possible violation. The evidence of noncompliance is established by the above-mentioned certification, which is transmitted to the President. Only upon receipt of such a certification may the President direct the Secretary of the Treasury to resort to import prohibitions against the offending country. While the domestic enquiry is in progress, the foreign state is served a warning, *i.e.*, diplomatic representations are made to make it aware of the threat that is hanging over its fisheries or wildlife products. The offending state is thus given a chance to mend its ways. Upon signing Public Law 96-61, President Carter stated in part:

This bill . . . amends section 8 of the Fisherman's Protec-

> tive Act of 1967 to specifically require the Secretaries of Commerce and the Interior, as appropriate, to promptly investigate and act upon any actions by foreign nations that might be cause for certification. . . .
>
> With regard to . . . the Pelly Amendment, the Secretaries of Commerce and Interior should work with the Secretary of State to take prompt action to ensure that all avenues of negotiation are fully exhausted before certification is made against any foreign nation. However, in those negotiations all nations will be informed of . . . the determination of this Government to use them if remedial action is not undertaken. Certification under this act will, of course, take place only to further the purposes of this act, that is, to provide strong support for the International Convention for the Regulation of Whaling and for the conservation of the whales.[86]

These rules have proved effective. When Japan and Russia announced in 1973 their intention to disregard the whaling quotas set by the International Whaling Commission (IWC), the Secretary of Commerce certified after the 1973-1974 whaling season that these nations had harvested sperm, fin and mink whales in excess of IWC quotas and that such practices were diminishing the effectiveness of the IWC's conservation program. At the 1974 meeting of the IWC, both nations agreed to abide by the decisions of the IWC. As a result, President Ford decided not to impose an embargo on their fishery products. In 1978, similar steps were taken against the governments of Chile, Korea, and Peru, and at the June 1978 meeting of the IWC all three indicated their intention to join the IWC by its July 1979 meeting.[87] However, in a case concerning the Tuna Convention Act of 1950, the Department of State in an Aide-Mémoire to the Embassy of Spain called attention on September 8, 1975, to problems arising from Spanish fishing boats operating in the yellow fin tuna regulatory area of the Inter-American Tropical Tuna Commission (IATTC). The department recognized that Spain was not a member of the IATTC, but it held that, as a party to the 1958 Geneva

[86] *U.S. Digest* 1979, p. 1641.

[87] H.R. Rept. 95-1029, 95th Cong., 2d sess. (1978), pp. 8-11; [1978] *U.S. Code Cong. and Adm. News*, Vol. 3 (1979), p. 1773; *U.S. Digest* 1979, p. 1637.

Convention on Fishing and Conservation of the Living Resources of the High Seas, Spain had to cooperate in conservation matters. The department suggested that, in order to avoid an embargo, effective measures be taken, including withdrawal of the boats operating in the regulatory area at the time. One month later, following Spain's failure to comply with the "suggestion," a ban was imposed on imports into the United States of yellow fin tuna directly or indirectly received from Spain.[88] Five years later, the Spanish Government objected to the IWC's quota of 143 fin whales from the Spain-Portugal-British Isles stock. Referring to recent statements by a visiting Spanish official that the Spanish whaling industry would not abide by the 143 whale quota and that the Spanish government intended "unilaterally to establish a national quota for take from this stock at a level comparable to that of catches in recent years," the Department of State expressed its concern about those plans and noted "the strong possibility, under such circumstance, of certification of Spain by the U.S. Secretary of Commerce under . . . the Pelly Amendment." After further discussions between officials of the Spanish embassy and the department, the Spanish government accepted the commission's decision to limit the quota of fin whales to 143.[89]

Procedural safeguards also exist during the implementation of the measure. The Secretary of Commerce or the Secretary of the Interior is required to periodically review the activities of the nationals of the offending country, and, if the reasons for which the import prohibitions were imposed no longer prevail, the secretary concerned terminates the certification and publishes notice thereof in the Federal Register.[90] It is difficult, therefore, to view the measure as a punishment.

3. Adequacy

The purpose of the Pelly Amendment, as well as the Antihijacking Act, is not to inflict a punishment, *i.e.*, a true sanction

[88] See *U.S. Digest* 1975, pp. 518-519.
[89] *U.S. Digest* 1979, p. 1649.
[90] 22 U.S.C. § 1978(d) (1982).

on the offending state, but merely to exercise enough pressure to prevent a foreign state from jeopardizing specific collective interests. To what extent are such measures adequate?

Such a question is not easy to answer because it raises psychological issues such as the concept of deterrence, which legal scholars may have some difficulty evaluating. Reparation of particular injuries involves no psychological considerations. The measurement of the injury sustained and the compensation to be paid are not open to doubt. Psychological evaluations are beyond the scope of this study. From a legal point of view, however, certain observations must be made.

In its report on the Pelly Amendment, the Committee on Merchant Marine Fisheries emphasized a point that deserves some consideration. During the hearings, department witnesses frequently preceded the concept of "international conservation measure" by the term "widely held." The committee rightly pointed out that such wording apparently suggested that the U.S. right to impose "sanction" for the breach of the international program depended on the number of states that had acceded to it. Ruling out the wording, the committee stated: "[A]ll multilateral convention agreements, be there 3 or 15 signatory nations, stand on an equal footing. The key to the application of this legislation is not the number of signatories but whether the conservation measure is in force pursuant to the agreement's terms."[91] The committee's position was well founded insofar as the compliance with a multilateral convention by third states is not, as already mentioned, necessarily linked to the emergence of a customary rule.[92] Enforcement measures in that particular case are linked to the consequences deriving from the legal existence of the multilateral convention. As to third states, the international program is merely invoked against them just as it is invoked against any objecting contracting party. As a result, the committee was right to point out that the number of signatory nations was irrelevant in the case.

Bearing in mind such an approach, the subsequent legislative

[91] H.R. No. 92-468, *supra* n. 69, at 2416.
[92] See *supra*, p. 69.

developments of the Pelly Amendment are quite relevant. On February 9, 1978, a bill (H.R. 10878) was introduced to provide additional protection to endangered and threatened species of fish and wildlife. At the time it was noted that the United States, as a signatory to the Convention on International Trade in Endangered Species of Wild Fauna and Flora, had no means of persuading other nations to comply with the convention unless the illegally traded articles were imported into the United States. Following the United States' successful use of the Pelly Amendment in the conservation of whales, Congress intended to give the United States the same leverage for the conservation of endangered and threatened species. The Committee on Merchant Marine and Fisheries explained that "H.R. 10878 would provide the President with the authority to embargo *only wildlife products* from the offending nation. He could not decide to embargo *other products* even if the Secretary found that the offending country was diminishing the effectiveness of the Convention."[93]

Why was such a restriction on the President's authority imposed? This is a fundamental legal issue relating to the legal concept of countermeasures; namely, the power of a state following a breach of an international obligation, not to perform vis-à-vis the offending state an international obligation different from the breached obligation. Still, Congress did not grant the President such broad authority. It refused to allow the President to direct an embargo on *different* products from the offending country. In short, the President was not authorized to take steps outside the field of the offense. The same solution prevailed with the Antihijacking Act of 1974. In response to any direct or indirect support given to terrorist activities and viewed as inconsistent with the Convention for the Suppression of Unlawful Seizure of Aircraft, that act authorized the President only to suspend air services to any foreign nation which he determined was encouraging aircraft hijacking by acting in a manner inconsistent with the convention. In both cases, the response was confined to the same substantive field (wildlife products or avia-

[93] H.R. Rept. 95-1029, 95th Congress, 2d sess. (1978), p. 11; [1978] *U.S. Code Cong. and Adm. News,* Vol. 3 (1979), p. 1775 (emphasis added).

tion matters). These pieces of legislation are of the utmost interest. Interestingly, they seem to apply to countermeasures a requirement deriving from the *exceptio non adimpleti contractus*. However, the *exceptio* is barely at stake here since action may be taken against third states. Still, to what extent is such a constraint necessary? It is submitted that two complementary answers may be given to the problem.

A first approach may be found in the necessity to tailor a response which stands the proportionality test. Indeed, the Pelly Amendment response is well adjusted to its goal, which is to stop the unlawful depletion, insofar as it seeks to deprive the offenders of any enrichment from their misdeeds. It is interesting to note that when the Pelly Amendment was under discussion because of, *inter alia*, the objection of Denmark to the Atlantic salmon ban, the Committee on Merchant Marine and Fisheries weighed the problem of whether the President should be limited to declaring an embargo only on Danish salmon. The committee was of the opinion that:

> The President may embargo all Danish fishery products. . . . The monetary value of a single specie of fish may be insignificant thus nullifying the purpose of this legislation. . . . In the case of Atlantic Salmon, Danish exports to the United States totalled 54,365 pounds in 1970 worth $63,844.00. Imports of all Danish fish products totalled 31,656,000 lbs. valued at $10,543,298. The impact of losing a 10 million dollar market as opposed to a 63 thousand dollar market is obvious.[94]

The willingness to cause harm only to Danish fishermen and fishing industry (the direct beneficiaries of the offense) is not disputable. Similarly, but in a more oblique approach, the 1974 Antihijacking Act seeks to prevent the airline companies of the offending country from making a profit connected with the unlawful activities. These benficiary-oriented measures represent an attractive means to provide for responses which fit the prin-

[94] H.R. No. 92-468, *supra* n. 69, at 2414.

ciple of proportionality.[95] But it must be emphasized that confining the response to the substantive field of the treaty has nothing in common with an obligation to act by way of reciprocity. The responding state is not facing a problem of reparation, but a problem of enforcement; it is not trying to obtain redress for a damage suffered, but to find the most appropriate means to have the treaty complied with. In both cases, it turns out that the harm inflicted upon those who make a profit from the breach is connected with the substance of the treaty and therefore the substance of the offense. But in both cases redress is sought not as a matter of reparation, but primarily as a matter of law and order *(ordre public)*.

A second approach to explain the restricted scope of these actions could be proposed as merely tentative. It could be articulated in reasoning *a contrario:* Would the United States have adopted the same constraint if the breached treaty rule had turned into a customary rule? There are good reasons to believe that it would not because a customary rule is not only invocable, but also binding. As a result, one may wonder whether actions for "invocability" are not bound to remain within the field of the invoked rule, whereas actions for compliance with customary law may be taken outside the field of the offense. In other words, actions for the enforcement of treaty rules which have not become customary in nature could be subject to specific limits. However, should such limits prove to be compulsory, the problem is that actions for "invocability" may well be partially ineffective. International fishery programs, for example, are not actually enforced against third states which do not import the benefits of their misdeeds into the territory of the United States. As long as their fish or fish-related products do not enter United States territory, these states may deplete marine resources without being

[95] Interestingly enough, the same approach may also be taken as regards particular injuries. Under Section 301 of the Trade Act, the United States retaliation may strike in the sector which is the focus of the unfair trade practice. But it may also target the trade interests of these foreign individuals or corporations which benefit from the unfair trade practice. In her analysis of Section 301 (*supra* chap. 1, n.209, at VII-17), Jeanne S. Archibald notes: "For example, assume foreign insurance firms are restricted in the areas in which they can compete with domestic firms. Assume further that the parent companies of these domestic insurance firms engage in shipping to the U.S. Retaliation may be directed to those shipping activities."

vexed in any manner. To some extent, it is the domestic legislation rather than the international program that is actually, as a matter of fact, enforced against them.

Whatever, there is no doubt that whenever a treaty rule has become customary in nature, the possible steps states may take to ensure compliance with that rule are not limited to the substantive field of the offense.[96] They may resort to genuine reprisals. But in such a case, since universal customary rules are by nature and by definition binding on every state of the international community, the injury sustained, regardless of whether it follows a breach of a multilateral convention, is not collective but universal.

[96] See also Anthony D'Amato, "The Concept of Human Rights in International Law," *supra*, Chap. 1, n. 206, at 1120.

3

Remedies for Universal Injuries

A universal injury has to be defined as an injury affecting the entire international community. It is generally agreed at the present time that certain international obligations are fundamental for international society, since their violation may give rise to international concern. Such obligations are often referred to as obligations *erga omnes,* in accordance with a statement made by the International Court of Justice in the *Barcelona Traction* (Judgment):

> [A]n essential distinction should be drawn between the obligations of a State towards the international community as a whole, and those arising vis-à-vis another state. . . . By their very nature the former are the concern of all states. In view of the importance of the rights involved all states can be held to have a legal interest in their protection; they are obligations *erga omnes*.[1]

These obligations have received special attention in the draft Articles on State Responsibility, prepared by the International Law Commission. The first part of the draft articles includes a provision that

[1] I.C.J. *Reports* 1970, p. 32, § 33. Such obligations, however, may not be adjudicated by international tribunals as a matter of procedure when there are no grounds for the applicant to institute proceedings. Its right to do so may derive from treaty law (*e.g.* the right of each state which is a party to the European Convention on Human Rights to lodge a complaint against any other contracting state for violation of the convention, irrespective of the nationality of the victim), or from customary law (the right of each state to protect its nationals), *ibid.*, p. 47, § 91. Apart from these two possibilities, "all states are interested—have an interest" (*South West Africa* (Judgment), I.C.J. *Report* 1966, p. 34, § 50) or "have a legal interest" *(Barcelona Traction, supra)* in the protection of such obligations.

> [a]n internationally wrongful act which results from the breach by a state of an obligation so essential for the protection of fundamental interests of the international community that its breach is recognized as a crime by that community as a whole, constitutes an international crime (Article 19(2)).

As for examples of such crimes, the draft expressly provides that

> . . . an international crime may result, *inter alia,* from: . . . (c) a serious breach on a widespread scale of an international obligation of essential importance for safeguarding the human being, such as those prohibiting slavery, genocide and *apartheid* (Article 19(3)).[2]

To draw up a list of obligations *erga omnes* is no easy task. In the *Barcelona Traction* (Judgment) case, the court mentioned some of them, such as the prohibition of genocide and slavery. But beyond such obvious examples, a number of doubts may be cast on the exact content of other possible obligations *erga omnes*. However, whereas that content is merely a question of uncertainty, the remedies which may be contemplated following a violation have become a political issue. It is less a question of deciding whether states may take steps against such violations than whether they can act alone. In particular, several Third World members of the International Law Commission have already strongly opposed any unilateral action by states in such cases and favored the intervention of the international community organized as a whole in the United Nations organization.[3] It is not the purpose of this study to settle that dispute.[4] However, insofar as the United States has enacted in its domestic law statutory provisions aimed at providing remedies for such universal injuries, these provisions are directly relevant.

The great majority of United States remedies for universal injuries relating to the protection of human rights are to be found in Title 22 of the U.S. Code (Foreign Relations). There are, however, other provisions scattered in different titles which,

[2] *Report of the International Law Commission,* 33 G.A.O.R. 10, A/33/10 at 193 (1976).
[3] See, for example, *Yrbk. I.L.C.*, (1977), Vol. II(2), p. 119, § 12.13.
[4] For some answers, see E. Zoller, *Peacetime,* at 118-120.

though not directly covering human rights issues, may nevertheless be resorted to, in order to provide remedies for related universal injuries. Such provisions are obviously difficult to single out, since their implementation for human rights purposes is a matter of practice. For instance, following the imposition of martial law in Poland in December 1981, President Reagan, in a nationwide televised statement, announced his intention *inter alia* to suspend Polish civil aviation privileges in the United States as "a warning to the Government of Poland that free men cannot and will not stand idly by in the face of brutal repression."[5] Three days later, the Civil Aeronautics Board issued an order suspending the permit of Polskie Linie Lotnicze (LOT) under Section 102(a) (5) of the Federal Aviation Act of 1958 as amended.[6] That section, however, does not specifically refer to "brutal repression," but only instructs the board to consider the needs of the national defense in the exercise of its powers and duties. On the other hand, a statute such as the Export Administration Act of 1979 does not include the protection of international human rights among the factors to be taken into consideration by the export regulations. However, Public Law 95-495, approved on October 10, 1978, added an amendment to Section 4 of that act imposing a total embargo on exports to Uganda (except cereal grains and additional food products) as an "exceptional response" to an "international crime of genocide."[7] Similarly the same Export Administration Act was used when the United States sought to make it clear to the Soviet Union that Soviet support for the declaration of martial law in Poland was not acceptable. Two regulations were issued on December 30, 1981, by the Department of Commerce. The first extended the existing oil and gas controls on goods and technology to the transportation, exploration and production of petroleum and natural gas.[8] The second suspended the processing of validated license applications for all exports to the Soviet Union.[9] In that respect the Reagan administration followed to

[5] See 76 *A.J.I.L.*, 381 (1982).
[6] 49 App. U.S.C. § 1302(a) (5) (1982).
[7] 92 Stat. 1051.
[8] 15 C.F.R. § § 379, 385, 399 (1982).
[9] 15 C.F.R. § 390 (1982).

some extent the Carter administration, which responded to the Soviet invasion of Afghanistan by suspending *inter alia* all licenses for high technology and strategic exports to the Soviet Union, pending review.[10] Besides violations of internationally recognized human rights,[11] the United States also considers as sources of injury for the entire international community any refuge given to individuals committing acts of international terrorism such as hijacking aircraft, and several statutory provisions aim at providing remedies against international terrorism.

Unlike the statutes which provide remedies for violations of multilateral conventions, these statutes do not always refer to international instruments. There are two exceptions: Section 502 B of the Foreign Assistance Act of 1961 as amended[12] and Section 1 of the Arms Export Control Act of 1968.[13] Both expressly refer to the Charter of the United Nations and, more specifically, either to its "international obligations," or to its "purposes and principles." Since those two statutes, provisions relating to international human rights have dropped all reference to the UN Charter. Even Public Law 95.435, approved on October 10, 1978,[14] which imposed a trade embargo on Uganda as a measure against an international crime of genocide, did not refer to the UN Charter.[15] This is significant in that, although a party to the UN Charter, the United States is not a party to most of the human rights treaties promulgated by the United Nations or by organizations associated with it.[16]

[10] 45 F.R. 3027 (Jan. 16, 1980).

[11] The U.S. concern for international human rights has been spreading abroad. During the negotiations between the European Community and 66 African, Caribbean, and Pacific countries to replace Lomé II, Community negotiators for the first time succeeded in including a human rights clause in Lomé III, which many ACP nations had previously refused.

[12] 22 U.S.C. § 230(a) (1) (1982).

[13] 22 U.S.C. § 2751 (1982).

[14] 92 Stat. 1051.

[15] Section 111(b) of Pub. L. 95-88 (95 Stat. 1533), which added a subsection to Section 116 of the International Development and Food Assistance Act of 1975 [22 U.S.C. § 2151n(e) (1982)], refers to the Universal Declaration of Human Rights. However, it concerns not suspension of assistance but of funds made available for studies or activities to encourage or promote increased adherence to political and civil rights.

[16] See Paul C. Szasz, "The International Legal Aspects of the Human Rights Program of the United States," 12 *Cornell Int'l L.J.*, 161, 167-169 (1979). The official list of treaties and other international agreements of the United States in force on January 1, 1984, does not even include among multilateral treaties a heading relating to "human rights." Apart from conventions on the rules of warfare, the most relevant headings are "slavery" and "traffic in women and children."

In the circumstances, the United States clearly has no treaty entitlement, *i.e.* legal ground, to provide remedies for violations of international human rights in multilateral conventions to which it is not a party. This is no place to determine whether those international instruments have become part of substantive customary law. But in this respect there are two facts to consider. First, when Congress started to express concern for international human rights, it referred not only to the UN Charter, but also to "the constitutional heritage and traditions of the United States."[17] Secondly, regarding the multilateral conventions to which the United States is a party, it should be noted that the official *Digest of United States Practice in International Law* includes to date an interesting heading: "Jurisdiction Based on Universal and Other States Interests." In 1973 that heading covered "crimes conventions," in particular the Tokyo Convention on Offenses and Certain Other Acts Committed on Board Aircraft (1963), the Hague Convention for the Suppression of Unlawful Seizure of Aircraft (1970), and the Montreal Convention for the Suppression of Unlawful Acts against the safety of Civil Aviation (1971).[18] There is no doubt that this universal jurisdiction bears on individuals, but it is unclear whether it also bears on states.[19]

United States remedies for universal injuries illustrate in many respects the faltering international rules in that field. To be sure, the United States has not yet gone as far as Mr. Willem Riphagen, Special Rapporteur on State Responsibility, who proposed to the international Law Commission a provision reading as follows: "An international crime entails *all* the legal consequences of an

[17] Pub. L. 93-559, § 46, Dec. 30, 1974, 88 Stat. 1815. State legislation is evidence of the material source of custom, cf. *The Scotia* (1871) 14 Wallace 170.

[18] *U.S. Digest* 1973, 200-203. After 1973, the scope of this heading was extended. It includes to date issues of extraterritoriality relating to antitrust laws (*U.S. Digest* 1977, 465-471) or to drug abuse prevention and control (*U.S. Digest* 1979, 822-827), criminal offenses not having effect in the United States *(ibid.,* 827-831) and service of process outside the United States *(ibid.,* 831-838).

[19] The notion of "universal jurisdiction" has been embodied in the Tentative Draft No. 2 on the *Restatement of the Law* [*Foreign Relations Law of the United States (revised)*] at Section 404. Such jurisdiction is apparently to be applied only to individuals who commit an "offense" against international law. But, significantly, the reporter also referred to the notion of "international crime" (as defined by the International Law Commission as an act of a state) and asserted: "An international crime is presumably subject to universal jurisdiction" (Sec. 404, reporter's note, § 1 *in fine* at 117).

internationally wrongful act.''[20] In particular, the bulk of its remedies for universal injuries are simple measures and not countermeasures.

I. Measures

1. Substance

The very first step taken by the United States to remedy universal injuries took place in one of the most discretionary fields, that of bilateral assistance. Indeed, bilateral foreign assistance is always a voluntary appropriation. At the outset, concern was rather limited in scope since Section 32 of the Foreign Assistance Act of 1973 provided that:

> It is the sense of Congress that the President should deny any economic or military assistance to the government of any foreign country which practices the internment or imprisonment of that country's citizens for political purposes.[21]

One year later, the scope was extended from political imprisonment to cover

> a consistent pattern of gross violations of internationally recognized human rights, including torture or cruel, inhuman or degrading treatment or punishment; prolonged detention without charges; or other flagrant denials of the right to life, liberty, and the security of the person.[22]

But the response was restricted to the reduction or termination of ''security assistance.'' Since then, the ''consistent pattern'' model has been continuously enlarged. It includes today, in addition to the criteria set forth in 1974, the right to trial, disappearance of persons by abduction, and clandestine detention.[23] As to the field of the response, it has been extended from the

[20] A/CN.4/380 at 8 (emphasis added). See also 39 G.A.O.R. 10, A/39/10 at 239 (1984).
[21] Pub. L. 93-189, 87 Stat. 714, approved Dec. 17, 1983. Indeed, the provision was primarily directed against Chile and the policy followed by General Pinochet's government. See *International Protection of Human Rights, The Work of International Organizations and the Role of U.S. Foreign Policy,* Hearings Before the Subcommittee on International Organizations and Movements of the Committee on Foreign Affairs, House of Representatives, 93rd Cong., 1st session, pp. 529-556, esp. at 554.
[22] Pub. L. 93-559, 88 Stat. 1815, approved Dec. 30, 1974.
[23] 22 U.S.C. § 2304(d) (1982).

reduction or termination of military assistance, to cover prohibition of security assistance, and exports of crime control and detection instruments,[24] the prohibition of development assistance,[25] and the prohibition of agricultural commodities agreements.[26]

Occasionally the measure is less drastic, especially when United States corporations and business may benefit from the activity subject to regulations. For instance, Eximbank is not precluded from giving credit in support of United States exports to countries that violate human rights, but it is invited to deny such credit if "such action would clearly and importantly advance United States policy in such areas as international terrorism and human rights;"[27] or OPIC (Overseas Private Investment Corporation) is not barred from insuring investment or from guaranteeing loans of American investors with respect to projects to be implemented in a developing country that violates fundamental human rights, but the corporation shall take into account, in the conduct of its programs in a country, all available information about observance of human rights and fundamental freedoms in that country;[28] or arms sales are not prohibited to human rights violators, but such sales shall be approved only when they are consistent with the foreign policy interests of the United States, and with the purposes of the 1961 Foreign Assistance Act.[29] There is ample evidence, therefore, that human rights and business do not mix well. In 1981, Congress deleted a paragraph of Section 1 of the Arms Export Control Act which provided that arms sales could not be approved when they had the effect of arming military dictators who were denying fundamental rights

[24] 22 U.S.C. § 2304(a) (2) (1982).
[25] 22 U.S.C. § 2151n(a) (1982).
[26] 7 U.S.C. § 1712(a) (1982).
[27] 12 U.S.C. § 635(b) (1) (B) (1982). In order to assess the true effectiveness of the consideration given to the status of human rights in the country receiving the exports, it must be borne in mind that the Eximbank Board of Directors also has to take into account under the 1954 act such economic factors as adverse effects on the competitive position of United States industry, on materials in short supply in the United States, and on domestic employment. See *U.S. Digest* 1977, p. 226.
[28] 22 U.S.C. § 2199(i) (1982).
[29] 22 U.S.C. § 2751 (1982). By contrast, arms sales are not to be made or credits and guarantees are not to be extended to any foreign country which discriminates on the basis of race, religion, national origin or sex against any United States person [22 U.S.C. 2755(a) (1982)].

or social progress to their own people.[30] But unlike human rights violations, which essentially bear on the population of the country concerned, international terrorism has worldwide consequences which justify the prohibition of arms sales credits and guarantees to countries granting sanctuary to international terrorists.[31]

International terrorism is no doubt a major concern for the United States, especially when supported by states which are not dependent on its economic or military assistance. That is apparently why international terrorism is countered by remedies that are not resorted to against human rights violators, such as in the field of the United States' Generalized System of Preferences, the ineligibility for designation as a beneficiary of any country granting sanctuary to international terrorists,[32] or in the field of export regulations, the use of export controls to encourage foreign countries to prevent the use of their territories as havens for international terrorists.[33]

Finally, it should be noted that violations of internationally recognized human rights seldom have direct effect on United States nationals. They do, however, when a foreign country imposes a boycott against any company regardless of its nationality if this company is owned or managed by individuals of a particular race or religion. As a response to the Arab boycott, the Ribicoff Amendment of the Tax Reform Act of 1976[34] denies certain tax benefits to taxpayers which "participate in, or cooperate with" such boycotts. Foreign source income attributable to boycott-related activity loses the tax benefits of the foreign tax credit [Domestic International Sales Corporations (DISC)],[35] and the deferral of United States tax on foreign source income.[36] This situation is, however, a borderline case as far as the present study is concerned because the Arab boycott was imposed by states which were at war with Israel.

[30] Pub. L. 97-113, Title VII, § 734(a) (10), Dec. 29, 1981, 95 Stat. 1560.
[31] 22 U.S.C. § 2753(f) (1982).
[32] 19 U.S.C. § 2462(b) (7) (1982).
[33] Export Administration Act of 1979, 93 Stat. 504 codified at 50 App. U.S.C. § 2402(8) (Suppl. V, 1981).
[34] Pub. L. 94-455, Title X, § 1064(a), Oct. 4, 1976, 90 Stat. 1520.
[35] 26 U.S.C. § 999(b) (1) (1982).
[36] 26 U.S.C. § 908(a) (1982).

2. Procedures

A major problem raised by violations of fundamental rules of international law is to be found in the establishment of evidence. Allegations of such violations cannot be based on a limited record. They have to rely on a thorough study and investigation. This is especially true with regard to violations of human rights. In that respect it should be noted that in wartime, although the same requirements prevail, the problems are less daunting than in peacetime because at the end of hostilities, the entrance of the victorious power into the territory of the defeated power makes it easier to collect evidence or hear witnesses. Moreover, the archives of the alleged "criminal state" may still be available. That in substance was what happened after the Second World War at the Nuremberg and Tokyo trials, although in both cases only individuals were tried and convicted. But in peacetime, evidence cannot be so easily collected.[37] A particularly interesting aspect of United States law relating to the protection of internationally recognized human rights is to be found in an attempt to overcome such difficulties. The United States has decided to promote human rights in the whole world, but it has at least tried to subject its own policy to a set of procedural safeguards.

A first safeguard is to be found in the concept of "consistent pattern of gross violations of internationally recognized human rights." No ordinary violation can give rise to action. On that specific point, United States law has reflected United Nations resolutions, which require similar criteria to justify international concern.[38] Section 502 B(a) of the Foreign Assistance Act of 1961 as amended sets out specific examples of gross violations such as torture, inhuman treatment or punishment, prolonged detention without charge or trial, abduction, flagrant denial of the right to life, liberty, or the security of person. These examples

[37] As a result, there may be clear differences in the way a government and a nongovernmental organization may look at the human rights situation in various selected countries. See, for example, the discrepancies between the Netherlands government and Amnesty International as far as the human rights situation was concerned in thirteen countries receiving the Netherlands development aid in Peter R. Baehr, "Concern for Development Aid and Fundamental Human Rights: The Dilemma as Faced by the Netherlands," 4 *H. Rts. Q*. 39, 49 (1982).

[38] See Oscar Schachter, Book Review on *Human Rights in International Law and the Helsinki Accord* [Th. Buergenthal, ed.] in 17 *Colum. J. Trans. L.*, 531, 534 (1978).

evoke the habeas corpus safeguards and exclude any social or economic rights. Should only civil and political rights be at stake, it must be pointed out that violations will not call for action unless their accumulation amounts to a ''*consistent* pattern of *gross* violations.'' The term ''consistent'' refers to a continuous practice; it excludes occasional violations such as unfortunate but inevitable incidents occurring during a political emergency. In short, that wording opens the door to possible lawful derogations in the case of public emergencies (*e.g.*, Article 15 of the European Convention on Human Rights, Article 4 of the International Covenant on Civil and Political Rights). To that extent, most of the ''sanctions'' against Poland implemented not even three weeks after the imposition of martial law are controversial. However, there is no doubt that there can be no derogation from such rights as the right to life, the prohibition of torture, the ban on slavery, and the prohibition of the retroactive imposition of criminal penalties.[39] The term ''gross violations'' has been elaborated upon by the Legal Adviser of the Department of State. On March 19, 1975, he expressed the view that ''gross'' cannot be less than ''grave breaches'' described in the 1949 Geneva Convention for the Protection of War Victims. He further emphasized that ''with respect to patterns of human rights violations, it seems reasonable to consider that we are talking *both* about the consistency over a relevant and significant period of time and about a significant range of the kinds of governmental acts or omissions that may violate human rights.'' According to him, a determination made by an international independent body such as the United Nations Human Rights Commission, or a finding by the Inter-American Commission on Human Rights, the European Commission or the International Court of Justice could be regarded to that effect as authoritative.[40] Significantly, Section 116 of the Foreign Assistance Act of 1961 as amended enumerates among the factors to be considered ''the extent of cooperation of (the) government in permitting an unimpeded

[39] See especially Joan F. Hartman, ''Derogations from Human Rights Treaties in Public Emergencies,'' 22 *Harv. J. Int'l. L.*, 1 (1981).
[40] *U.S. Digest* 1975, pp. 221-223.

investigation . . . by appropriate international organizations, including the International Committee of the Red Cross, or groups or persons acting under the authority of the United Nations or of the Organization of American States.''[41] As for establishing the facts, the Secretary of State is required to transmit each year to Congress a full and complete report on practices regarding human rights not only in countries receiving development assistance, but in all other foreign countries which are members of the United Nations.[42] However, the overall survey of foreign practice is not required for security assistance purposes.[43] The difference may be explained by the fact that suspension of development assistance concerns a greater number of foreign countries than suspension of military assistance and that it may be decided on broader grounds. To that extent, a comparative analysis is requested to ensure more fairness in the determinations to be made. When suspension of military assistance is contemplated, the report of the Secretary of State is prepared with the help of the Assistant Secretary of State for Human Rights and Humanitarian Affairs. Nevertheless and in any case, the relevant reports make use of the information collected by the human rights officer to be found in each United States embassy, usually in the political section.[44]

These procedures have been steadily improved. The Secretary of State was required to collect information on human rights situations in countries receiving development assistance two years after the adoption of the International Development and Food Assistance Act of 1975.[45] Initially, the President was only required to report to Congress on the steps taken to promote human rights. Under present law the Secretary of State has to submit to Congress each year a full and complete report that first establishes the status of human rights in countries receiving development assistance and that secondly records the steps taken to change United States programs because of human rights con-

[41] 22 U.S.C. § 2151n(c) (1) (1982); see also 22 U.S.C. § 2304(b) (1982).
[42] 22 U.S.C. § 2151n(d) (1) (1982).
[43] 22 U.S.C. § 2304(b) (1982).
[44] *U.S. Digest* 1979, p. 622.
[45] See Pub. L. 95-88, Section III(a), Aug. 3, 1977, 91 Stat. 537.

siderations. The Secretary of State is helped in his task by a number of administrative organs, in particular the Bureau of Human Rights and Humanitarian Affairs, which keeps a continuous flow of information on human rights practices from different sources, *e.g.* other State Department bureaus, the Central Intelligence Agency and nongovernmental organizations.[46]

As for security assistance, Congress goes even further, since it may request the Secretary of State to submit to its relevant committees within thirty days all the available information about respect for human rights and fundamental freedoms in the country concerned.[47] In order to continue to supply military aid to countries such as Argentina, Chile, and El Salvador, the President had to "certify" to Congress that the governments of those countries had made significant progress in complying with internationally recognized rights.[48] As a matter of procedure, such requirements have to be connected with the "certifications" provided by the Pelly Amendment. It has been alleged, especially for El Salvador, that "the certification provision is unsound law," ending up in "hollow certification" because certifications were issues *pro forma* and unjustified on the record.[49] But that is a matter of fact, not a matter of law. An administration's willingness, for political reasons, to certify regardless of the circumstances does not mean that the provision is necessarily "unsound law." Rather, it means only that the factual implementation of the provision needs to be improved. For the purposes of this study, such a provision is additional evidence of the efforts by Congress to base its decisions on established facts and not merely on allegations.

The statutory requirements rely on the usual practice of congressional enquiries as illustrated by the numerous hearings

[46] On the administrative process, see D.R. Carter & F.D. Brogan, "United States Human Rights Policy: Effect on Exports," 9 *Ga. J. Int. & Comp. L.*, 287, 308-311 (1979).
[47] 22 U.S.C. § 2304(c) (1) (A) (1982).
[48] Sections 725(b) and (c), 726(b), 728 of the 1981 International Security and Development Cooperation Act (Pub. L. 97-113, Dec. 29, 1981, 95 Stat. 1544) set as a note under 22 U.S.C. § 2370 (1982).
[49] See Richard B. Nash, "Certifying Human Rights: Military Assistance to El Salvador and the International Security and Development Cooperation Act of 1981," 14 *Colum. H. Rts. L. Rev.*, 275, 296-298 (1982-3).

convened by the Senate Foreign Relations Committee or the Foreign Affairs Committee of the House of Representatives.[50]

[50] The following list illustrates the groups represented before congressional hearings on topics related to human rights:

1) *Human Rights in Guatemala*
    - State Department
    - a private citizen
    - professors from Arizona State University and the University of North Carolina
    - Amnesty International
    - The Newspaper Guild

   See Human Rights in Guatemala. Hearing before the subcommittees on Human Rights and International Organizations and on Inter-American Affairs of the House Committee on Foreign Affairs, 97th Cong., 1st Sess. (1981).

2) *U.S. Policy Towards South Africa*
    - State Department
    - Defense Department
    - professors from the University of California at Berkeley, Wesleyan University, the Massachusetts Institute of Technology, and Georgetown University
    - The *New York Times* editorial board
    - The South African Foundation
    - Lawyers Committee for Civil Rights Under Law
    - Opportunities Industrialization Centers of America
    - Investor Responsibility Research Center
    - Ford Motor Company
    - Rexnord
    - Mobil Oil Company
    - General Motors
    - Citicorp
    - Coca-Cola Company
    - AFL-CIO
    - Interfaith Center on Corporate Responsibility
    - Washington Office on Africa
    - National Bar Association
    - TransAfrica

   See U.S. Policy Toward South Africa. Hearings before the subcommittees on International Economic Policy and Trade on Africa and on International Organizations of the House Committee on Foreign Affairs, 96th Cong., 2d Sess. (1980).

3) *Human Rights in Nicaragua*
    - International League for Human Rights
    - a professor of history, Georgetown University
    - MISURA (Indians Organization of Nicaragua)
    - Council for Inter-American Security

   See Human Rights in Nicaragua. Hearing before the Subcommittee on Human Rights and International Organizations of the House Committee on Foreign Affairs, 98th Cong., 1st Sess. (1983).

4) *Economic Sanctions Against Rhodesia*
    - Washington Office on Africa
    - Amnesty International
    - American Conservative Union
    - House of Lords, United Kingdom
    - Freedom House
    - United Steelworkers of America
    - United States Catholic Conference
    - Congressional Black Caucus
    - National Association for the Advancement of Colored People (NAACP)
    - president of Denison University and former U.S. Ambassador to Zambia
    - former U.S. Ambassador to Sierra Leone

   See Economic Sanctions Against Rhodesia. Hearings before the subcommittees on Africa and on International Organizations of the House Committee on Foreign Affairs, 96th Cong., 1st Sess. (1979).

5) *Human Rights in Asia: Noncommunist Countries*
    - The International League for Human Rights

Many witnesses may testify at these hearings: governmental officers, academics, scientists, independent researchers, even representatives of the country concerned. In a lecture given on November 17, 1978, the Chairman of the Subcommittee on International Organizations stated that since 1974 the subcommittee had held more than 150 hearings on human rights problems in over 40 countries.[51] These hearings make sense because they counterbalance the shortcomings of the annual report made by the Department of State. Indeed, as Mr. Fraser acknowledged: "[T]he report is one of the few ways to get a window on what's going on. Everything else is done by cables marked 'confidential,' and we rarely have a full picture of what is happening."[52] For instance, before adopting the trade embargo against Uganda, congressional committees heard, *inter alia,* the Assistant Secretary of State for Human Rights and Humanitarian Affairs, the Assistant Secretary of State for Economic and Business Affairs, the Director of the Central Intelligence Agency, the Director of the Office of Export Administration for the Commerce Department, the Executive Secretary of the Committee on Uganda, a professor of African studies from Brooklyn College, a professor of Political Science from the University of Michigan, the President of the National Coffee Association, a vice president of General Food Corporation, and a former minister of the Ugandan government. Some of these witnesses claimed that the reports

North American Coalition for Human Rights in Korea
National Council of Churches
State Department
Center for International Policy

See Human Rights in Asia: Noncommunist Countries. Hearings before the subcommittees on Asian and Pacific Affairs and on International Organizations of the House Committee on Foreign Affairs, 96th Cong., 2d Sess. (1980).

6) *Forced Labor in the Soviet Union*
AFL-CIO
International Human Rights Law Group
International Society for Human Rights
a former Soviet political prisoner
Treasury Department
U.S. Customs Service
State Department

See Forced Labor in the Soviet Union. Hearing before the Subcommittee on Human Rights and International Organizations of the Senate Committee on Foreign Relations, 98th Cong., 1st Sess. (1983).

[51] See Donald M. Fraser, "Human Rights and U.S. Foreign Policy," 23 *Int'l Stud. Q.*, 174, 178 (1979).

[52] *Ibid.*, at 180.

were based on misinformation and hearsay, that the situation was more anarchic than despotic. Conversely, others testified that the Amin regime was the cruelest, most barbaric in recent memory, that forced labor had been imposed on farms and in industry, and that thousands of people had been killed.[53] On the whole, these debates are certainly not without shortcomings and deficiencies, but their mere existence is a conspicuous addition to the record in establishing evidence regarding universal injuries.[54]

The various aspects of these procedural requirements and safeguards certainly meant that the appropriation process was the subject of "long hours of careful legislative decision."[55] In the event, it must at least be acknowledged that the United States search for remedies to universal injuries has been accompanied by extensive procedural guarantees. Admittedly the United States is monitoring international human rights with respect to the due process principle. To that extent, even if these procedures are not perfect and are often cumbersome, they are better than no safeguards at all, as in the case of the "sanctions" against Poland and the Soviet Union. The controversial aspects of these measures are the result of hasty action rather than a matter of substance.

3. Adequacy

No doubt none of statutory provisions relating to the protection of human rights is a true sanction. They are not penalties, since they can always be lifted or reversed following a change of

[53] See United States-Uganda Relations: Hearings Before the Subcommission on Africa, International Organizations and International Economic Policy and Trade of the House Committee on International Relations, 95th Cong., 2d Sess. (1978); Uganda: The Human Rights Situation: Hearings Before the Subcommission on Foreign Economic Policy of the Senate Committee on Foreign Relations, 95th Congress, 2d Sess. (1978) and Comment "United States Trade Sanctions Against Uganda: Legality Under International Law," 11 *Law & Pol'y. Int'l. Bus.* 1149 (1979).

[54] These hearings should not be confused with the personal lobbying that may be undertaken by senior officials of the country concerned. On September 22, 1981, President Duarte of El Salvador visited Capitol Hill and wrote to the Chairman of the Senate Foreign Relations Committee to protest against the conditions imposed on "a government friendly to the United States and fully committed to fulfill its pledge," 39 *Cong. Q. Weekly Rep.* 1829 (Sept. 26, 1981). From a more general point of view, it should be noted that foreign government lobbying is a very common practice. See Thomas M. Franck & Edward Weisband, *Foreign Policy by Congress* (1979) 180-186.

[55] According to the statement made by a professional staff member of the Senate Foreign Relations Committee. See Paul Albert, "The Undermining of the Legal Standards for Human Rights Violations in the United States Foreign Policy: The Case of 'Improvement' in Guatemala," 14 *Colum. H. Rts. L. Rev.*, 231, 240 (n. 60) (1982-1983).

behavior by the offending country. More specifically, military assistance may be resumed to any country which has improved its human rights records.[56] The suspension of all military assistance to Turkey following the invasion of Cyprus, as required under Section 22 of the Foreign Assistance Act of 1974, was repealed *de facto* by presidential action under Section 13 of the International Security Assistance Act of 1978.[57] As for other countries, and in particular under the Reagan administration,[58] suspension of military assistance has often been contemplated but seldom implemented. In the case of Argentina, Chile and El Salvador, threatened by suspension of military assistance in 1981, a certification of the President to the Speaker of the House or the Chairman of the Senate Foreign Relations Committee, determining that these three countries were "making significant progress in complying with internationally recognized principles of human rights" was enough.[59] Apparently the President made the certification only for assistance to El Salvador.[60] For Argentina and Chile, the President delegated his functions to the Secretary of State.[61] In any case, the more discretionary the presidential powers, the more uncertain the response to the breach. Congress was obviously aware of this problem when in 1976 it restricted the power of the President to resume military assistance for extraordinary circumstances.[62] With respect to subsequent practice, that congressional limitation on the presidential powers apparently did not prove all that effective.

As far as development assistance is concerned, the measure provided is even less stringent than the suspension of military assistance because economic assistance cannot be suspended if "such assistance will directly benefit the needy people" in the

[56] 22 U.S.C. § 2304(e) (1982).
[57] See *U.S. Digest* 1978, pp. 1602-1608; *U.S. Digest* 1975, pp. 829-832.
[58] During the Carter administration, all military aid to Chile, Paraguay, Uruguay and Argentina was suspended either by action of the executive branch or by Congress. See Robert Cohen, "Human Rights Diplomacy: The Carter Administration and the Southern Cone," 4 *H. Rts. Q.*, 212, 225-226 (1982).
[59] See *supra* p. 110.
[60] Determination of the President, No. 82-4, Jan. 28, 1982, 47 F.R. 6417.
[61] Exec. Ord. No. 12163, Sept. 29, 1979, 44 F.R. 56673, set out as a note under Section 2381 of Title 22 of the U.S. Code.
[62] Pub. L. 94-329, Title III, § 301(a), 90 Stat. 798 approved June 30, 1976.

country.[63] A similar restriction bars the President from contemplating the possibility of not entering into an agricultural commodity agreement with any foreign country engaged in a consistent pattern of gross violations of internationally recognizable human rights.[64] That humanitarian prerequisite should be related to other humanitarian considerations limiting U.S. responses against foreign nations which violate international rules.[65] Like the reparation of particular injuries, remedies for universal injuries have to abide by certain standards of civilization. However, such restrictions, especially as applied to the suspension of economic assistance, also make the contemplated measure less effective because it is illusory to imagine a form of development assistance that would not be accorded to people in need. The essential purpose of development assistance is precisely to provide relief to those in need. On the other hand and however serious the alleged human rights violations, the inevitably odious nature of a suspension of development assistance to a starving and homeless people turns a formidable weapon into an unenforceable measure. That is why, unlike military assistance, suspension of economic assistance has seldom been used in practice. But military assistance is not the same as economic assistance; it does not serve the same purpose nor benefit the same people. In a laudable effort to separate the wheat from the chaff, Section 116(b) of the International Development and Food Assistance Act of 1975[66] provides in substance that congressional committees may require the administration to submit in writing information demonstrating that such assistance will directly benefit the needy people in the country. Such a requirement is by nature an ''unfulfillable'' condition because it implies earmarking of United States assistance in the budget of the receiving

[63] 22 U.S.C. § 2151n(a) (1982).
[64] 7 U.S.C. § 1712(a) (1982).
[65] See the Right to Food Resolution, (Senate Concurrent Resolution 138) passed by the Senate on September 16, 1976 which expressed Congress' view that every person has the right to a nutritionally adequate diet; that the need to combat hunger at home and abroad should be a fundamental objective of the United States policy; and that the United States should expand and emphasize its support of self-help development efforts in countries most seriously affected by hunger and malnutrition. The House of Representatives passed a similar resolution (House Concurrent Resolution 737) on September 21, 1976; *U.S. Digest* 1976, p. 568.
[66] 22 U.S.C. § 2151n(b) (1982).

state, an unrealistic practice either because most developing countries do not have a budgetary law comparable to that in force in Western countries, or because if they do, the principle of budgetary universality with its collateral rule of the prohibition to earmark resources to outlays makes such a requirement unfeasible. Thus in 1969, Section 303(a) of Public Law 91-175[67] had to repeal a provision allowing the President to terminate assistance when he found it was being diverted to cover military expenditure.

As a result, the potential leverage of the suspension of development assistance proves impracticable. It is indeed worth noting that when measures were contemplated against Uganda for the alleged international crime of genocide, suspension of development assistance was unfeasible, and Congress had to adopt an *ad hoc* legislation imposing a trade embargo. Assistance to Uganda had been shrinking well before the discovery of the atrocities, *i.e.*, already in 1973, when a number of problems led successively to the termination of Peace Corps and AID programs and ultimately to the closing of the embassy in Kampala and the withdrawal of all United States official personnel.[68] As for Nicaragua, before the fall of the Somoza regime, on July 17, 1979, the Carter administration had started reducing military assistance in 1977 and stopped it altogether in early 1979; however, Congress still released a $75,000,000 economic aid package on September 12, 1980.[69]

Initially, human rights statutes applied suspension of assistance only in relation to military matters. Such was the purpose of Public Law 93-559 approved on December 30, 1974.[70] Only one year later was suspension of assistance extended to development programs by Public Law 94-161 approved on December 20,

[67] 83 Stat. 820.
[68] See *U.S. Digest* 1978 pp. 80-81.
[69] See "Western Hemisphere: Nicaragua," *Department of State Bulletin* 66 (May 1979); *N.Y. Times* Sept. 13, 1980, at 2 Col. 1. See Comments, "The Legitimacy of Economic Coercion: The Carter Foreign Aid Policy and Nicaragua," 5 *Loy. L.A. Int'l & Comp. L.J.*, 101, 102-106 (1982).
[70] 88 Stat. 1815.

1975.[71] The reasons for such an extension are not clear.[72] It was probably felt that suspension of assistance, especially under the Hickenlooper Amendment, had been an efficient means of exerting pressure on foreign countries and that since it had been applied to military aid, it would be rather "natural" to apply it also to development assistance and economic aid. On the other hand, it is often believed that economic assistance consolidates and perpetuates repressive regimes. For instance, it has been alleged that in the case of Chile, economic assistance provided before 1979 did not benefit the people who suffered from repression, except when these persons could receive assistance "through *direct funding* from foreign governments or private organizations."[73]

In any event the grounds for assimilation of military aid and economic assistance are quite doubtful.[74] There are indeed basic substantive and symbolic differences between military and development assistance. Unlike development aid, military assistance relates to the *imperium* insofar as it directly benefits the rulers and only indirectly the people. Weapons have little to do with charity. The rationale is quite different in the two cases. As for the Hickenlooper Amendment, a sword of Damocles threatening any developing country seeking its own economic independence without regard for the vested rights of United States corporations, it must be borne in mind that this statutory provision was meant as a remedy for particular injuries. But particular injuries follow different standards from universal injuries. A particular injury calls for compensatory damages, which have to be tailored to the loss actually incurred. To that extent the shortcomings of the Hickenlooper Amendment derive less from

[71] 89 Stat. 860.

[72] One may wonder whether they are not to be found in the legislation which Congress adopted in 1973 against Chile in an attempt to kill two birds with one stone, *i.e.* to respond to the nationalization of United States copper mines by the Allende government, which had not provided adequate compensation, and to respond to the political imprisonments by the military junta which replaced the socialist government after the coup of September 11, 1973. Whatever, the procedural aspects followed by the Harkin Amendment have been thoroughly described by Franck & Weisband, *supra* n.54,at 84-89.

[73] Antonio Cassese, "Foreign Economic Assistance and Respect for Civil and Political Rights: Chile—A Case Study," 14 *Tex. Int'l L.J.*, 251, 260 (1979) (italics in the text).

[74] See Edwin M. Martin, "Should Observance of Basic Human Rights Be a Prerequisite for Aid?" 16 *Atl. Comm'y. Q.*, 216, esp. at 218-219 (1978); and Baehr, *supra* n. 37, at 40-42.

its underlying principle—*i.e. restitutio in integrum*—than from its unlimited scope, which covers all the assistance to the offending country. By contrast, universal injuries call not for monetary compensation but for redress. Universal injuries entail no monetary loss, *i.e.*, no economic impoverishment, but immaterial harm. In short, whereas particular injuries generally cause material damage, universal injuries cause "moral" damage. It is doubtful that both kinds of damages should be subject to the same standards.

In any event, the suspension of economic assistance as a reaction to the violation of fundamental human rights admittedly does not stand the proportionality test. But above all, such a remedy, because it is practically unfeasible, cannot effectively make the "criminal state" comply with the law.[75] It may, therefore, be necessary to go beyond such inoffensive displays of enmity and encroach upon certain international obligations which are binding between the responding and the offending states.

II. Countermeasures

All provisions of the United States Code surveyed so far show ample evidence of a steady commitment to the need and the right to take strong measures against offending states. Concerning countermeasures against alleged "criminal states," that commitment seems to be somewhat inconsistent. There is no other field where so much hesitation and contradiction is apparent.

There is no doubt, however, that a universal injury enables any individual state to resort to countermeasures against the offender. As long as the fundamental character of the obligation is universally recognized and the breach is indisputable, there is theoretically no rule that cannot be the subject of counter-

[75] At a Conference on "Economic Sanctions as an Instrument of United States Strategic and Foreign Policy" which took place at the University of Pennsylvania Law School on Oct. 16, 1982, Mr. Lee R. Marks, Former Deputy Legal Adviser of the State Department made these suggestive remarks: "I share your view about Argentina. It is basically a despicable regime and I am all for cutting off military assistance to it. I feel that economic assistance is quite different. I worked on human rights problems in the Carter Administration, and think that the human rights legislation passed by Congress is largely ineffective in promoting human rights. It was impossible to administer by the State Department as seen by an endless series of irrational *ad hoc* decisions, almost any one of which was indefensible when compared with another one." in 6 *J. Comp. Bus. & Cap. M.L.*, 55, 78-79 (1984).

measures. To that extent, Mr. Willem Riphagen, Special Rapporteur on State Responsibility, rightly put forward at the International Law Commission a provision that "an international crime entails all the legal consequences of an internationally wrongful act."[76] However, in the case of certain rules, noncompliance would not be legitimate under contemporary international law. Humanitarian rules are an obvious example. But one may ask whether other rules are not also subject to the same exception, in particular the provisions of a Headquarters Agreement between an international organization and a reacting state, which would have undertaken not to impose any impediment to transit to or from the organization headquarters.[77] However, that kind of exception derives not from the fundamental character of the obligation at stake, but from the unlawfulness of any countermeasure affecting the rights of third parties.[78]

Apart from such exceptions, a criminal state is properly speaking an "outlaw;" it places itself outside the law and cannot claim any of the rights which international law bestows on other states. Theoretically such a state has no rights regardless of their customary or treaty origin, provided that the rights do not stem from humanitarian rules. Indeed, in order to distinguish between the legal consequences of international crimes and delicts, it is necessary to consider that the criminal state is as it were even further

[76] See *supra*, n. 20.

[77] See the problems faced by the United States government when, in response to the shooting down of the South Korean passenger aircraft by a Soviet military jet on Sept. 1, 1983, the governors of New York and New Jersey ordered the Port Authority of New York and New Jersey not to grant clearance for the landing of the Soviet plane carrying Soviet Foreign Minister Andrei Gromyko to the annual meeting of the United Nations General Assembly. Such action would have been inconsistent with Article IV, Section 11, of the agreement between the United Nations and the United States regarding the headquarters of the United Nations (T.I.A.S., 1676), whereby the United States agreed that "federal, state or local authorities shall not impose any impediment to transit" to or from United Nations Headquarters on representatives to the United Nations. Moreover Section 12 of the article provides that this obligation applies without regard to the status of relations between the United States and the other government involved.

To save face, the United States argued that it had not breached the agreement because there was no requirement that a delegation be allowed to land wherever it desired. . . . But the most important point is that the United States had to allow Mr. Gromyko to land at a nearby air base. See Note, "Act by State Governments Affecting Foreign Relations," 25 *Harv. J. Int'l. L.*, 200-205 (1984). Significantly, in 1978, the administration rejected proposals to restrict the travel of Ugandan officials accredited to the United Nations and to deny Ugandan aircraft landing rights in U.S. territory. See Comment, *supra* n.53, at 1152.

[78] See *infra*, pp. 128-131.

away from law compliance than the delictual state. Whereas the latter could admittedly be exposed to countermeasures relating to the field of the delict, the former, by reason of the gravity of the violation, should be deprived of responses relating to specific fields. This is so less because international crimes may not be countered by reciprocal actions than because if such differences between the consequences of the breach are not made, the difference between crime and delict would be purely semantic. To some extent this analysis shows as a matter of pure logic that the concept of ''international crime'' leads to a stalemate because reprisals taken against a delictual state already entail temporary nonperformance of any nonhumanitarian obligation short of force between the victim and the offender.[79] Insofar as the major limitation on responses to international delicts is the unlawfulness of the use of force, one may wonder whether the so-called international crime does not entail a dispensation from such a prohibition.

Although the consequences of violations of fundamental international obligations are not commonly perceived, they are, however, confirmed by international practice. For instance, under contemporary customary international law, there is no doubt that the slave trade, though not extinct, is illegal.[80] As a result, any state is still entitled to visit, search and seize foreign vessels engaging in the slave trade, whatever the nationality of the offender or the flag flown by the ship.[81] Similarly, a crime of genocide entitles any state to dispense temporarily with the obligation to respect the territorial sovereign integrity of the offender in order to put a stop to the atrocities. The lack of any international protest following the intervention of Tanzania in Uganda in 1979 is a point of great significance. *A fortiori*, a state is not bound to respect the independence of a criminal state and the courts of one country are not compelled to grant sovereign

[79] See the *Naulilaa* Award, 2 *U.N.R.I.A.A.* 1026 (1928); Hans Kelsen, ''Unrecht and Unrechtsfolge im Völkerrecht,'' 12 *Z.a.ö.R.V.*, 575-576 (1932); E. Zoller, *Peacetime*, at 41-42.

[80] See Arnold D. McNair, *The Law of Treaties* (1961), 227.

[81] Compare *The Enterprise*, *The Hermosa* and *The Creole* (British-United States Claims Commission, 1853), in John B. Moore, *International Arbitrations*, Vol. I, p. 409, Vol. 4, p. 4349 to *The Lawrence* (1855, same Commission, *ibid*, Vol. 3, p. 2824). See also A. de La Pradelle & N. Politis, *Recueil des Arbitrages Internationaux*, Vol. I, pp. 703-705, 740-741.

immunity to such a state for a criminal act—even *jure imperii* acts—committed within its own territory. This particular legal aspect of the consequences of an international crime may well be overlooked because national courts are more likely to rely on domestic law and the exception of public policy (*ordre public*) than on international law to refuse to give effects in the *forum* to ''criminal'' foreign pieces of legislation. In *Letelier v. Republic of Chile* (1980), the U.S. District Court (DC) rightly held that:

> [T]here is no discretion to commit, or to have one's officers or agents commit, an illegal act. Whatever policy options may exist for a foreign country, it has no ''discretion'' to perpetrate conduct designed to result in the assassination of an individual or individuals, action that is clearly contrary to the precepts of humanity as recognized in both national and international law. Accordingly there would be no 'discretion' . . . to order or to aid in an assassination and were it to be demonstrated that a foreign state has undertaken any such act in this country, that foreign state could not be accorded sovereign immunity.[82]

This important judicial statement makes it clear that sovereign immunity is not to be granted to a foreign ''criminal'' state. The court's reservation related to the effects of the crime ''in this country;'' *i.e.*, within the jurisdiction of the United States, must not be viewed as an exception to the principle, but merely as a precondition for a United States court to assert its jurisdiction *ratione materiae*. However, as far as practical results are concerned, this is a very important point. As in other foreign states, the powers of the courts in the United States do not derive from international law, but from municipal law, and more specifically from the Constitution. Municipal courts are therefore very sensitive to the limits which their own municipal legal order has assigned to their powers.[83] No national judge will ever consider himself as directly vested with international powers unless the Constitution or a statutory provision actually says so. That is

[82] 488 F. Supp. 665, 673 (1980).

[83] See Paul Reuter, ''Le droit international et la place du juge français dans l'ordre constitutionnel national,'' in *L'application du droit international par le juge français* (1972), 17, 23.

why whenever municipal law requires national judges to give effect to international rules only when definite prerequisites are met, these prerequisites will always determine the potential effects of international rules in the *forum*. Whether procedural or substantive, they may be weighed differently by the national judges, in particular when the law-making or law-finding authorities have not yet asserted the proper scope of obscure or controversial provisions. Such is the case in the United States with Section 1350 of the Alien Tort Statute.[84] Section 1350 provides that a district court shall have original jurisdiction over civil actions "by an alien for a tort only, committed in violation of the law of nations or a treaty of the United States." In *Filartiga v. Peña-Irala*, the Second Circuit did not feel the need to attach to Section 1350 other requirements than those deriving from international law, probably because the suit was only brought against an individual.[85] However, in *Hanoch Tel-Oren v. Libyan Arab Republic* where the suit was brought against the Palestine Liberation Organization (PLO), the Libyan Arab Republic, the Palestine Information Office, the National Association of Arab Americans, and the Palestine Congress of North America, the district court (DCC) construed Section 1350 as compelling plaintiffs to invoke a "cause of action" which, if given to them by the law of nations or by treaties of the United States, would permit the court to grant relief.[86] The court of appeal dismissed the application in a brief *per curiam* opinion based upon three separate concurring opinions.[87] Whereas the core of Judge Bork's opinion consisted in extending the municipal concept of self-executing treaties[88] to the rules of customary international law,[89]

[84]28 U.S.C. § 1350 (1982).
[85]630 F.2d 876 (1980).
[86]517 F. Supp. 542, 549 (1981).
[87]726 F.2d 774 (1984).
[88]As Stefan A. Riesenfeld rightly puts it: "Strictly speaking, the term 'self-executing' is not a notion whose meaning is determined by international law. The self-executing nature of a treaty provision is a product of international and domestic *constitutional rules*." (emphasis added), in "The Doctrine of Self-Executing Treaties and *U.S. v. Postal*: Win at Any Price," 74 *A.J.I.L.* 892, 900 (1980). Unlike United States courts, European courts are more generous in recognizing the direct effect of international treaties; see the thorough analysis made by Michel Waelbroeck, *Traités internationaux et jurisdictions internes dans les pays du Marché Commun* (1969), 161-188.
[89]For a criticism, see Anthony D'Amato, "Judge Bork's Concept of the Law of Nations Is Seriously Mistaken," 79 *A.J.I.L.*, 92-105 (1985) followed by a rebuttal from Alfred P. Rubin, *ibid.*, at 105-112 and a reply from Anthony D'Amato, *ibid.*, at 112-113.

Judge Edwards refused to read Section 1350 as covering torture by non-state actors, failing any guidance from the Supreme Court on the statute's use of the term "law of nations," and Judge Robb argued that the case was a nonjusticiable "political question." Whatever the merits of these opinions, all three are significantly founded on municipal legal requirements, just as in the *Letelier* case, the court emphasized the effects of the crime in the country. Similarly, in *Siderman v. Republic of Argentina*, although in a judgment by default of September 28, 1984, the district court (DCC) first refused to grant sovereign immunity to Argentina for acts of torture committed by the former military junta against Joseph Siderman eight years before,[90] the same court vacated the default judgment on March 7, 1985, precisely because a condition of municipal law was not actually fulfilled in the case: "With respect to the Foreign Sovereign Immunities Act, none of the enumerated exceptions to immunity listed in 28 U.S.C. § 1605 apply herein."[91]

On the other hand, just as, internationally speaking, foreign sovereign immunity cannot protect criminal states, so the Act of State doctrine should not apply to them.[92] Indeed, as a matter of fact the Act of State doctrine entails the very same effect as foreign sovereign immunity: It exempts foreign states from the jurisdiction of municipal courts. However, should it be indeed legitimate to regard a foreign state as "criminal," the logic of international crime inevitably places such state outside the protection of any nonhumanitarian rule. This state must therefore be deprived of the Act of State doctrine as a last resort to its avoiding conviction even if this would appear feasible only as a matter of declaratory judgment. In short, whenever a suit is brought against a criminal state in a United States court, there is under international law no need for a treaty or another agreement between the United States and such foreign country to

[90] *Siderman v. Republic of Argentina* DCC (9th Cir.), September 28, 1984, No. CV 82-1772-RMT (MCx), Judgment by default.

[91] *Siderman v. Republic of Argentina*, DCC (9th Cir.), March 7, 1985, No. CV 82-1772-RMT (MCx), order vacating default judgment and dismissing action.

[92] For similar views, see Jordan J. Paust, "Federal Jurisdiction Over Extraterritorial Acts of Terrorism and Nonimmunity for Foreign Violators of International Law Under the FSIA and the Act of State Doctrine," 23 *Va. J. Int'l. L.*, 191, 242-247 (1983).

justify an exception to the Act of State doctrine, provided that the suit is entirely related to a violation of a fundamental internationally recognized human right.[93] However, like foreign sovereign immunity, the Act of State doctrine is part of municipal law. As the Supreme Court held in *Banco National de Cuba v. Sabbatino*, it is "a principle of decision *binding* on federal and state courts alike."[94] Despite the fact that it is not "compelled" by the Constitution, it has "constitutional underpinnings."[95] Therefore, the chances that judges may discard it and directly apply international law are slight unless the foreign piece of legislation squarely involves genuine "persecutions."[96]

Nevertheless, the authority granted by international law to each state to remedy universal injuries is very broad. Any noncompliance with a nonhumanitarian international obligation that may lead the "criminal state" to comply with the law, is permissible. The only limit is to be found in the impossibility of "punishing" the offending foreign state. Final measures should, therefore, be excluded because in peacetime no state is entitled to punish another, since no state is superior to another.[97]

Nevertheless, the principal that a criminal state places itself outside the law is not seriously disputable. The real problem, however, is to know the extent of the freedom of foreign states with respect to such crimes. In contemporary international law, solidarity mainly exists in matters relating to peace and international security, although the failure of the Security Council of the United Nations in the maintenance of peace has considerably devalued the solidarity created by the UN Charter. When the particular interests of a state are not affected, that state rarely feels under an obligation to take strong action against the of-

[93]To that extent, it is doubtful that rights in property fall within this category (see *Siderman v. Republic of Argentina*, DDC (9th Cir.), September 28, 1984) unless the deprivation of property is unambiguously linked to the denial of fundamental human rights as in case of "persecution(s);" see the *Bernstein* exception (*Bernstein v. N. V. Nederlandsche-Amerikaansche Stoomvaart-Maatschappij*, 210 F.2d 375, 2nd Cir. 1954).
[94]376 U.S. 398, 427 (emphasis added).
[95]*Ibid.*, at 427 (quotation marks in the text).
[96]See *supra*, n. 93 and *infra*, Chap. 4, p. 158, n. 65.
[97]See E. Zoller, *Peacetime*, p. 61-62, and for an implicit confirmation, see Section 4(a) of the 1976 Foreign Sovereign Immunities Act, which rules out the possibility of declaring a foreign state liable for punitive damages (28 U.S.C. 1606 (1982)).

fender, as is illustrated by the scarcity of the United States statutes providing for countermeasures against states which violate fundamental rules of international law.

1. The Content

Several United States statutes provide for countermeasures against states which violate fundamental international obligations. However, with respect to the principle of relativity prevailing in international law, the determination of the fundamental character of the breached obligation may be subject to different interpretations. In some cases the question is indisputable. Violations of the basic rights of the human person, such as genocide, slavery or racial discrimination, are doubtless breaches of fundamental obligations. The International Court of Justice expressly referred to them in the *Barcelona Traction* case.[98] Such is also the case of acts of torture, as illustrated by the *Filartiga v. Peña-Irala*,case (1980), although it concerned an act of torture committed by an individual.[99] But there are some domestic equal qualifications which seem controversial. For instance, it is doubtful that a ban on emigration amounts to a breach of a fundamental international obligation. Neither the UN Charter, nor the Universal Declaration of Human Rights—especially Article 13—requires a state to let its citizens emigrate, *i.e.*, to leave the country once and for all. The following analysis will hold to the statement of Section 402 of the Trade Act (1974), which regards as a ''fundamental human right,'' ''the right or opportunity to emigrate''[100] and denies nondiscriminatory treatment to any non-market-economy country which fails to recognize that right of its own citizens. Apart from basic human rights, a fundamental obligation is certainly to be found in the obligations of states not to support terrorist activities directed against the security of for-

[98]I.C.J. *Reports* 1970, p. 32, § 34.

[99]630 F.2d 876, 883-884.

[100]19 U.S.C. § 2432(a) (1982). Section 409 of the Trade Act considers even as a ''fundamental human right,'' ''the right or opportunity to join permanently through emigration, a very close relative in the United States such as a spouse, parent, child, brother or sister'' [19 U.S.C. 2439(a) (1982)]. However, the denial of such right by a non-market-economy country only gives rise to a simple measure: the refusal of credit guarantees and commercial agreements.

eign air carriers; any air carrier from such states is liable to have its air permit over United States territory suspended.[101]

As for procedures which may be attached to United States countermeasures for universal injuries, no statute provides for safeguards as stringent as those relating to the suspension of assistance. But the procedures which established evidence of a consistent pattern of gross violations of internationally recognized human rights indirectly cover the countermeasures in response to such violations.

Curiously enough, there are only two statutory provisions of general application which provide for countermeasures against states committing violations of fundamental obligations. The first is to be found in the 1977 International Financial Institutions Act, which requires United States executive directors of various international financial institutions to oppose any loan, extension of financial assistance or technical assistance to any country whose government either engages in a consistent pattern of gross violation of internationally recognized human rights, or provides refuge to individuals committing acts of international terrorism by hijacking aircraft.[102] The second is an amendment added to the 1958 Federal Aviation Act, which provides for the suspension of any foreign air carrier permit, the national state of which is a sanctuary for an international terrorist organization.[103] All other statutes are directed at one state or a group of states and therefore, somewhat awkwardly, the United States redresses universal injuries mostly with case-by-case remedies.

2. Adequacy

Unlike the remedies for particular and collective injuries, United States countermeasures for universal injuries have no inherent logic. When one brings them together in order to discover their common features, the contradictions which arise are large enough to suggest that they have not been fully considered. As a result, their relevance to the injuries they seek to redress is rather doubtful.

[101] 49 App. U.S.C. § 1514(a) (1982).
[102] 22 U.S.C. § 262d (1982).
[103] 49 App. U.S.C. § 1514(a) (1982).

The first striking feature of United States countermeasures is their unequal distribution. Some violators of fundamental international obligations are "more equal than others." For instance, if racial discrimination and the prohibition of emigration are both violations of fundamental human rights, both should be put on an equal footing and be subject to countermeasures. In actual fact, apartheid gives rise only to unfriendliness—*e.g.*, Eximbank shall not guarantee, insure or extend credit in support of any export to the government of South Africa[104]—whereas restrictions on emigration are sanctioned by a genuine countermeasure, the impossibility of receiving nondiscriminatory treatment.[105] In the latter case, the infringement of the international customary rule of nondiscrimination derives less from substance than from factual implementation. It must be borne in mind that the United States does not distinguish between nondiscriminatory treatment and most-favored-nation treatment. Both have been put into the same category, as can be seen from the rates set forth in column 1 of the United States Tariff schedules. A foreign state cannot therefore complain of discrimination if it is not granted most-favored-nation treatment. However, discrimination does exist when nondiscriminatory treatment is not equally applied. Such is precisely the case of Section 402 of the Trade Act, which denies that treatment on a discriminatory basis, *i.e.*, to non-market-economy countries alone. Similarly, if apartheid, like genocide, violates a fundamental obligation, the imposition of an arms embargo in one case[106] and of a total trade embargo in the other[107] does not make legal sense. Still, if an officially ordered political assassination is as serious a breach as the dissolution of and the prohibition against membership in unions, there should be no legal reason to take simple measures in one case[108] and stringent countermeasures in the other,[109] unless the life of one individual is worth less than the freedom of many.

[104]12 U.S.C. § 635(b)(a) (1982).
[105]19 U.S.C. § 2432(a) (1982).
[106]See *U.S. Digest* 1973, pp. 542-544.
[107]Act of Oct. 10, 1978, Pub. 1. No. 95-435, § 5, 92 Stat. 1051.
[108]See *U.S. Digest* 1979, pp. 50-51.
[109]See 76 *A.J.I.L.*, 379-384 (1982).

It is true that discrimination is also a common feature of the simple measures taken against violators of fundamental human rights. As to foreign assistance, country-specific statutes contrast with general legislation. Such statutes apply only to the countries which they designate. But discrimination as applied to measures is not legally similar to discrimination as applied to countermeasures because the action in the first case bears on privileges or advantages, whereas in the second it encroaches on legal entitlements. On June 23, 1977, the House of Representatives approved a bill (H.R. 7797) which would have prevented funds appropriated for international financial institutions from being used "directly or indirectly" for, *inter alia*, seven specific countries (Uganda, Cambodia, Laos, Vietnam, Mozambique, Angola and Cuba). No doubt such a step was motivated not only by the intention to remedy for universal injuries. But the restrictions under H.R. 7797 would have required the institutions to discriminate by denying funds to specific countries. Thus the bill was inconsistent with the charters of those institutions, which typically go on to state that considerations relevant to their decisions "shall be weighed *impartially*."[110] Eventually the House had to leave out the reference to the seven countries.[111]

In addition to their unequal distribution, most U.S. countermeasures for universal injuries have been ill-conceived insofar as they usually affect the rights of innocent third parties.[112] Such is the case of Section 701 of the International Financial Institutions Act, which instructs the executive directors of various international financial institutions to oppose any loan, any extension of financial or technical assistance to any country engaged in a consistent pattern of gross violations of internationally recognized human rights, or which provides refuge to individuals committing acts of international terrorism by hijacking air-

[110]Article 36, Section 2 of the African Development Bank (emphasis added); see also Article IV, Section 10 of the International Bank for Reconstruction and Development, Article V, Section 6 of the International Development Association.

[111]See *U.S. Digest* 1977, pp. 754-763.

[112]However, when the United States is affected as a third party by the remedies of foreign states, it does not fail to protect its sovereign rights, as illustrated by the antiboycott provisions of the Export Administration Act of 1979, Pub. L. 96-72, approved on September 29, 1979, 93 Stat. 503, 521 codified at 50 App. U.S.C. § 2407 (Suppl. V, 1981).

crafts.[113] Since fundamental international obligations are by nature *erga omnes*, all subjects of international law are bound at least not to assist or aid a violator of such obligations. This duty to abstain applies to international organizations as well as to states. However, a member state must respect the international legal personality of the international organization, *i.e.*, its rights to establish its position vis-à-vis other states or any subject of international law. Therefore it cannot prejudge the position that the international organization will see fit to adopt against a "criminal state," certainly at least not before that organization has had a chance to do so. In short, the international legal personality of an international organization precludes a member state from taking preventive steps which affect the decision-making function of the competent organs.[114] If the international organization fails to respond, a member state should theoretically be able to dissociate itself from abstention. Similarly, the United States does not respect the budgetary autonomy of an international agency when it imposes, as a prerequisite to its contributions to the United Nations Relief and Works Agency, the condition that the agency take all possible measures to assure that no part of its contribution shall be used to furnish assistance to any refugee receiving military training from a guerilla or terrorist type organization.[115] The agency is no doubt under the

[113] 22 U.S.C. § 262d(f) (1982).

[114] Significantly, Pub. L. 96-544, Dec. 17, 1980 (94 Stat. 3213) provided that at the International Monetary Fund "it shall be the policy of the United States: (1) that the Palestine Liberation Organization should not be given membership in the Fund or be given observer status or any other official status at any meeting sponsored by or associated with the Fund; . . . (3) that in the event that the Fund provides either membership, observer status, or any other official status to the Palestine Liberation Organization, such action would result in a serious diminution of U.S. support." [22 U.S.C. § 286e note (1982)]. But see the opinion of Robert H. Mundheim, General Counsel of the Department of the Treasury submitted to Secretary of the Treasury, Michael W. Blumenthal, in a memorandum on the legality of international development lending institutions accepting U.S. earmarked contributions or subscriptions in *U.S. Digest* 1977, pp. 755-760, especially at 757. However, Oscar Schachter has argued that: "Since it is a proper objective of the banks to meet human needs, conditions which interfere with that aim and prevent large groups of population from receiving their proportionate share could not be regarded as irrelevant to the decisions of the banks. One must, therefore, conclude that there may be circumstances under which a pattern of gross violations of human rights will be sufficiently related to economic considerations so as to constitute a proper ground for decisions on the making of loans," in "International Law Implications of U.S. Human Rights Policies," 24 *N.Y.L. Sch'l. L. Rev.*, 63, 86-87 (1978).

[114] 22 U.S.C. § 2221(c) (1982).

obligation not to give assistance to terrorist activities, but a member state cannot prejudge the legal position taken by the agency on such an issue. The rights of third states are also affected when the United States threatens to suspend the right of any foreign air carrier whose national state is maintaining air service between itself and a foreign nation that is a sanctuary for any terrorist organization,[116] without giving that country the opportunity to take action on its own against the offender. The rights of third states are also affected by Section 3 of the 1979 Export Administration Act, which provides in substance for the use of export controls to encourage other countries to take immediate steps to prevent the use of their territories as sanctuary to persons involved in acts of international terrorism,[117] without giving the third party time to take any measures. This is actually a consistent pattern of U.S. remedies for internationally wrongful acts: a long-standing failure to take into account the rights of third parties. In international law there is no such thing as a ''full-faith and credit clause'' that would be attached to the acts, records or administrative decisions of the United States or any other foreign country.[118] This trend certainly culminated in the so-called pipeline sanctions issued on December 30, 1981, by the Commerce Department under the 1979 Export Administration Act. The amendments to these regulations issued on June 22, 1982, extended licensing to the export of foreign goods and technical data by companies owned or controlled by U.S. citizens. They also applied to foreign-produced goods whose production depended on U.S. technology licensed by a company subject to U.S. jurisdiction.[119] The infringement on the territorial sovereignty of European states was so blatantly unjustified that the sweeping extraterritorial control program had to be withdrawn. As a result, all legal issues became moot in mid-December since all related enforcement proceedings were terminated.[120] The pipeline dis-

[116]49 App U.S.C. § 1514(a) (1982).

[117]50 App U.S.C. § 2402(8) (Suppl. V, 1981).

[118]According to the wording of Article IV, Section 1 of the Constitution of the United States (September 17, 1787).

[119]47 F.R. 27250 (June 24, 1982).

[120]47 F.R. 51858 (November 18, 1982). See also *Dresser Industries, Inc. v. Baldrige*, 549 F. Supp. 108 (Doc. 1982) (order denying preliminary injunction).

pute is only an episode of this consistent American policy. However, in response to universal injuries as opposed to particular or collective injuries, it may be asked whether such a policy does not have some legal justification insofar as universal injuries by nature arouse universal concern. This is an extremely difficult question to answer because it emphasizes an apparently insoluble contradiction between the atomized structure of international society and the generalized consequences of an universal injury. To some extent it is questionable that the concept of international crime is adequate for the contemporary structure of international society. In any event, the European states clearly did not regard Soviet support of the imposition of martial law in Poland as a universal injury.

Finally, a third feature of a particular statute deserves some consideration. The 1958 Federal Aviation Act as amended gives authority to the President to suspend the right of any air carrier or foreign air carrier to engage in foreign air transportation to and from any foreign nation that permits the use of its territory as a sanctuary for any terrorist organization that uses aircraft hijacking as an instrument of policy.[121] The remedy for such a universal injury is confined to the field of the crime (aviation matters). That specific feature in matters related to universal injury is certainly not a requirement, since a criminal state puts itself quite literally outside the law. However, the tradition of retaliation, which limits the response to the substantive field of the breach, is so well enshrined in the international opinion that alternatives have not yet been conceived.[122] In that respect, it is interesting to note that the Bonn Declaration on Hijacking has followed a similar path in expressing a resolution to take "immediate action" to cease all flights to any country[123] that refuses extradition or prosecution of those who have hijacked an aircraft and/or does not return such aircraft.

[121] 49 App U.S.C. § 1514(a) (1982).

[122] See for instance the wording used by Mr. Kevin Chamberlain, Legal Counsellor of the Foreign & Commonwealth Office: "It is submitted that the right to take *retaliatory measures in response to a fundamental breach* of the Chicago Convention exists . . . ," in "Collective Suspension of Air Services With States Which Harbour Hijackers," 32 *I.C.L.Q., 616, 631 (n.30) (1983).*

[123] *Ibid.* at 627.

In conclusion, it may be said that the United States countermeasures contemplated in the case of universal injuries have far less strength and uniformity than countermeasures in response to particular injuries. This is hardly surprising, since redress for universal injuries belongs to a field where politics still prevails over law.

However, even if foreign policy considerations are left aside, it must be recognized that regulating and administering the dosage of remedies for universal injuries is no easy task. The major reason is that so-called international crimes establish an opposition between the usual individualized imputability of the breach and the inevitable collective impact of the remedies generally available. International crimes are in the great majority of cases attributable to a person or group of persons, *i.e.* the ruler(s), whereas the system of collective responsibility that permeates the institution of reprisals is by definition not individualized. Therefore, any impersonal action taken in response to an international crime is likely to be viewed as hateful insofar as, especially in the face of a consistent pattern of gross violations of internationally recognized human rights, innocent people are punished twice: first by their own leaders and then by the responding foreign country.

In any event, one may wonder whether any attempt to redress violations of fundamental human rights is not an attempt to square the circle. The action has to bear especially on the culprit, and peacetime remedies do not provide many devices to achieve this end as long as most of them are beleaguered by collective responsibility. Interestingly enough, the very first step taken by Congress against Uganda, even before the imposition of a trade embargo, was to urge the President to "prohibit the export of military, paramilitary and police equipment to Uganda."[124] Similar steps could not have been taken against Kampuchea (Cambodia), with which the United States had no military or economic ties. However, in both cases, Congress found that such events required not only "special notice" and "condemnation by out-

[124]Sec. 610(d)(1) of Pub. L. 95-426, approved Oct. 7, 1978 [92 Stat. 963; 22 U.S.C. 2151 note (1982)]; *U.S. Digest* 1978, p. 465.

side observers,'' but also support to multilateral action by the UN and encouragement to bilateral action by countries having more extensive relations with such countries in order to put an end to the brutal and inhumane practices.[125] Actually Congress took measures which were similar to those listed by the Special Rapporteur on State Responsibility in the draft articles put forward in its fifth report to the International Law Commission, which reads as follows:

> An international crime committed by a state entails an obligation for every other state:
> (a) not to recognize as legal the situation created by such crime; and
> (b) not to render aid or assistance to the state which has committed such crime in maintaining the situation created by such crime; and
> (c) to join other states in affording mutual assistance in carrying out the obligations under subparagraphs (a) and (b).[126]

If it proves impossible to go beyond such inoffensive measures, the concept of international crime is likely to be no more than a legal nicety. An interesting aspect of the United States law is that it has endeavored to provide other remedies, even though they do not all fit the crime, and alternatives do exist. There are remedies which bear on the government and not on the population of the state as a whole. The hostages crisis, for instance, showed that the freeze of Iranian governmental assets did succeed in getting the Iranian government to mend its ways and release the American hostages.[127] Other remedies also exist in the field of diplomatic privileges, as opposed to diplomatic immunities, or in the field of trade matters, where certain commodities may be owned by public official agencies and exploited for the benefit

[125]Sec. 610(a)(b) of Pub. L. 95-426, *Ibid., U.S. Digest* 1978, p. 464.

[126]*Report of the International Law Commission*, 39 G.A.O.R. 10, A/39/10 at 240 (1984).

[127]See, however, in that respect the surprising motivation of Executive Order 12211 ''Future Prohibitions on Transactions with Iran,'' signed by the President on April 17, 1980. The text provides for additional steps against Iran ''to deal with . . . [*inter alia*] . . . the added unusual and extraordinary threat to the national security, foreign policy and economy of the United States created by subsequent events in Iran and neighboring countries, including the *Soviet invasion of Afghanistan*,'' 45 F.R. 26685-26686 (emphasis added).

of the leaders (*e.g.* coffee in Uganda). Without resorting to a ban on imports as sweeping and probably excessive as that on Cuban sugar, the imposition of reasonable quotas or adequate tariff increases may help ensure compliance with the obligation not to render assistance to the officials who have committed such "crimes." There is little doubt that a uniform measure applicable to all criminal leaders would be impracticable. Such measures have to be tailored on a case-by-case basis, and therefore factual discrimination is inevitable. But discrimination in fact does not have the same significance as discrimination in law, which is what is currently being applied.

In that respect, to improve international remedies against violations of fundamental international human rights, it would appear that the United States should first and foremost abandon the astonishing discrepancy between the measures taken against apartheid and those following the imposition of martial law in Poland. In short, redress for international crimes is subject to compliance with the principle of equality before the law. Either such violations are equally redressed, or the United States should renounce its leadership in the field. But the current international practice is inconsistent *mutatis mutandis* with its long-standing constitutional commitment to the equal protection clause, which precludes any suspect classifications.

4

Toward a General Theory of Unilateral Remedies for International Offenses

The variety of international remedies provided by the laws of the United States shows that violations of international obligations entail different kinds of offenses and therefore different kinds of situations. In international law as well as in municipal law, any breach of law disrupts the social order. In other words, any breach of law entails a wrong in the broadest sense; *i.e.* an injury calling for redress. The injury may take various forms, and in particular it may or may not entail a damage caused to a subject whose subjective right has been impaired. In that sense, there is no doubt that the existence of a damage is not a prerequisite to the existence of an internationally wrongful act. The International Law Commission which in that respect entirely followed its special rapporteur, Roberto Ago, explained in substance that breaches of human rights conventions or international labor conventions do not normally cause any damage, but yet constitute internationally wrongful acts.[1] In short, the damage is totally irrelevant to the existence of the internationally wrongful act.

But when turning to the consequences of the wrongful act, it is impossible to continue to disregard the occurrence of the damage. Complete unconcern with the occurrence of a damage and, therefore, with the different remedies that follow a wrongful act is actually a feature of primitive law and procedure. In primitive societies any wrong is subsumed under the single category of

[1]*Yrbk. I.L.C.*, 1973 (II), p. 183. See in particular Second Report on State Responsibility, by Roberto Ago, Special Rapporteur, Doc. A/CN-4/233, *Yrbk. I.L.C.*, 1970, Vol. II, p. 194, para. 53 and the criticism of Jean Combacau, "La responsabilité internationale," in Hubert Thierry, Jean Combacau, Serge Sur & Charles Vallée, *Droit International Public* (1981), 655, 656-669.

atonement, which makes no distinction between vengeance and restitution.[2] There is no question that international law is a primitive legal order; but it must be borne in mind that it is applied by subjects whose legal orders have long ago gone far beyond the primitive. That is why states do not usually feel free to do whatever they want when taking the law into their own hands. In other words, states, albeit in an unconscious manner, differentiate between remedies. All the international remedies laid down in the statutes of the United States give ample evidence of this in that they all are purposive in very definite manners.[3] It would be absurd to consider the aim the same when the United States withdraws a previously granted trade concession which was modified by a foreign country and when it bans the importation of any fish product from a foreign state which fails to abide by an international fishery program. The Pelly Amendment was never intended to seek compensation, whereas Section 125(d) of the Trade Act was precisely conceived for that purpose. The difference in purpose stems from a difference in motive. In one case the United States is seeking redress for damage directly caused to its economic or patrimonial interests; in the other, steps are taken to make the lawbreaker revert to law compliance. There is no question that where a damage has occurred, *i.e.* where an economic loss has been incurred, this element becomes a decisive factor in determining the choice and the priority of the remedies available to tackle the consequences of the wrongful act. A survey of the international remedies laid down in the laws of the United States shows that a clear distinction is made between remedies seeking reparation and remedies providing for retribution. In other words, United States remedies for international wrongs have already gone beyond a specific feature of primitive legal orders. This in itself casts some doubts on the commonplace assertion that international law, at least when exemplified by

[2]Max Weber, *Economy and Society* (1978), Vol. II, 647.

[3]Legal scholars indeed distinguish between civil and criminal sanctions as a matter of purpose. Emile Durkheim went further into this distinction when he drew a line between the concept of *restitutionary sanction* (which ''consiste seulement dans la remise des choses en l'état, dans le rétablissement des rapports troublés sous leur forme normale'') and the concept of *repressive sanction* (which ''consiste essentiellement dans une douleur infligée à l'agent''), in *De la division du travail social* (1902), 33.

state practice, is a primitive law. Moreover, insofar as none of the United States international remedies provides for final and definitive harm against the wrongdoer, a second feature stands out in the distinction between enforcement and punishment. It is therefore submitted that with respect to the practice of the United States, the purpose of international remedies may be threefold: reparation, enforcement and punishment. However, the margin of freedom which the United States avails itself of with respect to these three purposes is mostly dependent upon whether or not a damage has been sustained.

I. Reparation

Despite the well-known statement made by the Permanent Court of International Justice in the *Chorzów Factory* case,[4] there is no doubt that in exercising unilaterally their rights to obtain reparation for the breach of an international duty, states are always tempted to do more than is necessary to reestablish the equivalence of conditions between the parties, unless unilateral reparation is organized by the treaty itself, an uncommon practice in international law. However, that is the case for the contracting parties to the GATT and the Subsidies Code insofar as, in order to compensate the injury caused by unlawful subsidies, they are explicitly allowed to levy countervailing duties on foreign subsidized products, but not in excess of an amount *equal* to the estimated bounty or subsidy determined to have been granted.

Under classical international law, punishment prevailed over reparation, *i.e.*, reparation was not commensurate with the injury sustained. The traditional mode of redress known as ''retaliation'' is the best example of this conspicuous feature of unilateral remedies. In other words, unlike judicially adjudicated remedies,[5] unilateral remedies were more often than not tainted with an idea of revenge. Until recently, all the statutes enacted by the

[4]*Chorzów Factory* Case (Jurisdiction), P.C.I.J., Ser. A/8,21; *Chorzów Factory* Case (Merits) P.C.I.J., Ser. A/13,47.

[5]In arbitral awards, reparation is usually governed by the principle laid down by Umpire Parker in the *Lusitania* cases (Nov. 1, 1923): ''The fundamental concept of 'damages' is satisfaction, reparation for a *loss* suffered; a judicially ascertained *compensation* for wrong. The remedy should be commensurate with the loss, so that the injured party may be made whole.'' (italics in text), 7 *U.N.R.I.A.A.* 39 [footnotes omitted].

United States since the end of the 19th century to provide reparation for an internationally wrongful act did not limit the intensity of the response. It once seemed that in any event the United States remedy could be a measure in excess. This goes back to the 1887 Act that threatens to respond to any harassment of American fishermen in British North American waters with a total ban on imports from the British North American dominions;[6] or the 1916 Act that counters foreign bans on United States products with unlimited similar actions;[7] or the 1930 Tariff Act that responds to similar offenses with measures that can result in total exclusion of foreign products.[8] As late as 1962, for instance, Section 252(b) of the Trade Expansion Act authorized the President to suspend all the benefits of trade agreement concessions to products of any foreign country that engaged in discriminatory acts inconsistent with a trade agreement entered into with the United States.[9] The only limit attached to such actions related to the nature of the response insofar as the remedy, especially in trade matters, formerly took place within the field of the offense. In other words, the remedy was limited in substance, but not in intensity. When surveying the statutes in an historical perspective, there is no doubt that the measure in excess is progressively discarded, the trend being towards compensatory remedies. However, this evolution primarily affects reciprocal actions.

Among the recent United States statutes providing for reciprocal action, the great majority simply aim at reestablishing equality between the parties. For instance, taxation is to be "adjusted" to match the more burdensome foreign taxes;[10] or compensating charges on foreign air carriers have to be "equal" to the foreign excessive charges;[11] or foreign noncompetitive financing is "equalized" by similar financial arrangements;[12] or the trade concession to be withdrawn must be "substantially

[6]46 U.S.C. § 143 (1982).
[7]15 U.S.C. § 75 (1982).
[8]19 U.S.C. § 1351(a)(1)(B) (1982).
[9]Pub. L. 87-794, Oct. 11, 1962, 76 Stat. 879.
[10]26 U.S.C. § 896(b) (1982).
[11]49 App. U.S.C. § 1159a (1982).
[12]12 U.S.C. § 635a-3 (1982).

equivalent'' to the modified trade obligation.[13] In other words, whatever form it takes, reciprocity by identity or by equivalence is merely compensatory in purpose.

The most interesting aspect of this evolution is that compensatory purposes that were attached to some forms of nonreciprocal actions seem to have progressively dwindled. It used to be that the United States could take steps outside reciprocity as a device to obtain compensation for a damage actually sustained and not redressed. In *Banco National de Cuba v. Sabbatino*, the Supreme Court held that ''the freezing of Cuban assets exemplifies the capacity of the political branches to assure, through a variety of techniques, that the national interest is protected against a country which is thought to be improperly denying the rights of United States citizens.''[14] Further, the Court regarded that policy as aiming ''to assure that United States citizens who are harmed are *compensated* fairly.''[15] However, in *Dames & Moore v. Regan*, the Supreme Court turned the frozen assets into ''bargaining chips,''[16] depriving them of compensatory purposes and nullifying at the same time the legal expectations of United States plaintiffs against Iran. Moreover, that judicial statement was made without regard to the legal title of property at stake, *i.e.* without regard to the fact that the frozen assets were the property of the government of Iran. This reasoning by omission bears some significance insofar as it rules out the possibility of explaining the Supreme Court's standing by the customary immunity which protects any property of a foreign state from seizure or execution in peacetime.

Similarly, when turning to different forms of action outside reciprocity, it is clear that their purpose is also for the United States to avail itself of similar ''bargaining chips'' when dealing with foreign nations. For instance, the summary suspension of foreign air carriers permits as a response to anticompetitive actions by foreign governments is not a compensation, but a device

[13] 19 U.S.C. § 2135(d) (1982).
[14] 376 U.S. 398, 412.
[15] *Ibid.* at 431 (emphasis added). See also *Sardino v. Federal Reserve Bank of New York*, 361 F.2d, 106, 112-3 (1966).
[16] 453U.S. 654, 673.

"to counter such restrictions;"[17] or Section 301 of the Trade Act was not intended as "compensation" for the United States, but as a "negotiating leverage" resulting in "a credible threat of retaliation whenever a foreign nation treats the commerce of the United States unfairly."[18] By contrast, Section 125(d) of the same act was adopted to insure that the President would "obtain adequate and equivalent compensation when a foreign country withdraws trade agreement obligations of benefit[s] to the United States."[19] More specifically, it has been rightly pointed out that the purpose of Section 301 was "to serve as a means to eliminate an unfair trade practice, not as an end in itself. Action under Section 301 is expected to be remedial, *not compensatory*."[20]

It is submitted that these statements are very significant in that they explicitly question the possibility of a state's resorting to compensatory unilateral remedies outside reciprocity. In short, compensation appears to be legitimate only within reciprocity. This contention appears to be strongly reinforced by the final result of the Border Broadcasting dispute between the United States and Canada. In 1976, Canada passed a law forbidding business tax deductions on Canadian advertising aimed at Canadian audiences from United States television and radio stations. United States broadcasting stations claimed to have lost millions of dollars in revenue and in 1978 a group of border broadcasters filed a complaint under Section 301.[21] The United States Canadian Border Broadcasting dispute is one of the rare trade disputes in which the threat of Section 301 proved ineffective; Canada strongly maintained its position and in doing so helped force the United States to resort to unilateral action.[22] A con-

[17]Senate Report No. 96-329, 96th Congress, 2nd Sess. (1980); [1980] *U.S. Code Cong. & Adm. News*, Vol. 2 (1980), at 58.

[18]Senate Report No. 93-1298, 93rd Congress, 2nd Session (1974); [1974] *U.S. Code Cong. & Adm. News*, Vol. 2 (1980), at 58.

[19]*Ibid.* at 7242.

[20]Jeanne Archibald, "Section 301 of the Trade Act of 1974," *supra* chap. 1, n.209, at VII, 16 (emphasis added).

[21]See Fischer & Steinhardt, *supra* chap. 1, n.208, at 641-649.

[22]The Border Broadcasting dispute took place outside the GATT system, since neither broadcasting nor taxation is covered by the agreement. For U.S./Canadian disputes under the GATT and the threat of Section 301, see, for example, the *AFL-CIO et al.* (301-32) or the J.I. Case Company (301-34). In both cases, consultations with Canada under relevant GATT or Code provisions were entered into. Section 301 Table of Cases, Office of the U.S.T.R.

spicuous feature of the United States response is to be found in its entirely reciprocal character, insofar as Section 232 of the 1984 Trade and Tariff Act added a new provision to the Internal Revenue Code that merely ''mirrored'' Canadian legislation,[23] although the petitioners had not failed to recommend among other alternatives, a ''general-linkage'' response that would have reduced the allocation of Canadian fishing rights.[24]

Therefore, if the purpose of nonreciprocal action as laid down by the Supreme Court and Congress is not compensation, and if, in a case where theoretically the response could have been nonreciprocal, the final result was indeed a reciprocal action by identity, there are strong reasons to believe that the United States does not avail itself of the right to compensation in a unilateral manner outside reciprocity. Moreover, insofar as reciprocal actions are limited in their intensity to a response likely to be equal to the damage, reparation as a matter of unilateral remedy is less restitutionary than compensatory in character.[25] In short, the United States practice has reduced unilateral reparation to reciprocal compensation.

There would certainly be some exaggeration in stating that reciprocity always provides the aggrieved party with ''reparation in an adequate form.''[26] Reciprocity seldom succeeds in restoring the victim to the previous conditions because reciprocity does not achieve *restitutio in integrum*. Actually a distinction should be made in that respect depending on the link that may exist between response and breach on the one hand and response and damage on the other. When the response is tailored to the breach, the aggrieved party is not necessarily compensated nor is it necessarily restored to the conditions which existed prior to the breach. For instance, similar discriminatory taxes on foreigners are not a true compensation if United States corporations in the

[23]98 Stat. 2991. This response had been determined as the most appropriate by the President on August 1, 1980 (45 F.R. 51173).
[24]See Fisher & Steinhardt, *supra* Chap. 1, n.208, at 648.
[25]In that sense, the fact that both under the GATT and the Subsidies Code, for instance, a countervailing duty has to be *equal* to the net amount of the bounty or the grant is another evidence that under international law, reparation is sought as a matter of compensation and not restitution. The potential enrichment of the offender is not to be redressed, at least unilaterally.
[26]*Chorzów Factory case* (Jurisdiction), P.C.I.J., Ser. A/8, 21.

foreign country are more numerous than foreign corporations in the United States, or likewise if the amount of United States business realized abroad is far more important than the foreign business realized in the United States. Similarly, compensating charges on foreign air carriers are not an adequate compensation if U.S. air carriers are more numerous than foreign air carriers. In short, it may be said that in such cases, the United States action goes some way toward reestablishing equality between the parties. But it is a nominal or formal equality. It is not a substantive equality, as equivalence is. Moreover, in both cases, the United States is not necessarily assured that the wrongdoer will stop its reprehensible behavior. It may do so, but such a result will be always fortuitous. As long as the harm inflicted on the wrongdoer does not become unbearable, the foreign state has no incentive to return to law compliance. To that extent, the United States action may just freeze the foreign state's behavior and not curb its potential obstinacy. By contrast, when the response is tailored to the damage, the United States is fully compensated for actual losses. However, restitution is not necessarily achieved insofar as by definition the United States may not avail itself of a right to take additional steps based upon the possible gains of the lawbreaker, since the response has to remain within the field of equivalence. Such is precisely the stalemate that follows the withdrawal of substantially equivalent obligations as a response to a breach of a trade agreement.

Secondly, reciprocity is seldom adequate insofar as it can only apply between symmetrical or equivalent obligations. Symmetrical or identical obligations were once the norm in classical international intercourse when states were bound by the same obligations: trade concessions were exchanged for trade concessions; diplomatic privileges for diplomatic privileges. That is why retaliation was and still is the common law remedy of the international legal order. However, such obligations, important as they still are, have now been superseded by commitments which impose different obligations between the parties. For instance, a duty free treatment is exchanged for a particular protection of foreign investments. In such a case reciprocity by equivalence will reestablish a substantive equality between the parties, because the remedy open to the wronged party fits the missing *quid pro quo*, without, however, being necessarily tailored to the damage. But still that remedy is not restitutionary in substance. With respect to the practice followed by the United States, it seems that restitutionary remedies are not feasible as a matter of unilateral remedy. In other words regardless of their reciprocal or nonreciprocal character, United States remedies never go so far as unilaterally granting the country *restitutio in integrum*. As far as restitution is concerned, the United States avails itself only of the right to take steps through law enforcement measures, the effect of which is to accelerate in some way the restitution owed by the lawbreaker. This is consistent with Article 33 of the Charter of the United Nations. One may indeed wonder what would be left of the obligation of states to settle their disputes by negotiation if the aggrieved party could unilaterally ensure *restitutio in integrum*. The same can be said *a fortiori* of any reciprocal action within a treaty which embodies a provision for arbitral or judicial settlement of disputes. That is why as a matter of procedure, reciprocal action which merely reestablishes equality between the parties does not have to be preceded by preliminary diplomatic steps. The difference that exists in that respect between reciprocity by identity and reciprocity by equivalence in the laws of the United States apparently follows the differences in results that may be achieved through both these reciprocal actions. The more likely it is that substantive equality is restored between the parties, the less preliminary warning is needed, whereas the unpredictable similar result that follows identical actions gives some sense to prior diplomatic steps.

Thirdly, without consideration of their identical or equivalent nature, reciprocal measures are only adequate to redress particular injuries. The international remedies of the United States show that reciprocity is never brought into play as far as collective or universal injuries are concerned. This feature is important for two reasons. On the one hand, it proves *a contrario* that reciprocal actions, hence compensatory measures, are indeed the sole unilateral reparation open to the aggrieved party. In other words, compensation by identity or by equivalence is the only legitimate reparation that the victim state may unilaterally obtain. On the other, it shows that breaches of international rules which warrant the international concern of a group of states or of the entire international community do not raise problems of reparation, but problems of enforcement. That is why an injury which does not affect a state in particular cannot be redressed by reciprocity, less because the condition of reciprocity is usually not attached to the breached obligation than because reciprocity is not a measure of enforcement. In that respect, it would indeed be ludicrous to hold that international fishery programs lay down norms of fundamental character as if the value of endangered species could ethically be put on a par with the value of human life or dignity. Compliance with such international programs is certainly not to be guaranteed by reciprocal actions. But it would be excessive to claim that reciprocal depletion of Atlantic salmon, for instance, would result in an "international crime." In that particular case, reciprocity is inadequate simply because reciprocity does not make sense when it is a matter of enforcing international law.

II. Enforcement

The absence of any compulsory judicial settlement of disputes as well as the lack of any coercive apparatus in the international society have made the enforcement of international law an intricate problem. Moreover, the principle of equality between states, which precludes a state from unilaterally imposing its will upon another, has turned this problem into an attempt to try to square a circle. However, there are sound reasons to believe that states may be law enforcers in particular when they are on the receiving end of an international offense and are not spontaneously awarded the *restitutio in integrum* by the offender.[27] We have noted that the United States specifically refuses to consider enforcement measures as measures of reparation. Not only is this position consistent with the principle of the peaceful settlement

[27]See E. Zoller, *Peacetime*, at 70-75.

of international disputes, it also stresses the need to avoid allowing law enforcement to be determined by, or contingent upon, a damage. In other words, the United States avails itself of the right to enforce international norms whatever the effects of the violation on its own economic and patrimonial interests. Such is the case when it takes steps to enforce international fundamental human rights. As a result, unilateral remedies to enforce the law are in some ways self-sufficient and represent an autonomous legal category. Therefore, it would be pointless to split this autonomous concept into two distinctive categories according to the presence or the absence of a damage. The motive to enforce international law is to be found in "an earlier act contrary to the law of nations."[28] However, if the damage is irrelevant to the concept of law enforcement measures, should the same solution prevail regarding the framework in which such measures are included? The United States has apparently given a negative answer insofar as it makes a distinction between situations where damages have been caused to the country and those where mere interests are affected. In particular, in the second situation it seldom avails itself of the right to infringe the rights of violators of fundamental international obligations. One may entertain serious doubts as to the legitimacy of, or the need for, such self-restraint. Indeed, the distinction between rights and interests is totally relevant to "the obligation to make reparation."[29] However, the same distinction has little weight with respect to enforcement as long as enforcement measures do not entail measures of reparation. That is why law enforcement measures need to be analyzed as totally independent of the right of the injured state to demand reparation. This is so true that enforcement problems arise whether or not they are accompanied by a problem of reparation. That is apparently why in the *Barcelona Traction* (judgment), the International Court of Justice referred to the "legal interests"[30] of all states in the protection of obligations *erga omnes*. Unlike reparation, which is only to be ap-

[28]See *The Naulilaa Incident* (1928), 2 *U.N.R.I.A.A.* 1026.
[29]See *Barcelona Traction*, Judgment, I.C.J. *Reports* 1970, p. 36, § 46 and Brigitte Bollecker-Stern, *Le préjudice dans la théorie de la responsabilité internationale* (1973).
[30]*Id.* p. 32, § 33.

plied as to particular injuries, enforcement is a matter of concern in case of particular, collective and universal injuries. But as to particular injuries, the problem of enforcement ought to arise only if reparation has not been obtained in an adequate form. That is why, where compensation has been unilaterally attained through reciprocal action, any move beyond reciprocity ought not to be permissible under international law. For instance, the withdrawal of a trade obligation equivalent to the trade concession that was modified or suspended by a foreign state may not be followed or accompanied by measures of enforcement.[31] To that extent, enforcement measures no doubt make sense only in relation to international offenses of a continuous nature, but only for the kind of offenses for which compensatory remedies were unfeasible. Except where the offender refuses to make reparation in an adequate form, states may not enforce international norms against instantaneous offenses. As long as the power to enforce international rules is not an inherent power,[32] a law enforcement measure would be wrongful if it had not been preceded by an unfulfilled request which would not be necessarily a request for reparation, but which could be a request for compliance in case of collective or universal injuries.

Basically, a unilateral action taken by a state to enforce an international rule is a coercive measure. It consists in exerting pressure on the offender. Such remedies may be simple measures

[31]In that respect, the Argentina-United States dispute over cattle hides exports is quite meaningful (see *supra*, Chap. 1, p. 26). On October 20, 1981, the President proclaimed the reimposition or a one percent ad valorem duty on Argentinian bovine leather imports, a measure the effect of which was merely a return to the *status quo ante,* prior to the bilateral agreement [Proclamation No. 4876, 46 F.R. 51707 (1981)]. The measure was to remain in effect until such time as the U.S.T.R. determined that Argentina was in compliance with the agreement or had otherwise granted adequate compensation for the breach. However, at the same time, in October 1981, the Tanner's Council of America, Inc. filed a petition with the U.S.T.R. pursuant to Section 301 of the 1974 Trade Act. The trade association charged that U.S. commerce had been burdened and restricted by the failure of Argentina to honor the agreement. It was further alleged that Argentina's restraints were ''unreasonable'' and contributed to a sharp increase in U.S. leather imports and a corresponding decline in U.S. tanning production. After extensive negotiations between both countries, the Section 301 action had to be dropped since following mutual abrogation of the agreement, the United States announced that it would raise tariffs back to the pre-agreement level. In other words, the United States availed itself of the right to obtain compensation, but not restitution (see *U.S. Import Weekly*, Feb., 3, 1982, at 415-416 and *id.*, Nov. 3, 1982, at 153).

[32]See E. Zoller, *Peacetime*, at 93.

or countermeasures,[33] but in any event both the requirements imposed by international law and the practice followed by the United States show that they have to be purposive in character. In other words they must give the foreign state a chance to mend its ways. It is submitted that the best way to achieve such a result is to subject every unilateral action for law enforcement purposes to a measure of proportionality.

To some extent, the international legal order has had the misfortune to have first received the concept of proportionality in the law of warfare. This is most unfortunate because in international law, proportionality is inevitably connected with armed reprisals. Nevertheless the proportionality at stake in warfare is irrelevant to the proportionality involved by law enforcement measures in peacetime. In wartime, armed reprisals are not genuine measures of law enforcement. Their purpose is not to get the belligerent to revert to compliance with the law, but to inflict a punishment or a sanction as a way for the responding state to be compensated after a particular offense. Armed reprisals in wartime are first and foremost measures of revenge; they are retaliatory actions of the most primitive kind. It is commonly said that they must be proportionate to the offense. However, that particular proportionality is entirely backward-looking, whereas proportionality in matters of law enforcement is forward-looking. This is inevitable since unlike repression, the enforcement of the law is an entirely forward-looking process. As a result, the proportionality at stake in matters of enforcement is a relationship between the end and the means; *i.e.* an assessment of how adequate the response is to fulfill a given purpose.

The principle of proportionality is a creation of European administrative law.[34] It has received its most elaborate form in Germany and in Switzerland, but it is completely unknown at least *eo nomine* in the United Kingdom[35] and in the United

[33]See *supra* Introduction, p. 8.

[34]See Kay Hailbronner, "The Principle of Proportionality," *General Reports to the 10th International Congress of Comparative Law*, 831-843 (1981).

[35]In the United Kingdom, the starting point for judicial review of administrative action is that public authorities are restrained from exceeding their powers, *i.e.* acting *ultra vires*, see Stanley de Smith, *Constitutional and Administrative Law*, 4th Ed. (1983), Harry Street and Rodney Brazier, [Eds.], 560-566. However, the doctrines of reasonableness, estoppel and fettering of discretion embody similarities to the principle of proportionality, see Hailbronner, *supra* n.34, at 835.

States.[36] The Prussian Administrative Tribunal was the first to recognize and apply the principle of proportionality as a legal limit on the police power. To that extent, it is not surprising that proportionality has been introduced into the legal order by the Naulilaa Tribunal,[37] *i.e.*, an international tribunal of Swiss arbitrators adjudicating the legitimacy of an act by Germany.[38] Insofar as in municipal law the principle of proportionality was applied as a limit on police power, one may better understand the tribunal's reluctance to link that principle to acts of reprisals.[39] In the conduct of warfare, reprisals are not police acts; they are not aimed at reestablishing law and order or at preventing a public disturbance. But as mentioned before, reprisals are primarily acts of punishment. In some ways reprisals merely indulge a thirst for revenge. By contrast, police acts are not punitive measures, but enforcement measures insofar as—whether or not force is used—they are carried out in order to reestablish public order and to insure compliance with the law. Many European administrative legal systems embody the principle that in order to achieve such aims, the means applied by the police must not be out of proportion with the purpose of the police action. The

[36]In the United States, the demise of the substantive due process since 1937 has put an end to the legal developments that could have emerged from *Lochner v. New York*: "The act must have a more direct relation, as a means to an end, and the end itself must be appropriate and legitimate, before an act can be held valid which interferes with the general right of an individual to be free in his person . . ." 198 U.S. 45 (1905). In socio-economic matters, the collapse of *Lochner* soon gave way to virtually complete judicial abdication; see Lawrence H. Tribe, *American Constitutional Law* (1978), 450. Today, while due process still protects a person's liberty in society, the Supreme Court will protect only those liberties or rights of "fundamental" constitutional character as enshrined in the Bill of Rights. However, fundamental rights shall not be restricted by governmental action where no compelling or overriding interest commands to do so; see John E. Nowak, Ronald D. Rotunda, J. Nelson Young, *Constitutional Law* (1978), 410. With respect to congressional power in particular, fundamental rights are still protected by the traditional relationality test as fixed by Chief Justice Marshall in *McCulloch v. Maryland*: "Let the end be legitimate, let it be within the scope of the Constitution, and all means which are not prohibited, but consistent with the letter and the spirit of the Constitution, are constitutional." 17 U.S. (4 Wheat.) 316, 421 (1819).

[37]2 *U.N.R.I.A.A.* 1011, 1025-1026.

[38]The arbitrators were Alois de Meyron (Switzerland), Robert Guex (Switzerland), Robert Fazy (Switzerland).

[39]It is worth recalling that in the *Naulilaa Incident*, the tribunal addressed proportionality in a rather cautious manner. It noted that the opinions of learned writers were divided on the issue whether or not the reprisals should be proportionate to the wrong. In particular, the award found that the German reprisals in the case were wrongful, first and foremost because they had not been preceded by an unfulfilled demand and only secondarily because they were disproportionate to the alleged wrong, 2 *U.N.R.I.A.A.* 1025-1026.

effects of police action on individuals affected by the measure have to be weighed; they have to stand a proportionality test. Primarily designed as a safeguard against police power, the principle of proportionality has been extended in many European systems to administrative power in general and it has gradually become a basic legal principle binding the executive and judicial branches and even the legislative branch,[40] to the extent that the Court of Justice of the European Communities has made it an unwritten general principle of community law.[41]

Insofar as the principle of proportionality applies to any law enforcement measures, there should be no reason for restricting its application in the international sphere to countermeasures alone. Any international remedy aimed at enforcing an international obligation should be subject to proportionality. In that respect the refusal of the Arbitral Tribunal in the *United States/France Air Service Agreement* dispute to categorically limit the scope of proportionality to the measures that infringe the subjective rights of the offender is quite significant.[42] In order to sustain the fundamental unity of law enforcement measures, the principle of proportionality should cover measures as well as countermeasures.

When turning to the concrete implementation of the proportionality test in the international legal order, it would be wrong to assume that the principle is elusive. True, the assessment of

[40]See Hailbronner, *supra* n. 34, at 831.

[41]See *Fédération Charbonnière de Belgique (case 8/55), Recueil* Vol. II, 1955-56, p. 304; *Hauts Fourneaux de Chasse* (case 15/57), *Recueil* Vol. IV, 1958, p. 190. In the case 11/70: *Internationale Handelsgesellschaft mbH v. Einfuhr-und Vorratsstelle*, the questions with regard to the internal legality of the contested measures were all related to one and the same problem: "namely whether these measures do or do not reflect the principle of 'proportionateness," meaning that, in pursuit of the general interest, citizens can be burdened only with such obligations as are absolutely necessary to attain the objective" (Conclusions of Advocate General Alain Dutheillet de Lamothe). The court did not evade the proportionality test and stated: "[I]mport and export licenses . . . are a *necessary and appropriate means* to permit the authorities to choose the most effective interventions on the grain market" and "the burden resulting from the bond system is not *excessive*" [1971-1973], *C.M.R. Courts Decisions* ¶ 8126, at 7425-7426. See also the case 114/76: *Bela-Mühle v. Grows-Farm* in which the court ruled on a regulation related to the common organization of the market in milk and milk products: "Nor . . . was . . . (the) obligation necessary in order to attain the objective in view. . . . It could not therefore be justified for the purposes of attaining the objectives of the common agricultural policy" [1977-1978], *C.M.R., Court Decisions*, ¶ 8448, at 8090; see also case 119, 120/77 *Olmühle Hamburg v. Hauptzollamt, ibid.*, ¶ 8450, at 8135.

[42]18 *U.N.R.I.A.A.* 443, § 83.

proportionality is no "easy task."[43] But the invaluable experimental field of United States international remedies provides a first-hand opportunity to set up certain basic rules and in doing so to overcome the level of approximation.

One point is sure: a law enforcement measure has to be temporary in duration. The *ratione temporis* safeguard is essential because it draws the line between pressure or coercion and punishment.[44] But, a measure can be coercive in purpose only if there is something left to coerce. In that respect, a distinction must be made between instantaneous and continuous offenses. Whereas coercion always makes sense against the latter, it is conceivable against the former only where there has been no spontaneous redress. As mentioned earlier, enforcement cannot be set in motion without a prior request to the foreign state and an explicit or implicit refusal. Therefore enforcement is undoubtedly subject to preliminary diplomatic steps. Once enforcement has been initiated, the problem is to determine how long the pressure should be exercised. A pressure that is continued indefinitely becomes disproportionate, since the goal is not attained. In that respect, the blocking of Cuban accounts, in force for nearly twenty-five years, raises serious problems. In *Nielsen v. Secretary of Treasury* (1970), the United States Court of Appeals (DDC) was aware of this when it emphasized that a blocking of accounts may turn into a taking "if continued indefinitely." But the court in an interesting statement added: "While the question is not free from difficulty, we think the sound course *at the present juncture* is for the courts to treat the blocking of Cuban accounts as not yet shorn of its temporary or interlocutory character, and to avoid a fixing of our government's course, not yet adopted by the legislative or executive branch, in the direction of vesting the assets of aliens."[45]

Secondly, a law enforcement measure has to be adequate *ratione personae* insofar as it must bear primarily on the individual(s) (*i.e.*, the leaders) who are in a position to revert to law

[43] *Ibid.*
[44] See E. Zoller, *Peacetime*, at 72-74.
[45] 424 F.2d 833, 844.

compliance. At the outset, this second safeguard rules out the legitimacy of any enforcement measure affecting the rights or even the interests of innocent third subjects of law. A measure whose enforcing effects run counter to the territorial jurisdiction of third states,[46] or whose ultimate consequences actually flout certain provisions of constitutive charters of international organizations, is internationally unlawful. Both the organization of human collectivities in states and the system of collective responsibility which pervades the essence of reprisals make it inevitable for a law enforcement measure to bear in some way or other on innocent persons. However there is a difference between an action that indiscriminately affects the entire foreign nation (suspension of economic assistance) and a measure that bears only on certain individual or corporations (suspension of foreign air carrier permits, blocking of foreign accounts with or without a distinction between private and governmental assets). Moreover, the procedural safeguards that are often attached to such measures in the United States (in particular, preliminary hearings and judicial review) ought to rule out measures which are fundamentally disproportionate in substance, *i.e.* with excessive effects on certain fundamental rights. Hence the significance of the scrupulous concern of United States courts for the basic rights of aliens, and in particular for the right to due process. There is no question that the Fifth Amendment does not require a trial-type hearing in every conceivable case of governmental impairment of foreign private interests and that the Federal Administrative Procedures Act does not apply in matters relating to foreign affairs. But in some specific fields—which need not incidentally be connected with enforcement measures following a denial of just compensation for damages—the United States has provided for legal requirements and opportunities that illustrate the manner in which enforcement of international rules could be fairly adjudicated at the municipal law level. In particular, a notice reasonably intended to apprise foreign individuals and governments of the imminent action and to afford them an op-

[46]See especially Patrizio Merciai, ''The Euro-Siberian Gas Pipeline Dispute—A Compelling Case for the Adoption of Jurisdictional Codes of Conduct,'' 8 *Md. J. Int'l L. & T.*, 1-52 (1984).

portunity to present their objections could be regarded as an elementary and fundamental requirement of any international law enforcement procedure in the domestic sphere. Such steps may enable innocent foreigners to make a convincing showing that the measure is invalid because it is unjust and unreasonable in its consequences. This would require, however, that the foreigners or their counsel could establish the link between private and public interests. To some extent they could with the assistance of their governments intervening as *amicus curiae* raise the issue of the protection of their own personal interests. The interaction between private and public interests which characterizes modern societies would justify the development of such procedures.[47] In any event, it would be excessive to claim that the constitutional laws of all members of the international society include the guarantees flowing from the Bill of Rights.

Thirdly, a law enforcement measure has to be adequate *ratione materiae* insofar as it must be directed against the most appropriate field in order to attain the expected result. This by no means entails the need to resort to reciprocal actions, since countermeasures precisely give a right to affect the subjective rights of the wrongdoer in a field substantially different from the field of the breached obligation; for instance, to infringe on fishing rights in order to obtain compliance with trade obligations or to suspend certain trade agreement concessions to obtain compliance with an international program for the protection of endangered species. The same can be said *a fortiori* of simple measures. From a general point of view, it must be emphasized that as a

[47]With respect to United States practice, there is little doubt that foreign governments either are not aware of pre-decision proceedings or minimize their importance or usefulness. Most of the time, they stay away from these preliminary proceedings. In Section 301 proceedings, for instance, foreign governments do not generally participate in the hearings. These hearings are frequently attended by silent consulate representatives, and often by considerably less silent representatives of the foreign industry affected or attacked by the petition. This was the case in the Canadian Broadcasting Dispute (43 F.R. 39617) where Canadian broadcasters participated in the hearings, and in the Steel Subsidies case (47 F.R. 10107) where representatives of the French steel industry took part in the proceedings. True, foreign governments have other opportunities to present their positions. In particular, they may talk directly with the Trade Representative and may request that certain information be included in the record. In other words, it may be said that in the view of foreign governments, diplomatic channels are still prevalent in international intercourse. It is unfortunate that foreign governments are reluctant to intercede during these hearings, since their own nationals actually have to pay the price for their alleged misdeeds.

test for the legitimacy of law enforcement measures, the principle of proportionality is quite distinct from the concept of equivalence. Equivalence covers measures of reparation and is the test for the adequacy of compensatory remedies. Therefore equivalence makes sense only in relation to particular injuries. By contrast, proportionality is not to be compared with reparation, but with enforcement. As a result, a law enforcement measure is not bound to be proportionate if it is equivalent, nor is it necessarily equivalent if it is proportionate.[48] For instance, the Hickenlooper Amendment, which provides for the suspension of the entire economic assistance to a foreign country following the nationalization of United States property without regard to the relevant rules of international law, is no doubt an excessive measure with respect to equivalence. But it could still stand the proportionality test if, in affecting the entire foreign nation as a whole, it did not entail excessive effects in relation to its objective. A proportional measure entails only the amount of coercion necessary to accomplish its objective.[49] In other words, the intensity of the measure in terms of monetary standards is of little help to assess the proportionality of a law enforcement measure.[50] That is why in the 1978 *Air Service Agreement Award (United States/France)*, the tribunal was satisfied that: "[I]t will not suffice, in the present case, to compare the losses suffered

[48]The distinction between the two concepts is overlooked more often than not insofar as the word "proportionality" is commonly used with the meaning given to it by the Benthamite tradition. See, *e.g.*, the remarks on "proportionality" made by Mr. Ushakov in *Yrbk. I.L.C* 1982, Vol. I, p. 217, §§ 42-43.

[49]To that extent, such measures are subject to the same requirements that limit humanitarian interventions to protect a foreign state's own nationals or even the nationals of a third state. See Richard B. Lillich, "Forcible Self-help by States to Protect Human Rights," 53 *Iowa L. Rev.*, 325, 349-350 (1967).

[50]As a matter of fact, the legislative practice followed by the United States shows that reference to monetary standards is barely made outside compensatory purposes. See in particular the evolution of the legal strategy with respect to government programs of compensation and insurance of United States fishing vessels for losses to the fishing industry resulting from "illegal seizures, penalties and confiscations by coastal foreign states." By contrast with the Hickenlooper Amendment, Pub. L. 90-482 adopted by the Congress on August 12, 1968, directed the Secretary of State in case of a failure by the foreign country to pay the United States claim, to withhold an amount equal to the unpaid claim from the funds programmed for assistance. In such a case, a compensatory measure was used in place of an action for law enforcement merely on the grounds of a monetary evaluation of the contemplated response. To that extent, Richard B. Lillich was right in portraying the provision as an "enlightened approach to the sanctioning process" instead of "terminating all aid across the board," quoted by Meron, "The Fishermen's Protective Act," *supra* Chap. 1, p. 31, n.79, at 295.

by Pan Am on account of the suspension of the projected services with the losses which the French companies would have suffered as a result of the countermeasures.''[51] It turned out, however, that in this particular case, the parties did not provide the tribunal with evidence that would have enabled it to verify the proportionality of the United States response.[52]

Finally, since reparation and enforcement raise completely different legal issues, one may entertain serious doubts as to whether or not enforcement comes within the scope of international responsibility. In following its Special Rapporteur Roberto Ago who eliminated the damage as a distinctive feature of international responsibility,[53] the International Law Commission has opened a path leading inevitably to the recognition that besides the damage and the obligation to make reparation, there is room for enforcement action and perhaps punishment.[54]

III. Punishment

All municipal legal orders nowadays make a fundamental distinction between civil and criminal offenses. Civil offenses are taken into consideration only where they entail a damage primarily to economic or patrimonial interests and under certain circumstances to moral interests. In international law, the indemnification of the damage is less broad in scope. Theoretically, the damage caused as a result of the state's conduct toward a subject whose subjective right has been impaired involves an obligation to make reparation only insofar as the damage follows an internationally wrongful act.[55] But whatever the difference

[51]18 *U.N.R.I.A.A.* 443, § 83.

[52]*Ibid.* at 444. See also E. Zoller, *Peacetime*, at 135.

[53]See *Yrbk. I.L.C.*, 1970, II, p. 193, §§ 15-25 and *Yrbk. I.L.C.*, 1973, II, p. 183, § 12.

[54]See Paul Reuter, ''Le dommage comme condition de la responsabilité internationale,'' *Mélanges Miaja De La Muella*, Madrid (1978), 836, 844.

[55]Theoretically when there is no breach of an internationally recognized form, international responsibility provides no redress for the injury sustained. Some treaties however do provide for such redress. Under such treaties, which have been enacted mostly in economic matters, a contracting party may under certain circumstances be temporarily dispensed from complying with one of its obligations under a mechanism which is known as an ''escape clause'' (GATT). However, when no such clauses have been embodied in an international agreement, customary international law does not provide injured states with an indisputable remedy as long as the injury does not derive from a breach of an international obligation and is not imputable to a determined

between the two orders, there is no question that the application of the "damage-reparation" principle leads to the reestablishment of equality between the parties. By contrast, criminal offenses exist even if no damage has been caused. In any event, the criminal punishment is never inflicted for the benefit of the possible victims. Until the International Law Commission introduced the concept of "international crime," criminal punishment barely existed as a matter of public international law. Of course, individuals had been convicted and punished as war criminals; but the state itself, as a group of human beings organized into a community as a whole, had never been subject to criminal responsibility.[56] This is not the place to discuss whether this new concept is to become part of substantive law in the near future. But there is no doubt that remedies for such crimes shall not be unilateral in character. Punishment is inconceivable as a matter of individual concern for each member of the international society.[57] In that respect, it should be noted that all United States measures or countermeasures against violations of fundamental internationally recognized human rights are not within the scope of punishment, but of enforcement. Individual or collective pun-

foreign state. In its report on Part One of the draft articles on "state responsibility," the International Law Commission has endeavored to partially overcome these shortcomings of customary international remedies by including in the chapter relating to the circumstances that preclude international responsibility, such concepts as "force majeure" or state of necessity. However, it is difficult to view some of these notions as indisputable concepts of substantive international law. On the other hand, some aspects of the problem dealing with remedies for injuries resulting from lawful international actions could have been addressed by the International Law Commission in the topic "international liability for injurious consequences arising out of acts not prohibited by international law," which was included in the program of work in 1978. Such would have been the case if the commission had decided to lay down primarily rules of non-fault liability which would have been of general application. Although many of its members acknowledge that "the traditional rules of international responsibility for wrongful acts were no longer responsive to all of the international community's needs," the commission has now delineated the topic as covering only transboundary loss or injury arising as a physical consequence of activities within state territory or control, *i.e.* as merely addressing the element of a physical consequence producing transboundary effects. See *Report of the International Law Commission to the General Assembly*, 39 G.A.O.R./Suppl. No. 10, at 175 (1984).

[56]One may wonder, however, if the settlements that followed the Second World War, did not entail certain punitive steps against Germany. See E. Zoller, *Peacetime*, at 59.

[57]See, however, the contradictions which exist within the International Law Commission as to the capacity of states acting alone or unanimously with respect to such offenses in *Yrbk. I.L.C.* 1979, II (2), at 116, § 3: "The countermeasures with which this article is concerned are measures the object of which is, by definition, to inflict punishment" and at 119, § 3: "[T]he international community (has turned) towards a system which vests in international institutions other than states exclusive responsibility . . . for deciding what measures are to be taken" (in case of violations of obligations *erga omnes*).

ishment of international offenses has to be clearly distinguished from the alleged punitive component that may accompany unilateral remedies for reparation or for enforcement, *i.e.* from what is known in municipal law as "penalties in civil actions"[58] or "private-law penalties."[59] In other words, punishment may be twofold: it is public when it is exercised for the benefit of the entire community and private when it is inflicted in the interest of the victim state.

In international law, public punishment is definitively beyond the scope of unilateral remedies. The principle of equality between states precludes the possibility of a single state's being in charge of securing atonement for the crime in the international community's interest, or deterring others from similar misdeeds, or educating the offender. That is why the concept of "sanction" as embodying a chastisement of "exemplary character"[60] is inconceivable in the field of peacetime unilateral remedies.

Insofar as criminal punishment inflicted upon states is inevitably based on a system of collective responsibility which rules out the individualization of the crime, it is very doubtful that criminal punishment in international law would be adequate even if exercised through the mechanism of international institutions. Regardless of its individual or joint exercise, a criminal punishment based on collective responsibility is still an act of revenge in its most primitive expression. In any event, the exclusion of criminal sanctions from the scope of unilateral remedies first requires any coercive measures against an offender to be of a temporary duration. One may wonder, however, if as a matter of reparation for fundamental international offenses, compensatory unilateral remedies may not entail certain definitive consequences. This problem arises with respect to suits that private victims may bring before United States federal courts as a matter

[58]See Guenther H. Treitel, Remedies for Breach of Contract, 16-4 in *International Encyclopedia of Comparative Law*, Vol. VII: *Contracts in General*, Chap. 16, p. 4.

[59]See Hans Stoll, Consequences of Liability: Remedies, 8-103 in *International Encyclopedia of Comparative Law*, Vol. XI: *Torts*, Chap. 8, p. 95.

[60]In the *Air Service Agreement Award* (1978) the Arbitral Tribunal wondered whether the object pursued by the United States action could be assessed as having "beyond the French case, an exemplary character directed at other countries and, if so, did it have to some degree the character of a sanction," 18 *U.N.R.I.A.A.*, 442, § 78.

of civil proceedings against foreign nations which have breached fundamental international obligations to their detriment, for instance when an individual who has been tortured in the territory of a foreign state seeks damages from such a government in United States courts. Until recently, the problem had barely arisen as such since judgments had been given only against individuals either separately,[61] or jointly and severally,[62] although in the *Letelier* case the action was brought against individuals and the foreign state. If satisfactory evidence of such "crimes" is produced, plaintiffs would undoubtedly be entitled to compensation for pain and suffering, wrongful death damages, moral damages and even punitive damages, as long as such damages are awarded against individuals. But to what extent may similar damages be awarded against the foreign state and if they are, to what extent does the plaintiff have a right to execute the judgment against the foreign state's assets in the United States? Such are the complex problems raised by the *Siderman* case.

On September 28, 1984, the United States District Court (C.D. California) granted Joseph Siderman, who had been detained and tortured eight years before by the former military regime in Argentina, a $2.7 million judgment for damages against the Republic of Argentina and the Province of Tucuman. Although this judgment was vacated and the action dismissed by an order of March 7, 1985,[63] it may still be considered in two different ways for analysis purposes. Under the laws of the United States and especially under Section 4(a) of the Foreign Sovereign Immunities Act, which permits execution against the commercial property of a foreign state in the United States only when the execution relates to a judgment establishing rights in property,[64]

[61]*Filartiga v. Peña-Irala*, 630 F. 2d 876 (2d Cir. 1980).

[62]*Letelier v. Republic of Chile*, 488 F. Supp. 665, 674, *judgment awarded*, 502 F. Supp. 259 (DDC 1980).

[63]See *supra*, Chap. 3, p. 123.

[64]28 U.S.C. 1619 (1982). It goes without saying that commercial activities are irrelevant in the case. In the *Letelier* case, personal representatives of Letelier endeavored to have the default judgment against the Republic of Chile for compensatory and punitive damages enforced by executing it on the property interest held by the Republic of Chile in Chilean National Airline (LAN). The district court granted execution against LAN's assets [567 F. Supp. 1490 (S.D.N.Y.) and 575 F. Supp. 1217 (S.D.N.Y. 1983)]. However, the court of appeals disagreed with the district court's finding that LAN's assets were "used for the commercial activity upon which the claim is based" and found that LAN's unwitting participation in the assassination was not a "commercial activity" since a commercial activity is one that a private person may lawfully undertake [748 F. 2d 790]. "The court of appeals decision reflects a strict but textually correct view of execution immunity under 28 U.S.C. § 1610 (a) (2)" according to Monroe Leigh in 79 *A.J.I.L.*, 442, 448 (1985).

it seems doubtful that the *Siderman* judgment would ever have been enforced. It would, therefore, have remained merely declaratory in substance. Under international law, however, and from a theoretical point of view, Judge Takasugi was right to implicitly deprive Argentina of immunity from jurisdiction and execution, because an international crime severs the criminal state from the protection of any nonhumanitarian international rules. A criminal state is so to speak "outside the law." But, if it is to be protected by the humanitarian rules of international law, should it be also protected by municipal law and specifically by domestic legislation relating to foreign sovereign immunity?[65] Curiously enough, the United States favors a positive answer. In a suggestion of interest sent to the *Siderman* court, which *sua sponte* reconsidered the issue of foreign sovereign immunity, the United States held:

> The legislative history of the FSIA unequivocally states that the FSIA sets forth the sole and exclusive standards to be used by the courts in resolving questions of foreign sovereign immunity raised by foreign states. See 1976 U.S. Code Cong. & Ad. News 6610. Most recently, the Ninth Circuit held in *McKeel v. Islamic Republic of Iran*, 722 F.2d 582, 586-87 (9th Cir.), *cert. denied*, 105 S. Ct. 243 (Oct. 9, 1984), that jurisdiction over foreign states and their instrumentalities can only be obtained under the FSIA. Pur-

[65]In the United States, the Act of State doctrine should be irrelevant as to a claim by the victim of torture, at least for two reasons. First, in *Alfred Dunhill of London, Inc. v. Republic of Cuba* [425 U.S. 682 (1976)], the Supreme Court held that the Act of State doctrine applies only to *formal acts* of sovereign authority such as a decree, statute or comparable instrument. Secondly, in *Filartiga v. Peña-Irala* [630 F.2d 876, 889 (2d Cir. 1980)], the Court said: "We doubt whether action by state official in violation of the Constitution and laws of the Republic of Paraguay, and wholly unratified by that nation's government, could properly be characterized as an act of state." As a result, in case of violations of fundamental human rights, an act of state defense is conceivable only with respect to "criminal" pieces of legislation. But precisely in this particular case, the Act of State doctrine already does not protect the foreign state, as this is illustrated by the "Bernstein" exception; *Bernstein v. Van Heyghen Frères, S.A.* 163 F.2d 246 (2d Cir. 1947); *Bernstein v. N.V. Nederlandsche-Amerikaansche Stoomvaart-Maatschappij*, 173 F.2d 71 (2d Cir. 1949), amended 210 F.2d 375 (2nd Cir. 1954). See also *Restatement of the Law, Foreign Relations Law of the United States (Revised)*, Tentative Draft No. 4, § 428, Reporters' Notes, §§ 3, 4 and 6 at 7-9.

suant to 28 U.S.C. § 1604 of the FSIA, which codifies as federal law the restrictive theory of sovereign immunity, a foreign state is immune from the jurisdiction of the federal and state courts, except as provided in Sections 1605 and 1607. See *Verlinden B.V. v. Central Bank of Nigeria*, 461 U.S. 480, 488, 497 (1983). If one of the specified exceptions to sovereign immunity applies, a federal district court may exercise subject matter jurisdiction under 28 U.S.C. § 1330(a). However, if the claim against the foreign state does not fall within one of the exceptions, federal courts lack subject matter jurisdiction, as well as personal jurisdiction. *Verlinden, id.*[66]

On March 7, 1985, Judge Tagasuki yielded to these arguments and obediently held: ''With respect to the Foreign Sovereign Immunities Act, none of the enumerated exceptions to immunity listed in 28 U.S.C. § 1605 apply herein.'' But the correctness of this statement lies in the assumption that Congress has authority to bar United States courts from applying international law. There is no question that Congress may nullify, in whole or in part, a treaty commitment.[67] But it is doubtful that a similar power exists regarding customary international rules,[68] a problem

[66]United States District Court, Central District of California, *Siderman, et al. v. Republic of Argentina, et al.*, No. CV 82-1772-RMT (MCx) Suggestion of Interest of the United States (28 U.S.C. § 517). It is questionable that the *Verlinden* case should be construed as the Department of Justice seems to believe. The Supreme Court held indeed in this case: ''The District Court and the Court of Appeals both held that the Foreign Sovereign Immunities Act purports to allow a foreign plaintiff to sue a foreign sovereign in the courts of the United States, provided the substantive requirements of the Act are satisfied. We agree.'' [103 S. Ct. 1962, 1969 (1983)] However one may wonder whether this agreement will go as far as putting on a par purchases of cement and acts of torture. Interestingly, in response to the Supreme Court's invitation in reviewing petition for a writ of certiorari in the *Hanoch Tel Oren* case, the Department of Justice submitted a brief which supports *mutatis mutandis* the same views as those presented in the *Siderman* case: ''The Foreign Sovereign Immunities Act bars the exercise of jurisdiction over Libya . . . That ruling . . . is clearly correct. The 'noncommercial tort' exception to the Foreign Sovereign Immunities Act, 28 U.S.C. §1605 (a) (5), renders foreign sovereign immune from suit for all noncommercial tortious acts except those that cause 'personal injury or death, or damage to or loss of property, *occurring in the United States*' '' (italics in the text), XXIV *I.L.M.* 427,434 (1985). In short commercial activity and acts of torture are not on a par only when they take place within the territory of the United States. As Pascal pointed it: ''Vérité en-deçà des Pyrénées, erreur au-delà.''

[67]See, for example, *Diggs v. Schultz*, 470 F. 2d 461, 465 (1972).

[68]At least, when such rules are part of the fundamental principles of international law. It is doubtful that these principles are only those ''few principles of customary law or provisions of multilateral treaties that recognize rights for private persons, notably human rights,'' as Louis Henkin states in ''International Law as Law in the United States,'' *supra* Chap. 1, n.180, at 1569 (n.44). All the principles relating to the status of the state in the international legal order (sovereignty, equality, jurisdiction, responsibility) are customary in nature.

which incidentally was completely ignored by Judge Tagasuki in his order of March 7, 1985. To the extent that in the international legal order, the consequences of an international crime are first and foremost customary in substance, the enactment of the 1976 Foreign Sovereign Immunities Act cannot have resulted in the abrogation of customary rules relating to international crimes.[69] Therefore, insofar as customary international law is part of the law of the United States, U.S. courts are entitled to sever foreign states violating fundamental human rights from the protection of sovereign immunity.[70]

However, when turning to the practical consequences of such judicial power, it becomes clear that it may well end in deadlock. As illustrated by the *Siderman* case, there are indeed no other grounds, except collective responsibility, for Argentina and the Province of Tucuman to be held liable for the damages sustained by the victim. This ultimate consequence of the *Siderman* decision raises an issue that cannot be dealt with in legal terms alone.

[69]True, another solution should apply if the concept of international crime has to be viewed as progressive development of international law and not as codification of existing international rules. But such an assertion would be inconsistent with the practice of states against countries which, for example, engaged in slave trade during the last century or are violating fundamental human rights in this century. In that sense, the growing concern of European states for fundamental human rights as illustrated in Lomé III is meaningful. See *supra* chap. 3, p. 102, n.11.

[70]It could be argued that human rights treaties which provide specific procedures against violators of fundamental rights have abrogated customary law in the field; in short, treaty remedies should be exclusive. But this is very doubtful for at least three reasons. First, none of these treaties deals with sovereign immunity. Secondly, the United States is not a party to the majority of them. Thirdly, the law of international responsibility is not the other side of the law of treaties. See in particular E. Zoller, *Peacetime*, at 114-118. Last but not least, few of these treaties provide the victim with a remedy similar in result to the redress which may follow a domestic civil suit. In the *Siderman* case, Judge Tagasuki held: ''The Organization of American States ('OAS') through the American Convention on Human Rights has set up the Inter-American Commission on Human Rights. After exhausting domestic remedies, or waiver thereof, an individual can bring a case against a state before the Commission. If the Commission is unsuccessful in settling the case, it can bring the matter before the Inter-American Court of Human Rights. As such, the OAS appears to provide plaintiffs with their remedy'' (Order of March 7, 1985). The correctness of this careful statement lies in the assumption that the international remedy may give the private plaintiff the *restitutio in integrum* for the damage sustained. Whenever the international remedy may lead to such a result, there is no doubt that the principle *Non bis in idem* should apply. But whenever the international remedy falls short of providing the victim with indemnification of the damage, possible precedence of this remedy over domestic suits is questionable. The American Convention on Human Rights, for instance, neither enables the commission to award compensatory damages, nor authorizes an individual to submit a case to the court. However, exhaustion of local remedies should certainly be a prerequisite for a domestic foreign court to assert subject-matter jurisdiction in case of a violation of fundamental internationally recognized human rights.

Collective responsibility is a highly rational institution in the absence of political institutions;[71] but it also illustrates the central reality of primitive law, the passive solidarity of the kinship group. There is no doubt that the practice of collective responsibility has rendered and still renders great service to international law.[72] However, if such principle is not mitigated (without being necessarily superseded) by the conception of fault, it may turn into an instrument justifying any act of revenge. It was Grotius who introduced the concept of fault—the *culpa* theory—in international law against the Germanic doctrine of reprisals: "A civil community, like any other community, is not bound by the act of an individual member thereof, without some act of its own, or some omission."[73] This "act of its own" lies in *patientia* or *receptus, i.e.*, in the sharing in the crime by "allowing" or "receiving."[74] The positivist doctrine dealt a death-blow to the principle of *culpa* in holding that responsibility is created not by the fault (*culpa*), but by a fact contrary to international law.[75] There is no question that the doctrine of absolute liability derived from the difficulties in dealing with the international responsibility of several South American countries for acts of their agents or mob actions in the course of revolutions occurring within their borders. Absolute responsibility is nowadays the common law of international responsibility.[76] However, with respect to certain internationally wrongful acts such as violations of fundamental human rights, absolute responsibility fails to make ethical, if not legal, sense. That doctrine results in holding a national community responsible as a whole for the misdeeds of leaders who often have seized and kept power by force against the will of the people. That is why criminal punishment of a state community

[71]See *supra*, Introduction, pp. 6-7.

[72]See, for example, J. Goebel, "The International Responsibility of States for Injuries Sustained by Aliens on Account of Mob Violence, Insurrections and Civil Wars," 8 *A.J.I.L.* 802, 804-808 (1914).

[73]Grotius, *De Jure Belli ac Pacis*, Lib. II, XXI, p. 342. See also Sir Hersch Lauterpacht, *Private Law Sources and Analogies of International Law* (1970), 135-6.

[74]See Lauterpacht, *supra* n.73 at 135.

[75]See D. Anzilotti, "La responsabilité internationale des Etats à raison des dommages soufferts par des étrangers," XIII *R.G.D.I.P*, 5-29, 285-309 (1906), esp. at 291.

[76]See Articles 1 and 3 of the Draft Articles on State Responsibility, *Yrbk. I.L.C.*, 1973, Vol. II, p. 173 and p. 176.

as a whole raises daunting prospects and is in complete opposition to the consistent pattern of the civilization process that has gradually led to an individualized approach to criminal responsibility and therefore to criminal punishment.[77]

By contrast with public punishment, private law penalties involve a punitive component that is not self-sufficient. As a result, such penalties are very different from the primitive private punishment as embodied in the archaic system of private revenge, which involved a complete subordination of the wrongdoer to the victim. Subordination was so extensive in primitive law that it has been viewed as entailing for the victim a genuine right *in rem* over the person of the tort feasor.[78]

In principle, damages are compensatory insofar as they shall not as a general rule exceed full compensation and enrich the victim. The latter shall not be entitled to recover more than his loss. However, several modern legal systems embody under different designations various institutions the effect of which is to add "something more" to the strict compensation for the injury done. These institutions are known as private law penalties, although their punitive character follows more their effects than their purposes. They are indeed viewed as punitive because they go, as it were, beyond the mere reestablishment of monetary equivalence between the wrongdoer and the victim. However, their purpose is not systematically punitive in substance. Sometimes they provide a substitute for the reparation of injuries that cannot be evaluated by monetary standards, such as injured feelings; in such case they give satisfaction for moral damages. Sometimes their primary purpose is to punish the wrongdoer and to make him atone for his wrong, but also to withdraw the possible enrichment gained by the wrongdoer and to deter him, and others, from similar future offenses; such are the many func-

[77]See in particular, R. Saleilles, *L'individualisation de la peine*, 22-49 (1898); Paul Fauconnet, *La Responsabilité, Etude de sociologie* (1920), 67-90. The evolution is also to be found in the Bible. In that respect, compare *Exodus* 20:5: "I the Lord your God am a jealous God, visiting the iniquity of the fathers upon the children to the third and the fourth generation," to *Deuteronomy* 24:16: "The fathers shall not be put to death for the children, nor shall the children be put to death for the fathers; every man shall be put to death for his own sin." See also *Joshua* 7:22-25; 2 *Kings* 14:6.

[78]See P. Ourliac & J. de Malafosse, *Histoire du droit privé*, vol. 1 (1969), at 381.

tions of punitive or exemplary damages. Finally, some private law penalties are merely remedial in purpose insofar as they mainly serve the interest of the aggrieved party in compelling the wrongdoer to abide, not by legal obligations as such, but by certain judgments based on such obligations; such is the purpose of fines levied in contempt proceedings, the effect of which is to compel a recalcitrant defendant to comply with an order for specific performance or an injunction. However, although labelled by the Supreme Court in a leading case as punishment,[79] compensatory fines are not always within the scope of punishment.

When turning to the consequences of an internationally wrongful act, the problem is knowing the extent to which, if at all, international law allows similar additional steps to be attached to the unilateral remedies made available to the victim state.

In international law, it can be said that every material damage involves an immaterial offense insofar as any breach of an international obligation affects the sovereignty of the victim state. Whatever their connection with a material damage, immaterial offenses are afforded reparation by international law through the mechanism of satisfaction.[80] Satisfaction may take several forms; it may even involve some punitive steps, but only insofar as they are taken against private individuals, especially when the injured state requires the other state to prosecute and to sentence the individuals responsible for the breach. With respect to the principle of equality between states, a satisfaction that would involve a punishment against the foreign state is not permissible. To that extent, the unanimous refusal by the International Court of Justice in the *Corfu Channel* case (1949) to award Albania any satisfaction other than a declaratory judgment bears great significance.[81] As a result, there is serious reason to believe that unilateral remedies may not entail additional steps to full com-

[79]*Gompers v. Buck's Stove & Range Co.*, 221 U.S. 418, 441 (1911).

[80]F. Przetacznik, "La responsabilité internationale de l'Etat à raison des préjudices de caractère moral et politique causés à un autre Etat," 78 *R.G.D.I.P.*, 919, 943-974 (1974).

[81]"The Court, unanimously, gives judgment that by reason of the acts of the British Navy in Albanian waters in the course of the operation of November 12th and 13th, 1946, the United Kingdom violated the sovereignty of the People's Republic of Albania, and that this declaration by the Court constitutes in itself appropriate satisfaction," I.C.J. *Reports* 1949, p. 36.

pensation in order to provide redress for non-material injuries. Moreover whenever the immaterial offense is unconnected to a material damage, the statement of the court ought to preclude the injured state from seeking redress unilaterally at once, *i.e.*, before the wrongdoer has been given a chance to provide adequate satisfaction. In other words, immaterial offenses *per se* are not subject to compensatory unilateral remedies.

Punitive damages, as possibly included in unilateral remedies, raise more intricate problems. On the one hand they involve for the victim a unilateral power to punish the wrongdoer, which as such does not have a better legal basis than where it is invoked as a ground to obtain redress for non-material injuries. Despite the strong admonitions of famous international scholars such as Sir Hersch Lauterpacht,[82] international tribunals have been extremely reluctant to award punitive damages, and the above-mentioned statement of the International Court of Justice in the *Corfu Channel* case seems to have dealt a deathblow to this theory.

However, insofar as the modern legal systems which recognize the possibility of a penal surcharge upon compensatory damages generally draw a line in that respect between the law of torts and the law of contracts, one may wonder whether international law does or should leave room for similar distinctions. The concept of punitive damages is mostly confined to common law countries, but the general rule that punitive damages shall not be awarded for breach of contract is rarely subject to exceptions.[83] Indeed punishment does not make sense in relation to the economic risk that generally pervades contractual relationships.

In international law, the origin of the breached obligation (*e.g.*, a treaty rule or a customary obligation) has no bearing either on the characterization of the breach as an internationally wrongful act, or on the regime of the international responsibility generated by such act.[84] In other words, international law does not distin-

[82]Sir Hersch Lauterpacht, *Collected Papers* [E. Lauterpacht (Ed.)], Vol. 1: The General Works (1970), at 390-397.
[83]See Treitel, *supra*, n.58, at 16-45, pp. 25-26.
[84]See Article 17 of the Draft Articles on State Responsibility, *Yrbk. I.L.C.* 1976, Vol. II (2), pp. 79-87.

guish between contractual and extra-contractual responsibility. However, with respect to the consequences of the breach, the law of treaties is still distinct from the law of international responsibility, inasmuch as the latter embodies unilateral remedies which are alien to the former. This distinction should be explained, not by the origin of the breached obligation,[85] but by the consequences of the violation. It is indeed the injury or the damage not redressed that gives a state the right to take additional steps beyond reciprocity, whereas the presence or the absence of such an injury or a damage is irrelevant with respect to the right to act in a reciprocal manner. In short, reciprocity is a unilateral remedy both in the law of treaties and in the law of international responsibility. Therefore it is logical in every respect that, as previously explained,[86] whenever reciprocity by identity or by equivalence gives an adequate compensation to the aggrieved party, additional steps should not be permissible. That is why the International Law Commission wisely emphasized that

> the fact that it has suffered a breach of an international obligation committed by another State does not, *in all cases*, purely and simply authorize the injured state in its turn to breach an international obligation towards the state which has committed the initial breach. What is legitimate in some cases does not become legitimate in others.[87]

However, with respect to these additional steps taken in peacetime by one state against another, especially when they follow a request for reparation that has not been honored, it is doubtful that such steps are intrinsically similar to the "punitive damages" existing in international legal orders. Such is the case of countermeasures, for they precisely rule out the lawfulness of punitive components. As a result, they ought to be more related to certain fines that are levied on recalcitrant defendants in order to enforce judgments against them.

The fines that many legal systems provide in contempt pro-

[85] *Contra* W. Riphagen, A/CN.4/366/Add. 1, §§ 41-56.
[86] *supra*, pp. 140-141.
[87] *Yrbk. I.L.C.* 1979, Vol. II (2), p. 116, § 4 (italics in the text).

ceedings are essentially law enforcement measures. Their primary purpose is neither to punish the defendant, not to enrich the plaintiff, but basically to insure the enforcement of a judgment. Internal remedies may present some characteristics that should by analogy provide a better understanding of the essence of law enforcement measures under international law.

A number of municipal legal systems provide coercive devices for the enforcement of certain types of judgments. In France, an *astreinte* imposes a coercive penalty upon the judgment debtor in case of nonperformance. The debtor can be ordered to pay the creditor a substantial sum of money for every day (week, month) of noncompliance. The idea is not to compensate the damage caused by nonperformance; indeed the *astreinte* is different from compensatory damages. Its purpose is to lead the debtor to fulfill his obligation under the threat of an increasingly harmful fine.[88] In common law countries, law enforcement measures are to be found mostly within the field of equitable remedies, such as specific performance to enforce a positive obligation to do or to convey something and injunctions to enforce a negative obligation to forbear. In addition, noncompliance with a court's order of specific performance or of an injunction amounts to contempt of court, which is efficiently enforced. Contempt proceedings may be criminal or civil. The difference is in the proceedings that follow. Criminal contempt proceedings are punitive in character; their aim is to further the interests of society and act as a deterrent against violations of public authority; the punishment usually takes the form of an unconditional fine or a prison term. By contrast, civil contempt proceedings are either compensatory or compulsive in purpose. First a compensatory payment may be ordered in favor of the aggrieved party. But civil contempt proceedings may also take the form of a condi-

[88]Loi no. 72-626 du 5 juillet 1972, Loi no. 75-596 du 9 juillet 1975, see Article 509 du Nouveau Code de Procédure civile. See also Jean Carbonnier, *Droit Civil*, Vol. 4: Les Obligations, 566-567 (1976). Since 1980, the administrative courts and the *Conseil d'Etat* may apply the device of *astreinte* against ''*personnes morales de droit public*,'' a sweeping legal category which includes, for example, the state, governmental departments, administrative organs, public agencies, regions, *départements* (provinces), counties, or cities. See Loi no. 80-539 du 16 juillet 1980, *Dalloz* and *Bulletin Législatif Dalloz*, 1980, at 285.

tional fine or imprisonment which will not be paid or suffered by the contemner if he abides by the law.[89]

Except for conditional prison terms, civil contempt proceedings as they exist in the United States are indeed very similar in purpose to *astreintes* in France. Such institutions are a means of coercion rather than measures of chastisement. They are spuriously punitive in character less because they may compensate in some ways the aggrieved party for the loss caused by the contemner's obstruction than because they may be made conditional on the defendant's failure to comply within a reasonable time. In other words, such measures are primarily comminatory, *i.e.*, they work as threats.[90] They are covered neither by compensation, nor by punishment. Between both concepts, there is room for a third; namely enforcement.

When addressing international unilateral remedies, the analysis above is quite meaningful. There is no doubt that international law does not authorize the punishment of one state by another. But both the absence of any coercive apparatus in the international society and the demise of international collective procedures are more often than not turning states into law enforcers. States may indeed enforce international rules for their exclusive benefit, *i.e.*, whenever a damage caused to them has not been compensated in an adequate form, or for the benefit of collective and universal interests. However, unilateral remedies for law enforcement purposes have an originality of their own as being outside compensation and necessarily behind punishment.

[89]See R. H. Field, B. Kaplan & K. M. Clermont, *Civil Procedure* (1978), 14-15.

[90]See in French Law the distinction between *astreinte provisoire* and *astreinte définitive*: the *astreinte* is made final only in case of a contemner's persistent obstinacy, Loi n. 75-596 du 9 juillet 1975. In the United States, the fine *in terrorem, i.e.*, imposed only conditionally and dependent upon the contemner's future conduct, has been supported in *United States v. United Mine Workers*, 330 U.S. 258, 303-304 (1974); *Sunbeam Corp. v. Golden Rule Appliance Co.*, 252 F.2d 467, 472 (2d. Cir. 1958).

Conclusion

With respect to the object of this study, the experimental field provided by the international remedies of the United States has certainly proved useful as a starting point to elaborating a theory of international unilateral remedies. The United States has carved out a comprehensive system of enforcement procedures which, internationally speaking, is an exemplification of a specific and particular state practice. This system as a whole illustrates the sophisticated statutory scheme that a single nation can achieve in the field of unilateral remedies. Whether United States practice is superior or inferior to another is doubtless debatable. But one point is sure: Its elaborate articulation gives it an influence that others do not have.[1] Moreover, the key position of the United States in international politics considerably strengthens the impact of this legislation in the formation of a customary international law of state remedies.

In that respect, two observations need to be made. First, United States legislation is a referential test for international rules, rarely because it construes the rules in a disputable and disputed manner, as when the United States resorts to economic coercion against other American states,[2] more frequently because it shapes international rules and crystallizes them into custom. International anti-dumping and countervailing duty law, for example, emerged entirely from United States practice. Today it is difficult

[1]See, for similar views, Charles de Visscher, *Theory and Reality in Public International Law* (trans.), 149 (1957) and Anthony D'Amato, *The Concept of Custom, supra* Chap. 2, n.7, at 65 and 96.

[2]See, for instance, the economic "sanctions" against Nicaragua, XXIV *I.L.M.* 809-822 (1985).

to imagine that United States legislative initiatives, not to mention court decisions, regarding violations of fundamental internationally recognized human rights could not eventually affect the still faltering content of international law in that field. Secondly, United States practice has established elaborate procedures that enable every interested person to be protected in one way or another. These procedures may indeed vary, depending on the particular substantive field they are concerned with. Some of them are the mere transposition into domestic law of established and recognized international obligations such as those that derive from the exhaustion of local remedies. But some others are applied because they are exclusively germane to United States constitutional or legislative requirements. Preliminary hearings are conspicuous examples. Such cases invite speculation over their possible impact on the formation of new procedural international obligations. On September 17, 1984, the Council of the European Community adopted Regulation 2641/84 on the strengthening of the common commercial policy against illicit commercial practices.[3] This regulation is a counterpart to Section 301 of the 1974 Trade Act. But interestingly enough, it establishes preliminary procedures that closely parallel those in force under United States legislation. It would be interesting to inquire further into the content of possible customary international entitlements of foreigners to due process.

Be that as it may, United States legislation shows that, projected in the international sphere, there are three types of unilateral remedies, depending on their purpose.

First, unilateral remedies may seek reparation and realize by themselves the compensation owed to the aggrieved party. Thus they encompass reciprocity by identity and by equivalence; they are covered by the concept of equivalence.

Secondly, unilateral remedies may be aimed at enforcing an international obligation. They may be prompted by two different situations: either a damage that has not been redressed in an adequate form, or an injury caused to the detriment of collective

[3]*O.J.E.C.*, No. L. 252, 20.9.84, pp. 1-6. See Elisabeth Zoller, "Remedies for Unfair Trade: European and United States Views," 19 *Cornell Int'l L.J.* (1985; forthcoming).

and universal interests, *i.e.*, two situations in which an international obligation has been breached. In short, there must be a need for a state to enforce international law. The enforcement authority is not a freedom, but a power. Enforcement measures embody nonreciprocal actions which are covered by the concept of proportionality. In any event, such actions must remain purposive in character, *i.e.*, they must always give the offender a chance to mend its ways. Therefore, they are necessarily temporary in character and rule out the lawfulness of any action that would either achieve by itself the missing reparation for the damage sustained, or inflict a penalty on the lawbreaker. These countermeasures are, therefore, not effective, but merely dispositive. They are a legal illustration of the fact that you can lead a horse to water, but you cannot make it drink.

Thirdly, should unilateral remedies embody genuine punitive actions, such measures are doubtless outside the power of a state, at least in peacetime. This is not the place to discuss whether such a power is or is not vested in the international community organized as a whole within the United Nations, as the International Law Commission seems to believe. But one point is sure: Whatever the form under which punishment is implemented, whenever punitive actions are directed at states, they are necessarily based upon the passive solidarity of the community, *i.e.*, the system of collective responsibility. Whether the inclusion of such sanctions in substantive international law would represent progress for the international society is questionable.

There is little doubt that the international community as a whole has not reached a stage of development that would make subtle legal distinctions possible and feasible. The survey of the unilateral remedies open to the aggrieved party shows ample evidence of the backward position in which international responsibility is likely to remain confined for a long time. In particular, as international law stands, it would be illusory to seek a possible mitigating effect on the consequences of an international offense through the concept of fault (*culpa*). But so long as such a notion is rejected, the consequences of international responsibility will be based upon a system of collective responsibility. Therefore, just as they did in primitive societies, remedies for international offenses will continue to represent a risk the wrongdoer will always have to contend with, a risk inherent in sovereignty, a risk inherent in freedom.

Bibliography

Bibliography

"Act by State Governments Affecting Foreign Relations." 25 *Harv. J. Int'l. L.* 200-205 (1984).

Albert, Paul. "The Undermining of the Legal Standards for Human Rights Violations in the United States Foreign Policy: The Case of 'Improvement' in Guatemala." 14 *Colum. H. Rts. L. Rev.* 231-274 (1982-1983).

Anzilotti, D. "La responsabilité internationale des Etats à raison des dommages soufferts par des étrangers." XIII *R.G.D.I.P.* 5-29, 285-309 (1906).

Archibald, Jeanne S. "Section 301 of the Trade Act of 1974." In *Manual for the Practice of International Trade Law* (VII), William Kitchell Ince & Leslie Alan Glick [Ed.]. Federal Bar Association, Washington (1984).

Baehr, Peter R. "Concern for Development Aid and Fundamental Human Rights: The Dilemma as Faced by the Netherlands." 4 *H. Rts. Q.* 39-52 (1982).

Bernard, Claude. *Introduction à l'étude de la médecine expérimentale*. Paris, Baillière, 1865. Transl. Henry Copley Green, New York, The Macmillan Company (1927).

Bickel, Alexander. "The Supreme Court, 1960—Forward: The Passive Virtues." 75 *Harv. L. Rev.* 40-79 (1961).

Bin Cheng. *The Law of International Air Transport*. London, Stevens; N.Y., Oceana, 1962.

Blomeyer, Arwed. Types of Relief Available (Judicial Remedies). Chap. 4, Vol. XVI: Civil Procedure, *International Encyclopedia of Comparative Law*. J.C.B. Mohr, Tübingen; Martinus Nijhoff, The Hague (1982).

Bollecker-Stern, Brigitte. *Le préjudice dans la théorie de la responsabilité internationale*. Paris, Pedone, 1973.

Carbonnier, Jean. *Droit Civil*. Vol. 4: Les obligations. Paris, Presses Universitaires de France, Thémis (1976).

Cardozo, Michael H. ''Sovereign Immunity: The Plaintiff Deserves a Day in Court.'' 67 *Harv. L. Rev*. 608-618 (1954).

Carter, D. R. & Brogan, F. D. ''United States Human Rights Policy: Effect on Exports.'' 9 *Ga. J. Int. & Comp. L*. 287-331 (1979).

Cassese, Antonio. ''Foreign Economic Assistance and Respect of Civil and Political Rights: Chile—a Case Study.'' 14 *Tex. Int'l L. J*. 251-263 (1979).

Chamberlain, Kevin. ''Collective Suspension of Air Services With States Which Harbour Hijackers.'' 32 *I.C.L.Q*. 616-632 (1983).

Cline, William R. [Ed.]. *Trade Policy in the 1980s*. Institute for International Economics, Washington, MIT Press/Cambridge; London (1983).

Cofield, Shirley A. ''Using Section 301 of the Trade Act of 1974 as a Response to Foreign Government Trade Actions: When, Why and How.'' 6 *N.C. Int'l & Com. Reg*. 381-405 (1981).

Cohen, Roberta. ''Human Rights Diplomacy: The Carter Administration and the Southern Cone.'' 4 *H. Rts. Q*. 212-242 (1982).

D'Amato, Anthony A. *The Concept of Custom in International Law*. Cornell Univ. Press, Ithaca & London (1971).

——— ''The Concept of Human Rights in International Law.'' 82 *Colum. L. Rev*. 1110-1159 (1982).

——— ''Judge Bork's Concept of the Law of Nations Is Seriously Mistaken.'' 79 *A.J.I.L*. 92-105 (1985).

Del Bianco, Mark C. ''Execution and Attachment Under the Foreign Sovereign Immunities Act of 1976.'' 5 *Yale Studies in World Public Order* 109-146 (1979).

De Visscher, Charles. *Theory and Reality in Public International Law*. Percy Corbett (trans). Princeton University Press, 1957.

Dickinson, Edwin D. ''The Law of Nations as National Law:

'Political Questions'.'' 104 *U. of Pa. L. Rev.* 451-493 (1956).

Durkheim, Emile. *De la division du travail social*. 2 Ed. Paris, Felix Alcan (1902).

Dymock, Paul & Vogt, Donna. ''Protectionist Pressures in the U.S. Congress, A Review of the 97th Congress in 1982.'' 17 *J.W.T.L.* 496-512 (1983).

''Economic Sanctions as an Instrument of U.S. Strategic and Foreign Policy''. 6 *J. Comp. Bus. & Cap. M.L.* 55-80 (1984).

Fauconnet, Paul. *La Responsabilité, étude de sociologie*. Paris, Felix Alcan (1920).

Field, R. H.; Kaplan, B. & Clermont, K. M. *Civil Procedure*, 4th Ed. The Foundation Press (1978).

Fischer, Bart S.; & Steinhardt, Ralph G., III. ''Section 301 of the Trade Act of 1974: Protection for U.S. Exporters of Goods, Services, and Capital.'' 14 *Law & Pol'y. Int'l. Bus.* 569-691 (1982).

Franck, Thomas M.; & Weisband, Edward. *Foreign Policy by Congress*. Oxford Univ. Press (1979).

Fraser, Donald M. ''Human Rights and U.S. Foreign Policy.'' 23 *Int'l. Stud. Q.* 174-185 (1979).

Freeman, Alwyn V. *The International Responsibility of States for Denial of Justice*. Longmans, Green & Co., London (1938).

Gadbaw, R. Michael. ''Reciprocity and Its Implications for U.S. Trade Policy.'' 14 *Law & Pol'y. Int'l. Bus.* 691-746 (1982).

Galloway, L. Thomas. *''Star Industries, Inc. v. United States:* Sequel to the Chicken War.'' 6 *Int'l. Law.* 48-63 (1972).

Goebel, J. ''The International Responsibility of States for Injuries Sustained by Aliens on Account of Mob Violence, Insurrections and Civil Wars.'' 8 *A.J.I.L.* 802-852 (1916).

Gordon, Edward. ''The Blocking of Iranian Assets.'' 14 *Int'l. Law.* 659-688 (1980).

Grotius. *De Jure Belli ac Pacis*. Transl. Kelsey. Indianapolis, Bobbs-Merrill (1925).

Hailbronner, Kay. ''The Principle of Proportionality.'' *General*

Reports to the 10th International Congress of Comparative Law, 831-843. Akademiai Kiado (Zoltan Peteri, Vanda Lamin Ed.), Budapest (1981).

Hartman, Joan F. "Derogations from Human Rights Treaties in Public Emergencies." 22 *Harv. J. Int'l. L.* 1-52 (1981).

Hay, Keith A. J.; & Sulzenko, B. Andrei. "U.S. Trade Policy and 'Reciprocity'." 16 *J.W.T.L.* 471-479 (1982).

Henkin, Louis. *Foreign Affairs and the Constitution*. The Foundation Press (1972).

——— "International Law as Law in the United States." 82 *Mich. L. Rev.* 1555-1569 (1984).

Herod, Joseph Rogers. *Favored Nation Treatment, An Analysis of the Most Favored Nation Clause With Commentaries on Its Uses in Treaties of Commerce and Navigation*. New York, The Banks Law Publishing Co. (1901).

Hostie, Jean. "Contribution de la Cour Suprême des Etats-Unis au développement du droit des gens." 69 *R.C.A.D.I.* 273-348 (1939, II).

Hudec, Robert E. *The GATT Legal System and World Trade Diplomacy*. New York, Praeger Publishers (1975).

——— "Retaliation Against 'Unreasonable' Foreign Trade Practices: The New Section 301 and GATT Nullification and Impairment." 59 *Minn. L. Rev.* 461-539 (1975).

"IAM v. OPEC: 'Acts of States' and 'Passive Virtues'." 5 *Loy. L. A. Int'l. & Comp. L.* 159-171 (1982).

"International-Trade-Canada-United States Motor Carriers Reciprocity." 13 *G. J. Int'l. & Comp. L.* 857-864 (1985).

Jackson, John H. *Legal Problems of International Economic Relations*. West Publishing Co., St. Paul, Minn. (1977).

Kelsen, Hans. "Unrecht und Unrechtsfolge im Völkerrecht." 12 *Z.a.ö.R.V.* 567-608 (1932).

Khan, Mian Rashid Ahmad. *Islamic Jurisprudence*. Premier Book House, Katchery Road, Anarkali Lahore (no date of publication).

Lambert, Jeremiah D.; & Coston, William D. "Friendly Foes in the Iranian Assets Litigation." 7 *The Yale Journal of World Public Order* 88-113 (1980).

Lauterpacht, Hersch. *Private Law Sources and Analogies of International Law*. Archon Books (Reed. 1970).

——— *Collected Papers*. E. Lauterpacht (Ed.). Vol. I: The General Works. Cambridge Univ. Press (1970).

"The Legitimacy of Economic Coercion: The Carter Foreign Aid Policy and Nicaragua." 5 *Loy. L. A. Int'l. & Comp. L. J.* 101-127 (1982).

Leigh, Monroe; & Atkeson, Timothy. "Due Process in the Emerging Foreign Relations Law of the United States." 21 *Bus. Law*. 853-878 (1966) and 22 *Bus. Law*. 3-28 (1966).

Lillich, Richard B. "Forcible Self-Help by States to Protect Human Rights." 53 *Iowa L. Rev*. 325-351 (1967).

——— "The Protection of Foreign Investment and the Foreign Assistance Act of 1962." 17 *Rutgers L. Rev*. 405-427 (1963).

——— "Requiem for Hickenlooper." 69 *A.J.I.L.* 97-100 (1975).

Limpens, J. "De l'opposabilité des contrats à l'égard des tiers, Contribution à l'étude de la distinction entre les droits réels et personnels." *Mélanges ROUBIER*, Vol. II. Sirey, 89-104 (1962).

Lissitzyn, O. J. "The Legal Status of Executive Agreements on Air Transportation—Part II." 18 *J.A.L.C.* 12-32 (1951).

Martin, Edwin M. "Should Observance of Basic Human Rights Be a Prerequisite for Aid?." 16 *Atl. Comm'y. Q.* 216-221 (1978).

McNair, Arnold D. *The Law of Treaties*. Oxford Univ. Press (1961).

Merciai, Patrizio. "The Euro-Siberian Gas Pipeline Dispute—A Compelling Case for the Adoption of Jurisdictional Codes of Conduct." 8 *Md. J. Int'l. L. & T.* 1-52 (1984).

Meron, Theodor. "The Fishermen's Protective Act: A Case Study in Contemporary Legal Strategy of the United States." 69 *A.J.I.L.* 290-309 (1975).

Miller, William E. "The *Waterman* Doctrine Revisited." 54 *Geo. L. J.* 5-29 (1965).

Nash, Richard B. "Certifying Human Rights: Military Assistance to El Salvador and the International Security and Development Cooperation Act of 1981.'' 14 *Colum. H. Rts. L. Rev.* 275-310 (1982-3).

Nolde, Boris. ''Droit et technique des traités de commerce.'' 3 *R.C.A.D.I.* 295-462 (1924, II).

Nowak, John E.; Rotunda, Ronald D.; Young, J. Nelson. *Constitutional Law.* West Publishing Co., St. Paul Minn. (1978).

''Nuclear Non-Proliferation: Export of Nuclear Fuel to India.'' 22 *Harv. Int'l. L. J.* 227-233 (1981).

Ourliac, P.; & de Malafosse, J. *Histoire du droit privé*, Vol. 1. Paris, Presses Universitaires de France, Themis (1969).

Paradisi, Bruno. ''L'amitié internationale; les phases critiques de son ancienne histoire.'' 78 *R.C.A.D.I.* 329-378 (1951, I).

Paust, Jordan J. ''Federal Jurisdiction Over Extraterritorial Acts of Terrorism and Nonimmunity for Foreign Violators of International Law Under the FSIA and the Act of State Doctrine.'' 23 *Va. J. Int'l L.* 191-251 (1982).

Perrot, Roger. *Cours de voies d'éxécution.* Paris, Ed. Montchrestien, Cours de droit (1965-1966).

Potter, Pitman B. ''Relative Authority of International Law and National Law in the United States.'' 19 *A.J.I.L.* 315-326 (1922).

Przetacznik, F. ''La responsabilité internationale de l'Etat à raison des préjudices de caractère moral et politique causés à un autre Etat.'' 78 *R.G.D.I.P.* 919-974 (1974).

Reciprocity in Foreign Trade. CRS, Library of Congress, Archived 08/17/83, Issue Brief Number 1B82043 [Authors: Reifman, A.; & Ahearn, R.]

Reisman, W. Michael. ''Deterrence and International Law.'' In Miller, Arthur Selwyn; & Feinrider, Martin [Ed.]. *Nuclear Weapons and Law* 129-132. Greenwood Press, Westport (Conn.) (1984).

Restatement of the Law (Second revised). American Law Institute Publishers, St. Paul, Minn. (1965).

Restatement of the Law (Third, Tentative Draft). Foreign Relations Law of the United States, 5 vols. American Law Institute, Philadelphia (1980-1984).

Reuter, Paul. *Introduction au droit des traités*. Paris, A. Colin, Coll. U (1972).

——— "Le dommage comme condition de la responsabilité internationale." *Mélanges Miaja De La Muella*, Madrid, 837-846 (1978).

———. "Le droit international et la place du juge français dans l'ordre constitutionnel national." In *L'application du droit international par le juge français*. Paris, A. Colin (1972).

Riesenfeld, Stefan A. "The Doctrine of Self-Executing Treaties and *U.S. v. Postal*: Win at Any Price." 74 *A.J.I.L.* 892-904 (1980).

Rubin, Alfred P. "Professor D'Amato's Concept of American Jurisdiction Is Seriously Mistaken." 79 *A.J.I.L.* 105-112 (1985).

Saleilles, Raymond. *L'individualisation de la peine*. Paris, Félix Alcan (1898).

Schachter, Oscar. "The Enforcement of International Judicial and Arbitral Decisions." 54 *A.J.I.L.* 1-24 (1960).

———. Book Review on *Human Rights in International Law and the Helsinki Accord* [Th. Buergenthal (Ed.)]. In 17 *Colum. J. Trans. L.* 531-537 (1978).

———. "International Law Implications of U.S. Human Rights Policies." 24 *N.Y. Sch'l. L. Rev.* 63-87 (1978).

Schwebel, Stephen M. "The Compliance Process and the Future of International Law." 75 *A.S.I.L. Proceedings* 178-185 (1981).

Seagle, William. *The Quest for Law*. New York, A. Knopf (1941).

Sinclair, Ian. *The Vienna Convention on the Law of Treaties*. Second Edition. Manchester University Press (1984).

de Smith, Stanley. *Constitutional and Administrative Law*. 4th Ed. by Street, Harry; & Brazier, Rodney. London: Penguin Books (1983).

Sommerfield, Stanley L. "Treasury Regulations Affecting Trade With the Sino-Soviet Bloc and Cuba." 19 *Bus. Law*. 861-874 (1964).

Steiner, Henry J.; & Vagts, Detlev F. *Transnational Legal Problems*. The Foundation Press, Mineola, N.Y. (1976).

Stoll, Hans. Consequences of Liability: Remedies, Chap. 8, Vol. XI: Torts. *International Encyclopedia of Comparative Law*. J.C.B. Mohr, Tübingen; Martinus Nijhoff, The Hague (1971).

Szasz, Paul C. "Sanctions and International Nuclear Controls." 11 *Conn. L. Rev.* 545-581 (1979).

———. "The International Legal Aspects of the Human Rights Program of the United States." 12 *Cornell Int'l L. J.* 161-174 (1979).

Tasca, Henry J. *The Reciprocal Trade Policy of the United States, A Study in Trade Philosophy*. New York, Russell & Russell (1938).

"Testing Statutory Criteria for Foreign Policy: The Nuclear Non-Proliferation Act of 1978 and the Export of Nuclear Fuel to India." 14 *N.Y. Univ. J. Int'l L. & Pol.* 419-466 (1982).

Thierry, Hubert; Combacau, Jean; Sur, Serge; & Vallée, Charles. *Droit International Public*. Paris, Ed. Montchrestien, Précis Domat (1981).

Timberg, Sigmund. "Wanted: Administrative Safeguards for the Protection of the Individual in International Economic Regulation." 17 *Adm. L. Rev.* 159-172 (1965).

Treitel, Guenther H. Remedies for Breach of Contract, Chap. 16, Vol. VII: Contracts in General. *International Encyclopedia of Comparative Law*. J.C.B. Mohr, Tübingen; Martinus Nijhoff, The Hague (1976).

Tribe, Lawrence H. *American Constitutional Law*. The Foundation Press, Mineola, N.Y. (1978).

Turner, Brett R. "The Harvest of *Sabbatino: Vishipco Line v. Chase Manhattan Bank*." 8 *N.C.J. Int'l & Com. Reg.* 87-101 (1982).

"United States Trade Sanctions Against Uganda: Legality Under International Law." 11 *Law & Pol'y. Int'l. Bus.*, 1149-1191 (1979).

Viner, Jacob. *Dumping: A Problem in International Trade*. Reprints of Economic Classics, A. M. Kelley (1966).

Von Mehren, Robert B. "The Foreign Sovereign Immunities Act of 1976." 17 *Colum. J. Trans. L.* 33-66 (1978).

Waelbroeck, Michel. *Traités internationaux et juridictions internes dans les pays du Marché Commun.* Centre Interuniversitaire de droit comparé (C.I.D.C.), Bruxelles (1969).

Walker, H. "Dispute Settlement: The Chicken War." 58 *A.J.I.L.* 671-685 (1964).

Wallace, Don, Jr. "The President's Exclusive Foreign Affairs Powers Over Foreign Aid." *Duke L. J.* 293-328, 454-494 (1970).

Weber, Max. *Economy and Society*. Reed., Univ. of Calif. Press (1978).

Weiss, Leonard. "Reciprocity." In Rubin, Seymour J.; & Graham, Thomas R. [Ed.]. *Managing Trade Relations in the 1980's,* 165-259. Rowman and Allanheld (1983).

Wright, Quincy. *The Enforcement of International Law Through Municipal Law in the United States.* Univ. of Illinois, Urbana (1916).

———. *The Control of American Foreign Relations.* New York, Macmillan (1922).

Wright, Charles A.; Miller, Arthur R.; & Cooper, Edward H. *Federal Practice and Procedure.* Saint Paul, Minn., West Publishing Co. (1984).

Zoller, Elisabeth. "Quelques réflexions sur les contremesures." *Mélanges Colliard*, Paris, Pedone, 361-381 (1984).

———. *Peacetime Unilateral Remedies: An Analysis of Countermeasures.* Dobbs Ferry, N.Y., Transnational Publishers (1984).

———. "Remedies for Unfair Trade: European and United States Views." 19 *Cornell Int'l L.J.* (1985, forthcoming).

Index

Index